What People are Saying ab

My father, Ralph Turner, Sr. was one of the four key individuals who built the Bantam Reconnaissance Car (BRC) pilot model. His achievement remains one of our family's most treasured accomplishments. Paul Bruno has written a captivating story that describes what the American Bantam Car Company team experienced to build the BRC, as well depicts all the amazing events that led up to those fateful days in Butler, PA, during the late summer and early fall of 1940, when the fate of freedom hung in the balance and the first Jeep was built. —*Ralph Turner, Jr.*

This is a real thriller, just couldn't put it down. Paul Bruno's Project Management in History: The First Jeep tells the amazing story of how America's Jeep was born: it's regular guys beating impossible odds to create the vehicle that shaped freedom for our modern world. This book is the stuff of dreams and the fighting spirit that makes us winners. —*Martin Yate, NY Times bestselling author*

The First Jeep isn't just a list of chronological facts or a project process guide. It pulses with the passion of the times—and the resolve of the men who came together to create an all-terrain reconnaissance vehicle for a new kind of Army going into a new kind of fight. Paul Bruno is a storyteller. —*Joyce Faulkner, multi-award-winning author, former President of Military Writers Society of America, former Director of e-commerce for Consolidated Natural Gas*

As the long-time mayor of Roy Evans' and my hometown, Bartow, Georgia (Population 286), I am excited that Paul Bruno is publishing the story of Roy and the Jeep. Paul has captured the never say die attitude our hometown hero Roy instilled in his firm, the American Bantam Car Company, as well as chronicling in an action packed narrative the amazing events that led to the creation of the first Jeep.

The Roy Evans/Jeep exhibit draws the most interest from visitors to our City Museum and individuals from all the western world are enthralled by the story of "Small town boy makes good." I am sure *Project Management in History—The First Jeep* will be a hit and we thank Paul for honoring Bartow's own Roy Evans. —*Hubert Jordan, Past Mayor, Bartow Georgia*

Paul was one of my graduate students more than 25 years ago. I am delighted to see his new work that highlights an important part of our American history. He has a gift for keeping the flame alive and he has done so brilliantly in *Project Management in History: The First Jeep* showcasing an underdog story of triumph over all obstacles. —*William D. Danko, Ph.D.*

The Jeep—praised by Supreme Allied Commander General Dwight D. Eisenhower as one of three inventions that won World War II—remains one of the most recognized symbols of American ingenuity. Born in the waning days of the Great Depression from a failed company on a threadbare budget, the Jeep is a testament to individual achievement, heroic courage and the spirit of American enterprise in the face of adversity.

The American Bantam Car Company assembled much more than an extraordinary military vehicle that preserved the United States' freedom in World War II, they assembled a miracle. In telling the story of the Jeep, Paul has told the story of the American spirit, and his book is a tribute to Bantam's legacy of determination and perseverance.

Through Paul's comprehensive research and intricate detail, you will meet the men who changed not only automotive history, but American history as well. Retrace the story of small town Butler, Pennsylvania to the corridors of power in Washington, DC. The true story of the Jeep is far more powerful than any fictionalized account and holds valuable lessons for us all. *—Linda Harvey Burkley, Assistant Professor, Susquehanna University, Former President, Butler County Chamber of Commerce*

Project Management in History:

The First Jeep®

By Paul R. Bruno, PgMP, PMP

First Edition

PROJECT MANAGEMENT IN HISTORY SERIES
VOLUME 1: THE FIRST JEEP
FIRST EDITION

ISBN: 0-692-31802-X

EAN: 978-0-69-231802-7

Cover Design by M. Freedman & Imagine Communications
Published by MFP Enterprises LLC, Henderson, NV U.S.A.

Dedication

To the late Cathy E. Bruno, Ph.D, my beloved wife, companion and soul mate who supported me, and the telling of this story.

I am incredibly indebted to my parents, Miriam and Victor Bruno, and my brothers, Eric and Karl Bruno, for always being there for me and all my other family and friends who sustained me during the journey.

Acknowledgements

6th century B.C. Chinese philosopher Lao Tzu postulated that, "the journey of a thousand miles begins with one step." While the trek to write this book began with that initial stride, numerous individuals have walked with me along the away. I am indebted to the archivists at the United States Archives, College Park, Maryland who were always helpful and thoroughly professional. Robert Brandon of Butler, PA for sharing the rare photographs of the pilot model being built and Linda Burkley, also of Butler, PA for her support of telling this story over many years.

I wish to thank Manuel "Max" Freedman, writing mentor, businessman extraordinaire, and dear friend, for sharing his wisdom, conceiving and writing the entrepreneurial lessons, and for editing the book. Steven Hoese, best friend, and research partner. Hubert, Todd and the late Patsy Jordan, gracious hosts and my supporters in Bartow, Georgia, Roy Evans' hometown. Jack Lopez, archives researcher, who showed me the ropes at the College Park facility and Bill Mertens, another best friend and research partner. Linda Morales-Kennon, friend and supporter for many years, and Bill Norris for sharing key documentation.

I am grateful for Kim and Duncan Rolls, who graciously opened their home to Steven Hoese and me and for sharing their Bantam prototype recreation journey with us. Ralph Turner, Jr., namesake son of one of the four key individuals who built the first Jeep, for sharing documentation his father had kept and his own recollections of his dad's descriptions of events. Angela and Martin Yate, writing gurus, for sharing knowledge and wisdom on book publishing. Vincent Appel, Maxine "Max" Duvall, Glenn Krause, Morio Lurenz, and Paul "Randy" Petty for being there for me during my darkest hours in 2012, and for all the other friends who helped along the way, too many to name, who provided encouragement and support to keep going. Last but certainly not least, my nuclear family, Miriam and Victor Bruno, parents who helped me become who I am, and the best brothers anyone could ever have, Eric and Karl Bruno.

Finally, deep thanks to my late wife Cathy E. Bruno, Ph.D. It was her love, support and encouragement that made this book possible.

—Paul R. Bruno, PMP, PgMP, Henderson, Nevada – 2014

Contents

Paul R. Bruno

List of Figures

Entrepreneurial Lessons

List of Tables

Preface

Destiny. The dictionary defines it as, "a predetermined course of events often held to an irresistible power or agency," and "something to which a person or thing is destined." It is a concept that only hindsight tends to illuminate, and only when viewed in the rear view mirror of history.

The spring and summer of 1940 witnessed the resounding defeat of the French Army and British Expeditionary Force at the hands of a modernized German Army, designed to take advantage of the latest advances in technology. This included mobile vehicles, tanks used in formation to puncture enemy lines, as well as close air support of ground forces. The evacuation of the British from Dunkirk, and the final defeat of their French ally in June 1940, left only a thin line of English fighter planes between that island nation and total defeat.

While events unfolded rapidly in Europe, leaders of the United States Army, decimated by demobilization after World War I and budget cuts during the Great Depression, knew they were completely unprepared for this new type of mobile warfare, called blitzkrieg or "lightning war." Experts in the Army had worked from the end of World War I to develop a light weapons carrier / command and reconnaissance vehicle, but with limited success. In June 1940 a list of requirements was compiled for a revolutionary new truck to replace the cart and mule as the Army's primary method of moving troops and small payloads.

This book tells the story of the American Bantam Car Company, who dared to meet the challenge to build the pilot model in the unheard-of timeframe of forty-nine days. The ¼ ton truck 4 X 4 light project holds lessons for today's business leaders and project managers who face an environment of rapidly changing technology, volatile economic conditions and turbulent international relations, the same forces that assailed the U.S. Army throughout the period between World War I and World War II.

The macro analysis of the endeavor, viewed through the prism of the project management triple constraint model, reveals an effort with a revolutionary scope, undertaken by a firm with no resources, with an impossible delivery timeframe of forty-nine days, and the team had to get it right on the first try (quality). These limitations do not represent a recipe for success.

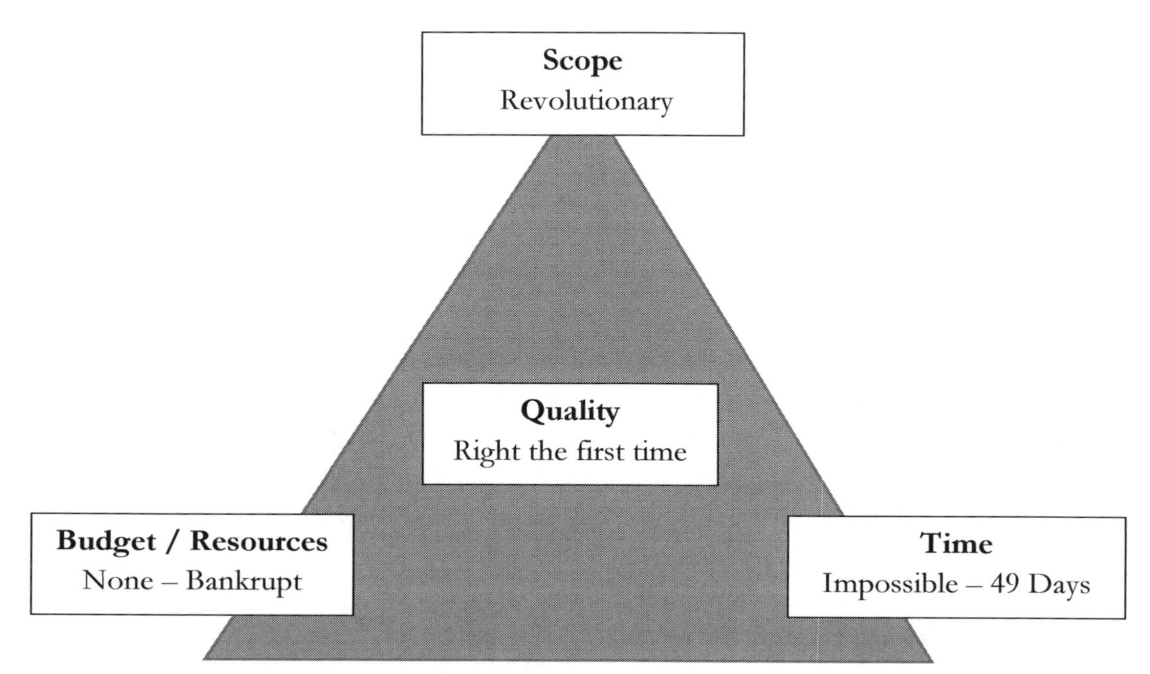

Triple Constraint for the First Jeep Project

This project, undertaken by a bankrupt company, located in a small western Pennsylvania city, by a group of individuals largely forgotten today, represents a classic case of the right people, in the right place, at the right time. The team grabbed ahold of the hand of destiny and built the Bantam Reconnaissance Car, better known today as the Jeep, a deliverable that would save the world and change history.

Introduction

The story of the creation of the first Jeep dates to the very beginnings of the automotive era in the early 20th century, long before the fateful events during the summer of 1940. This period was a free-wheeling time when numerous entrepreneurs were defining and redefining the industry. From 1900-1920 they established the industry, and during the next twenty years the business matured until their products became an indispensable part of daily life for millions around the world.

The story of the creation of the first Jeep, from the lineage that birthed it, to the final acceptance of the Jeep prototype in October 1940, represents the subject matter of this book. The story encapsulates the entrepreneurial spirit of the individuals who made up the early automobile industry, those hands-on, get-it-done, no-challenge-was-too-great personalities who were not afraid to get their hands dirty. We owe a debt to them for many of the wonders of the automobile we take for granted today.

The phases of the project lifecycle, from initiation to final product acceptance, provided the prism from which to view the extraordinary actions of the effort. Entrepreneurial Lessons interwoven within the text will provide insight and wisdom for use by today's project managers and business people. These were written by Manuel "Max" Freedman, a fifty year veteran of the commercial world, who has owned numerous businesses, including a graphics and publishing company and a screenwriting / movie consulting practice. Manuel's vast experience and exceptional writing ability made him uniquely qualified to cull the "teachable moments" from the fascinating events that led to the creation of the first Jeep.

Chapter 1: Company History and Leadership presents the history of the companies and individuals who contributed in some manner to the eventual development of the Jeep prototype. These range from Sir Herbert Austin and his vision for small cars, to Roy S. Evans, who single-handedly kept the firm which built the prototype afloat during the Great Depression, and instilled into that business the entrepreneurial and innovative culture that achieved the impossible.

Chapter 2: The Environment: The Great Depression and Early World War II examines the decades of the 1920s and 1930s, presenting the monumental changes that took place at the macro level, especially after the stock market crash of 1929 and the onset of the Great Depression. Project managers must understand the macro, as well as micro environments they operate within.

Chapter 3: The Stakeholder: The United States Army looks at the state of the American military during the interim between World War I and World War II. Understanding the needs and reality of the key stakeholders represents an important part of project management, and for the development of the first Jeep, the U.S. Army was the KEY stakeholder. There were various players within the Army including the Infantry, Cavalry, Artillery, and the Quartermaster branches, which all had their own agenda vis-à-vis the creation of a light vehicle.

Chapter 4: Project Genesis examines the various attempts by the United States Army to develop a light weapons carrier / reconnaissance and command car during the 1930s.

Chapter 5: Project Initiation: General Requirements tells the story of how the "general characteristics" were arrived upon within the Infantry and how these were documented in a now famous June 6, 1940 memo, recognized as the first "official" documentation of the Jeep prototype project.

Chapter 6: Project Initiation: Specific Requirements looks at how the Quartermaster Corps conducted an iterative process to turn the general requirements into specifications from which an automobile manufacturer could build a vehicle.

Chapter 7: Project Initiation: Bid documents how the Army determined the process they would use to choose a manufacturer to deliver a prototype and how the American Bantam Car Company won the award.

Chapter 8: Project Execution: Contract and Building the Prototype recounts the formalization of the agreement between the Army and the American Bantam Car Company, as well as the heroic efforts of the Butler small car manufacturer to hand build the pilot model in the incredibly short time of forty-nine days.

Chapter 9: Project Execution: Testing relates how the military put the Bantam Reconnaissance Car through a series of tests which the durable little vehicle successfully traversed, and the final acceptance of the Bantam product.

Chapter 10: The Prototype Redux presents the amazing story of Kim and Duncan Rolls who, during the first decade of the 21st century, undertook a project to recreate the pilot model.

Chapter 11: Epilogue looks at a final lesson from the story and presents evidence that might finally show how the ¼ ton truck 4 X 4 light became known as the Jeep.

Every project manager and entrepreneur hopes to make a difference. The summer of 1940 saw the bankrupt American Bantam Car Company in just that position. The lessons the story has to teach live on through the Jeep, and possibly into the future, if their experience inspires future entrepreneurs and project managers to attempt the impossible despite the odds!

Chapter 1: Company History and Leadership

Projects take place in a dynamic and ever-changing world. For every project a micro and macro environment exists, stakeholders have backgrounds and expectations, and the organization undertaking the endeavor has a history, culture and leadership that impacts success. For the firm that built the first Jeep, the history of the company, as well as the corporate culture developed through the personality of the institution's initial founder, Sir Herbert Austin, and his successor, Roy S. Evans, were critical for the eventual achievement of building the pilot model. Reviewing and examining this period, and the leadership of Austin and Evans, provides numerous lessons applicable today and demonstrates how singularly prepared this business was to undertake the seemingly impossible in the summer of 1940.

American Austin Car Company

Herbert Austin was born in England in 1866 to a farming family. He immigrated with his uncle to Australia in 1884 and his interest in mechanics and engineering led him to work at the Wolseley Sheep-Shearing Machine Company, Ltd. His talent at improving sheep hand clippers persuaded many Outback shepherds to put down their trusted tool in exchange for a mechanized version the English transplant had developed.[1] By the age of 27 Austin was the firm's manager and his success brought him to the attention of the company's directors. He was brought back to the mother country to oversee operations at the factory in Birmingham.[2]

Figure 1: Sir Herbert Austin

Austin's inquisitive mind led him to the fledgling automobile industry before the 19th century ended. By 1901 he had designed his first automobile and he continued to improve upon his designs over the next two years.[3] In 1905 Sir Herbert and the board of directors disagreed over the vision for the future of the motor car division, with the board believing that larger cars with heftier engines were the future, while Austin believed the opposite. After the two parted ways he had a change of heart and over the rest of the decade, and into the 1910s, he built a bigger car with more cylinders. On the eve of the First World War, Austin's company, the Austin Motor Car

> **Entrepreneurial Lesson 1**
> **Vision**
>
> Entrepreneurs are pioneers who put themselves out into the unknown without regard to whether or not anyone is following them. It is vision, intense and self-consuming vision that drives them out into the void. They do not follow trends. They are compelled to do what the vision drives them to do. Their visions create trends. To the entrepreneur, failure is not in the vocabulary. There are quite likely many years of struggle and seeming failures before breakthrough occurs, from sticking to the vision wherever it may take them.

Company of Birmingham, was building and shipping primarily four cylinder engines, about a thousand units a year.[4]

The war years saw Austin put his mechanical talents to use producing munitions, which resulted in knighthood. As the conflict ended Sir Herbert was ready to embrace his automotive future. His experience during the hostilities led him to conclude that mass production of one model was the wave of the future. He designed, manufactured, and marketed the Austin Twenty, which had modestly successful sales.[5]

Figure 2: 1926 Austin 7 Coupe—The Great Grandfather of the Jeep Prototype

With the British economy in the doldrums after the war, Sir Herbert decided that downsizing the vehicle was appropriate, and he marketed a new version, the Austin Twelve, which also had modest sales. The English economy of the early 1920s continued to languish and that fact, combined with labor and raw material problems, led him to think even smaller.[6] During this time the motorcycle with a sidecar became popular in England and the essence of a small vehicle which could transport a few people and baggage germinated in the mind of Sir Herbert to compete with that product. The high price of gasoline, short driving distances, and an exponential increase in passable roads, also provided fertile ground for smaller vehicles.[7]

His mechanical skills still sharp in his 50s, Austin designed a brilliant small car, the Austin Seven, which debuted in July 1922. This car, about the same size as a motorcycle with a sidecar, proved immensely popular.[8] The Austin Seven was a good fit for the English market with its high gasoline prices and the short driving distances. The Seven proved exportable to the European continent which had the same consumer dynamics. By the end of 1928 production in Germany and France had expanded the Seven's sales, but Sir Herbert had his eyes on an even bigger marketplace.[9]

The automobile industry in the United States had blossomed during the 1920s with--similar to Europe--an increase in traversable roads, but combined with two opposite dynamics than the Old World: low gasoline prices and long driving distances. Numerous manufacturers willingly produced vehicles for the motoring public and the general feeling of prosperity during the boom years following the 1921 – 1922 recession fueled rapid growth. The Ford Model T dominated the landscape, and later in the decade, the Model A would appear.[10]

General Motors and Chrysler would also grow dramatically during the decade and there were numerous niche players. With low gas prices and long driving distances large vehicles were the order of the day. In 1929 the American market did not have a small car offering and the demand for one seemed non-existent. However, all these facts did not deter the irrepressible Sir Herbert from attempting to bring the Austin Seven to the United States.[11]

January 1929 saw Sir Herbert and his bride, Lady Austin, in New York City with the intent to show off his products at the New York National Automobile Show. He intended to raise the financing and find the partners to manufacture and sell Austins in the United States under the banner of the American Austin Car Company, formed in February of that year. 1929 saw the peak of the stock market run-up on Wall Street during the 1920s, and American Austin's initial public offering sold briskly.[12]

Entrepreneurial Lesson 2
Foreign Markets

The best starting point is one's own natural market, in the backyard, so to speak. Before spreading out, it is best to learn how a product or service will do close to home. It gets complicated the farther away the market moves from its natural center. Yet there are many hugely successful worldwide businesses that do not ever reach the public's awareness.

Expanding across the globe comes with new costs: political, legal, lingual, economic, cultural, environmental, logistical, national and local within the target foreign country. Example: In Japan, advertising which depicts a setting sun is considered a deep insult to the country. The Japanese flag represents the rising sun.

Sensitivity to what is going on outside the entrepreneur's own world helps make the product or service better. Austin brought small cars from the UK to a foreign market, the USA. His successor, Roy S. Evans, coined the phrase small cars are going to be big, and went on to create the Jeep.

The search for a location for the home of the American Austin Car Company factory also proved fruitful with the selection of the small city of Butler, Pennsylvania. This city had a forward-thinking business community and a workforce with the skills to manufacture cars. Butler also possessed the additional advantage of having an idle automobile factory within its confines, the former home of the Standard Steel Car Company, which had gone bankrupt in 1923. The buildings were purchased and Arthur J. Brandt, a former General Motors executive, was chosen to direct the American Austin Car Company. The future appeared bright for a small car in the United States.[13]

At the time that Butler was ready to produce cars in 1929, the Austin models were not yet ready for American prime time. Although the vehicles' mechanical structure would resemble its European cousin, including the engine and chassis, the English styling needed Americanization. Alexis de Sakhnoffsky of the Hayes Body Company, a leading custom coachwork designer of the time, submitted a model that improved the lines of the Austin, which helped mask the smallness of the car, undoubtedly a concession to the tastes of the American consumer.[14] While the final touches to the vehicle were completed the company's infrastructure, including purchasing, marketing, production and engineering were put into place. All this effort took time, and 1929 slipped by without a single model rolling off the assembly line in Butler.[15]

1930 dawned and with it the cold winds of change. The American and world stock markets had crashed during the fall of 1929, dramatically altering the economic landscape. However, the transformed commercial conditions did not deter Sir Herbert, Brandt and the officers of the American Austin Car Company from visiting Butler on January 4th of that year to meet with city officials and inspect the factory.[16]

Three prototypes were displayed in New York City in February 1930 and dealers lined up to sign on to sell the new economy car. It would take another five months to bring production up to speed, but the assembly line began to hum in May and the first product was delivered to dealer showrooms in June.[17]

The vehicles delivered were masterpieces in small car engineering. The basic Austin specifications of a 75-inch wheelbase, 40-inch tread, 122- and 53-inch length and width, 60.5-inch coupe height, 8.75-inch ground clearance with a total weight of 1,130 pounds were maintained with American styling. The car was sixteen inches narrower and twenty-eight inches shorter than any vehicle on the American market and had an astonishing turning ratio of sixteen feet. These Austin basics would prove extremely valuable ten years later when the Army was looking for a small vehicle weighing a quarter ton. Priced at a competitive $445 f.o.b. Butler, the company appeared poised for success.[18]

Figure 3: 1931 American Austin Roadster—The Grandfather of the Jeep Prototype. Photo used with permission from Dale Lynn James.

American Austin had a product and a distribution network, but customers were another matter. With the market dynamics exactly opposite those of Europe (cheap gas and long driving distances) the leaders of the firm had to devise a compelling selling proposition for the American consumer.[19]

Their solution, which would remain consistent for the life of the company, was that the American Austin was not built to replace an individual's larger car, but to provide a cost-effective alternative for local driving. It was this vision that would attract Roy S. Evans to embrace the Austin line. The question remained, would the American buying public embrace the small car?[20]

The answer, similar to the 1970s during the initial oil crisis of the second half of the twentieth century, was a resounding no. Even though Sir Herbert announced in the summer of 1930 pre-orders of 184,117 units and 19,300 dealers applying to carry the brand, these numbers were not based upon fact.[21]

While the American Austin received extremely favorable public relations, word-of-mouth advertising, and became a household word during 1930, the bottom line was that the worsening Depression was having a major impact on the American and world economies. Auto sales for 1930 were dismal, and no matter how good the vision, advertising and public relations, the firm could not overcome economic reality. The America Austin Car Company sold only 8,558 units in 1930.[22]

It was at this juncture that the company made a fatal error, common to many automotive manufacturers in dire financial straits, when they invested their financial reserves into extending the model line of a product that was not selling. An additional coupe line was created (standard and deluxe), a business and cabriolet coupe were introduced, and the American Austin roadster was retained.[23]

This strategy proved futile in igniting demand. Along with fighting market fundamentals, such as the American public's reluctance to embrace small vehicles, the availability of cheap gas and the long driving distances, the stark fact was the American Austin Car Company had the unfortunate timing of entering the American market at the beginning of the worst economic crisis that country and world had faced to that date. While many still did not understand the magnitude of the disaster facing them in 1930 (chapter 2), there were at best, strong economic headwinds that Sir Herbert and his team were fighting in 1930 and 1931.[24]

Entrepreneurial Lesson 3
Evaluating Changes in Economic Conditions

One truth applies to all markets: They go up and down. The history of the United States is checkered with panics, depressions, recessions, ruined financial manipulators, and burst bubbles. Another truth: Easy money—isn't. Speculation triggered by the American Dream cratered in 1929 and 2008. Changes are usually swift once the point of no return has been passed. Savvy investors and entrepreneurs have to constantly and vigilantly monitor all the fundamentals and theoretical analyses that affect the world's economies, especially their own.

The entrepreneur needs to continually monitor economic and market conditions and be willing to adjust accordingly.

Sir Herbert and his team's oblivion to the changed economic landscape and alteration of their plans to fit the new reality was a fatal flaw for the American Austin Car Company.

American Austin sales tanked in 1931 to a paltry 1,279 units and as 1932 dawned liquidation of the company seemed the logical course. Reuben O. Gill was brought in to replace Brandt as President and General Manager, with his only duty being to preside over the organization's demise, including disposing of 1,500 unfinished vehicles. However, logic does not always sway a man with a vision, as well as the energy and the means to reach for that vision.[25]

American Bantam Car Company

The aforementioned Roy S. Evans was the consummate salesman. Born in 1900 at the dawn of the automotive industry, Evans grew up in the rural community of Bartow, Georgia, where he went to work at the age of eight due to the death of his father.[26] He started in newspapers, moved into shoe shines, then a peanut stand (a natural for Georgia!). In 1914 he started a taxi service where young Roy would transport passengers around Bartow in a borrowed Maxwell touring car in which he agreed to get his hands dirty maintaining and repairing the vehicle in exchange for using it. This was Evans' first brush with the automotive world.[27]

Figure 4: 1911 Maxwell Mascotte Touring Car.

The young entrepreneur graduated from high school, operated a "news butch" venture on passenger trains, and eventually became a clerk for the Central Bank of Georgia. He raced motorcycles for a short time, but they proved too dangerous. He sold his two-wheeler, and with the proceeds bought a Model T, rebuilt it and fell in love with the automobile. He became a used car salesman, and after graduating from Georgia Tech in the early 1920s, he opened a used car shop. After disastrous experiences during the Florida land bubble in the mid-1920s, Evans settled down into the car business, and with his indefatigable energy, was the largest automotive dealer in the South by 1932.[28]

With the deepening of the depression many businesses found themselves with excess inventory. While difficult times present numerous challenges, opportunity often lurks among the distressing news. Roy Evans had learned this lesson, having bounced back from the Sunshine State land speculation debacle. With money in the bank, a substantial credit line, and the network to distribute the merchandise, the Bartow entrepreneur was in perfect position to take advantage of large supply and low demand to buy in volume at low prices.[29]

Entrepreneurial Lesson 4
Niche Marketing

The early adopters of a visionary new product form its market, although the entrepreneur may not have intended to have customers and users from the market that launches it. If you are selling a product, the nature of the customer is unpredictable, but a sale is a sale is a sale. The visionary entrepreneur is not dissuaded. In fact, the early unexpected markets lead to other visions and inventions for serving them.

Evans had signed on early to sell the American Austin line and was, not surprisingly, the firm's biggest customer, accounting for eighty percent of sales. Evans noticed that when the American Austin appeared in 1930, the cars generated tremendous "buzz" among his customers. Most importantly, he truly believed in the small car concept for the American market and that the Austin was the car to fill that need. It was this belief that drove Evans to single-handedly keep the small car alive during the 1930s.[30]

The opportunistic car dealer struck a deal with Gill where he purchased the excess inventory of 1,500, had the vehicles completed, and sold the whole consignment at the bargain basement price of $295 per unit. Evans, the true believer in the small car, was willing to put his money where his belief was and agreed to assume management, as well as finance, the whole American Austin Car Company operation. Gill convinced suppliers that if the firm went under, their inventory would end up a total loss, as the components were unusable in any other vehicles. In the age old tradition of self-interest, they priced their merchandise competitively. The company had a pulse, if a faint one, and Roy Evans was all-in.[31]

Evans' resuscitation efforts appeared to pay off as sales in 1932 rebounded to 3,846 and 1933 saw a modest improvement to 4,726, truly remarkable figures given that the Great Depression bottomed out during those years. Franklin Delano Roosevelt assumed the Presidency of the United States in 1933 and his New Deal programs were in full swing as 1934 dawned and the future again appeared bright for the American Austin Car Company. However these sales levels proved unsustainable and purchases plummeted in 1934 to the point the money ran out and the firm declared bankruptcy in June. Production continued to the end of the year with 1,300 units completed. In less than two years the firm was back among the living dead.[32]

While some minor activity continued at the Butler factory maintaining the Austin market (parts and service), and the factory's excellent machine shop brought in some revenue filling odd jobs, the fact was the American Austin Car Company was once gain fated for oblivion, but fate hadn't met Roy Evans. The Bartow businessman remained committed to the vision of a small car in the driveway of every American, but was he willing to dive further into the deep end financially to keep that vision alive?[33]

The man who in 1926 had traded his last valuable possession to buy, refurbish and sell one car that was the genesis of his business empire, was willing to take a gamble and he rolled the dice. He arranged with the factory's mortgage holder to reduce the principle and interest as well as grant a two year mortgage extension, and negotiated with Butler city officials to have back taxes and interest forgiven.[34] Lastly, in the fall of 1935, the United States Federal Court accepted Evans' token payment of $5,000 on an asset valued at $10 million, and the Georgia entrepreneur had bought the factory! If Evans had gone all-in during 1932, he was now swimming in the deep end without a life jacket![35]

The Bartow entrepreneur, now working with his key lieutenant, William A. Ward Jr., went to Wall Street during 1936 to raise capital, and two brokers signed up to handle the sale of both common and preferred stock. It was during 1936 that a serendipitous association during the heyday of the early Austin models would enter history. When the initial cars appeared on the American market the term Bantam had become associated with the new vehicles, probably a reference to the miniature chickens of the same name, as the public viewed the cars as "miniatures."[36] The name stuck even though there was never an Austin Bantam. Evans, ever the pragmatist, decided to make lemonade out of lemons, and when he registered the new firm on June 2, 1936 he named it the American Bantam Car Company.[37]

Evans, installed as president and chairman of the board, went about creating an entirely new team to manufacture cars in Butler. Numerous individuals came and went, but one whom fate would slot for immortality was Harold Crist, plant manager and chief engineer. Crist was not averse to getting his hands dirty, which would prove beneficial during the hectic days building the Jeep prototype.[38]

However, before Crist would answer destiny's call, American Bantam had to sell cars as soon as possible. The enterprising Evans reached into his network of contacts, which once again brought Alexis de Sakhnoffsky, the preeminent coachwork designer who had created the original "American" look for the American Austin Car Company, back to Butler. De Sakhnoffsky created new designs in just three days and charged Evans just $300.00 to cover his expenses. With de Sakhnoffksy's designs relying completely on the original American Austin features, the Bantam team was able to retool to build the new models for a paltry $7,000. Evans and his team were making up the playbook during the game, and to say they were operating on a shoestring would insult the shoestring.[39]

Figure 5: 1939 American Bantam Roadster—The Father of the Jeep Prototype. Photo used with permission from Dale Lynn James.

While the Bantam team was frantically attempting to bring the factory on-line, bad news struck during the summer of 1937, when Evans found out that the two Wall Street brokers had swindled him by selling off the common stock assigned to them and absconding with their ill-gotten gains. With the company once again on the brink, Evans thought outside the box, and turned to the government for help.[40] He sent his trusted aide, Ward, to Washington, D.C. and secured a $250,000 loan from the Reconstruction Finance Corporation (RFC) with a lien against the factory to keep the lights on. The RFC was a major new development in the macroeconomic environment during the 1930s.[41]

The old adage states that, "necessity is the mother of invention" and necessity dictated that the American Bantam Car Company find every way to save money. This led Evans to the fateful decision of eliminating the use of exclusive parts, and building his vehicles from as many standard items as possible. It was this use of off-the-shelf parts that proved a critical skill when the Bantam team attempted to build the Jeep pilot model in 1940. Standardization would also rank as a major concern for the United States Army when they needed a new vehicle in the summer of 1940 (chapter 3).[42]

All the effort paid off in the fall of 1937 when the first American Bantam models entered the market. Production was ramped up, and by early 1938, the factory was functioning again. The Bantam, thanks to Harold Crist and his team, was a state-of-the-art small car, and the little company in Butler,

Pennsylvania was the unlikely, and singular depository of expertise on economy cars in the United States.[43]

Initial orders appeared strong, and there was discussion about entering foreign markets. The individuals who purchased Bantams, similar to their predecessors with the American Austin, raved about the vehicles; however, sales remained anemic in 1938 at a paltry 2,000 cars.[44]

Similar to the American Austin Car Company, the American Bantam firm was the victim of another case of bad timing. While the demand for small cars by the American buying public remained lukewarm at best, it did not help that the first Bantam models appeared during the recession of the late 1930s. As the Roosevelt Administration slowed government spending in 1937 to ostensibly balance the Federal government budget (chapter 2) the private sector United States economy had not grown enough during the middle 1930s to absorb the reduction in government spending. The ensuing recession would make Bantam's already dim prospects of success virtually impossible. However that would not stop Roy Evans from continuing to try.[45]

Figure 6: 1940 American Bantam Hollywood Convertible Developed by Alex Tremulis. Used with permission from Conceptcarz.com.

The story of how the Bantam Hollywood convertible model came to being in 1939 perfectly illustrates the innovative culture instilled by the personality of Roy Evans into the American Bantam Car Company that would prove so pivotal a year later. The Georgia businessman, among his many talents, was a pilot, having learned to fly in the 1920s. He used this skill to keep abreast of his far flung dealership network which included outlets in Los Angeles. On a visit in the last year of the 1930s he went to see one Alex Tremulis, a custom body expert operating out of Beverly Hills, to have side curtains installed on his Bantam Roadster. While Evans wanted curtains, the Californian had other ideas.[46]

When Evans saw Tremulis and asked for his curtains the enterprising body man countered by proposing a "Bantam Convertible" and he could make one by being supplied with a coupe from which he would shear off the roof! Evans' go-getter, can-do personality couldn't resist the challenge, and he had one delivered in an hour. The innovator spent just one night designing the convertible, and when he presented the plans the next day to Evans, the Chairman of the Board of the American Bantam Car Company approved them on the spot. Tremulis told Evans he could build the car in ten days. He immediately returned to his shop and cut off the roof of Evans' coupe. Later that afternoon Evans visited and was going to back out of the deal, but when he saw that his vehicle had no roof he rolled with the punches and changed his mind. Tremulis built the vehicle in ten days and delivered it to

Butler shortly thereafter.[47]

Evans ordered the new convertible into production. Harold Crist and others worked diligently during 1938 and 1939 to improve every aspect of the Bantam's line engineering. The firm had excellent, high quality products, which were state-of-the-art for small cars at the time, but nobody wanted them. Sales for 1939 were a meager 1,225 units, and while further aesthetic and mechanical improvements were made to the 1940 line, sales continued to plummet to only 800 units for 1940. By June of that year the firm was once again bankrupt. All seemed lost until Roy Evans decided to roll the dice one last time.[48]

During 1938 and 1939, while American Bantam focused primarily on the commercial market, they did begin to mine another consumer that the American Austin Car Company had only cursorily explored. American Austin had supplied some vehicles to the United States Army in 1932, but this initial effort was not followed up by either Austin, due to their bankruptcy, or the Army because of dire budget constraints caused by the Depression. In addition, since war was not imminent, there was no urgency to develop products for them.

However, as stated earlier, projects take place in a dynamic, ever changing world. Before examining the project that led to the creation of the first Jeep, a review of the macro environment, i.e. the economic malaise known as the Great Depression, and the United States' and world's response to it, along with an analysis of the state of the Jeep prototype's primary stakeholder, the United States Army, provides the backdrop to the events that unfolded during 1940.

Figure 7: Roy S. Evans (third from right and inserts) and the Bantam Team circa 1939. Sources (main): George Edward Domer, *Automotive Quarterly,* Fall 1976; (inserts): John W. Underwood, Heritage Press, 1965

Questions for Educators

Discuss the impact of a company's history on projects.

Evaluate the effect of different leadership styles on projects.

Examine how corporate culture impacts projects.

Discuss some of the pros and cons of Sir Herbert Austin's leadership style, or Evans' leadership methods.

Paul R. Bruno

Chapter 2: The Environment: The Depression and Early WWII

The environment that a project exits in, both macro and micro, impacts the effort from initiation to close. This can include at the macro level economic and political concerns to the fiscal health, organizational culture, and leadership of the organization undertaking the endeavor at the micro level. Understanding these issues, and managing their influence on the venture, represents a major challenge for the project manager and the project team.

> **Entrepreneurial Lesson 5**
> **Public Policy**
>
> Entrepreneurs may live in the clouds, but have their feet firmly on the ground. They must adapt to real world constraints, in order to achieve results. One impediment to the early development of the automobile was the virtually unusable old horse and buggy routes. This kept sales low. With the development of paved roads, sales increased manifold. In this way, the automotive visionaries, like Austin, adapted to real-world exigencies.

Numerous generations have believed that their time embodies a period of rapid change. Many denizens of the early 21st century suppose that unprecedented technological progress through information technology coupled with global economic and political instability ranks this period as one of the most unstable in history. However, citizens of prior epochs, the French Revolution, the United States Civil War, World War I or World War II, might also justly claim their world was turned upside down by unprecedented upheaval that ushered in a new era.

The Great Depression in the United States, the period in which both the American Austin and The American Bantam Car Company's operated, can lay claim to being a period of change on a massive scale. The first tepid responses of the Hoover Administration, followed by the more far-reaching actions enacted under Franklin Roosevelt's New Deal, saw legislation passed at breakneck speed that fundamentally altered the relationship between business and the United States Federal Government.

While the innovative, risk-taking culture of the American Bantam Car Company was primarily a product of the personality of Roy Evans and his team, the macro environment of massive change that the Butler company had to contend with during the decade also impacted the firm's operating style. The firm's remarkable manufacturing agility was also influenced by employing some of the most pioneering individuals working in the auto industry. Moreover, they built small cars for a market tepid to their products, which contributed to an innovative company environment. It forced them to react and adapt quickly to a constantly changing economic and political environment.

Sir Herbert Austin picked what appeared as the opportune year of 1929 to launch his initiative to sell an American version of the Austin 7. The prior decade had ostensibly seen, after a brief recession in the early 1920s, the greatest prosperity the United States and the world had known up to that time. The period was known as the New Economic Era, and similar to the 1990s, exhortations that the business cycle was conquered, and never-ending growth was the wave of the future, permeated the writings of the times.[49] Herbert Hoover had won election as President of the United States on the slogan, "A Chicken in Every Pot and Two Cars in Every Garage" and the English automaker was determined to make that second vehicle one of his small cars.[50]

Figure 8: Crowds Gather Outside Wall Street on October 29, 1929.

Entrepreneurial Lesson 6
Smoot-Hawley Tariff Act

Like with medicines, there are unintended side effects to the enactment of laws that affect the economies of companies and countries. Frequently the entrepreneur encounters any number of legal encumbrances. Although meant to prevent monopolies in the United States, restrictions of trade still hurt small entities, like farms, and storekeepers. When the laws are enacted, sometimes things get worse before they get better, as the lawmakers hoped would happen. Sometimes things never do get better.

The Great Depression of 1929 and the Great Recession of 2008 show the terrible consequences of head in the sand policies. The entrepreneur has to weather a lot of rocky seas to keep afloat as laws keep changing the rules of economic survival.

The New Economic Era lasted for a much shorter period of time than advertised and ended when the world and United States stock markets crashed in late 1929. The most precipitous day during this calamity was October 29, 1929 also known as "Black Tuesday." As described in chapter 1 Sir Herbert chose to ignore this major economic event and proceeded full-steam ahead with the launching of the American Austin in 1930. He may have believed, as did some other learned individuals of the time, that the dislocation was temporary and prosperity's return was just around the corner. However, business people of all stripes had to take notice of a game-changing piece of United States legislation passed in 1930 that altered the relationship of international trade, the Smoot-Hawley Tariff Act.[51]

Figure 9: Willis C. Hawley (left) and Reed Smoot, April 1929, shortly before the Tariff Act passed in the U.S. House.

Tariffs represent an economic policy used to artificially inflate the price of foreign goods by taxing them at the point of entry into a country to make them less attractive to domestic consumers and to, at least in theory, boost the sale of domestically made products. However, America's unilateral tariff increases led to retaliatory actions by other nations with a resulting large decrease in the overall volume of world trade by 1932. While the Butler car company was marketing its vehicles exclusively for the American market, the closing of possible foreign markets for their product, and the fact that the firm was operating in an environment of contracting economic activity, both domestically and internationally, did not bode well for the Pennsylvania auto manufacturer.[52]

Figure 10: An Unemployed Man Selling Apples at the Height of the Great Depression.

The auto industry was hit hard at the onset of the Depression. The Hoover Administration, contrary to conventional wisdom, did try a variety of measures to turn the economy around. These included an increase in spending for public works, assistance to the banking sector, and relief for the unemployed. However, the measures were far too limited to meet the emergency at hand. His effort at voluntary cooperation within the banking community, The National Credit Corporation, failed, and the Republican President set up the Reconstruction Finance Corporation (RFC) to replace it.[53]

The RFC provided $2 billion in aid to state and local governments, and made loans to businesses, including railroads, banks, and mortgage associations. This agency played a large role in the 1930s, and was the entity Roy Evans turned to when the American Bantam Car Company had difficulty raising capital in 1937. This intervention in the banking sector would foreshadow larger actions taken to regulate the financial industry later in the decade. Despite Hoover's actions and exhortations to have confidence in the economy, the Depression deepened throughout his term, bottoming out in the winter of 1932, taking the American Austin Car Company down with it.[54]

Figure 11: A "Bank Run" on a United States Bank Circa 1933.

Franklin Roosevelt promised Federal Government action to combat the calamity during his 1932 election campaign and upon taking office he inaugurated a series of sweeping reforms during 1933 and 1934, known by historians as the first New Deal. The first area addressed was the American banking system, which had deteriorated to the brink of collapse during the waning days of the Hoover Administration. The European banking system had failed in 1931 and England had gone off the gold standard that same year. Upon his inauguration on March 4, 1933, declaring "the only thing we have to fear is fear itself" Roosevelt initiated a five day bank holiday that closed all banks in the United States.[55]

Working with the newly elected Democratic Congressional majority, the Emergency Banking Relief Act of 1933 was passed in one day, March 9, 1933. This act was a stopgap measure that prevented a massive financial breakdown until the passage of the Banking Act of 1933, also known as the Glass-Steagall Act, in June. The latter legislation, among other stipulations, created the Federal Deposit Insurance Corporation and placed regulations on "speculation." In addition, Roosevelt also took the United States off the gold standard in June 1933. The President's first actions were considered conservative in nature because they did not nationalize the banking system. However, later initiatives would result in substantial change.[56]

The Administration's first foray into radical action to combat the Depression occurred in the agricultural arena, which FDR considered the root cause of the economic malaise. Reflecting a Jeffersonian belief in the integral nature of the "yeoman farmer" in American life, Congress, at Roosevelt's behest, passed the Agriculture Adjustment Act of 1933. This legislation had the expressed intent of propping up domestic farm prices, which had deflated drastically since the early 1920s.[57]

This was accomplished by paying farmers subsidies to leave fields fallow and by the killing of livestock. The act was successful in some respects; however, criticism of killing healthy animals (including six million piglets), as well as not growing food in the face of massive hunger in the nation, hampered the law's effectiveness. Whatever the merits of the bill, which was declared unconstitutional in 1936, this legislation signaled a new era of Federal intervention in the economic activity of the United States.[58]

Figure 12: The Dust Bowl Devastated U.S. Agriculture during the 1930s.

Roosevelt was determined to alter the fundamental relationship between the farmer and the land, as well as implement the delivery of electric power to rural areas. These desires led to the passage of the Tennessee Valley Authority (TVA) Act in May 1933. The law authorized a massive expansion of Federal intervention in the region for the purposes of economic development, including navigation, flood control, electricity generation, and fertilizer manufacturing. The use of Federal experts to assist small rural farmers in implementing more modern farming techniques, especially in land utilization, and providing for electric power through massive dam building, constituted the centerpieces of this effort.[59]

Entrepreneurial Lesson 7
Tennessee Valley Authority Act

We, the people of the USA, own via the federal government a bunch of corporations, like the TVA. What is more bewildering, however, is why we do not own all the other truly public ones, as well.

TVA was so successful at providing its key services that it felt like encroachment to the private corporations which competed to monopolize communities' power needs in the TVA region. What is more public than electrical power? Why should private enterprises own such things as water, gas, and natural rights-resources to generate electricity? They belong to all of us.

Taxes should go to what are truly public—power, water, telephone, infrastructure, internet, and other utilities that all people everywhere are entitled to have. Most of the medical industry is owned by Medicare. Usually it is the payer of last resort to doctors, pharmacies, hospitals and clinics. No question, nothing is wrong with private enterprise. Seems like the public owns what private enterprise should own and vice versa.

The TVA was an extremely ambitious project and, in the overall legacy of the New Deal, one of the more successful. The dams built provided much needed employment and reduced the number of catastrophic floods. The implementation of modern farming techniques drastically improved the agricultural sector in the region. The generation of electricity was so successful, and perceived as such a threat by private-sector electrical generators of the period, that they successfully blocked any further expansion of electricity generation based upon the law's model. The TVA met its objective to improve the living standards in one of the most impoverished areas in the southern United States, and continues to play a role in the region in the 21st century.[60]

A number of individuals in the Roosevelt Administration had experience with The War Industries Board, which was established in July, 1917 to coordinate the purchase of war materials during World War I. Many in the new government believed it had worked well, and was the model upon which to build the new relationship between business and the Federal Government. The New Dealers believed the laissez-faire capitalist system of the New Era had failed the American people, and drastic changes were needed. Their belief and the willingness of millions of citizens to go along with this realignment, led to the National Industrial Recovery Act (NIRA) passed in June 1933.[61]

Figure 13: Wilson Dam Was the First Dam Placed under TVA authority.

This act was a dramatic intervention into the economic life of the United States. The legislation authorized the President to regulate industry and permitted cartels and monopolies (effectively limiting competition and its deflationary effects) in order to encourage an economic rebound. The key to this limiting of competition and the creation of greater cooperation (similar to what

Figure 14: Blue Eagle NRA Poster Supporting the NIRA.

happened under the War Industries Board) was the implementation of "codes" among competitors in the same industry.[62]

The NIRA act also authorized the first large-scale use of a coordinated public works program to engender economic growth under the Public Works Administration. The idea of public works to "prime the pump" of economic expansion would see a massive increase under the Works Progress Act of 1935. The bill included a section, entitled Section 7(a), which impacted collective bargaining rights, and would be the forerunner of a much more comprehensive bill, the Wagner Act of 1935, which ushered in a massive wave of industrial unionism later in the decade.[63]

The implementation of the act from 1933 – 1935 saw the adoption of innumerable industry codes, the prohibition of thousands of business practices, and the issuance of thousands of administrative orders. These edicts, along with innumerable opinions and guides issued at the federal, state and local level, was, in essence, an infusion of massive bureaucracy into the American economy. The backlash was phenomenal and the Act was eventually, like the Agricultural Adjustment Act, declared unconstitutional in 1935. However, the precedent of massive Federal intervention into the United States economy was established.[64]

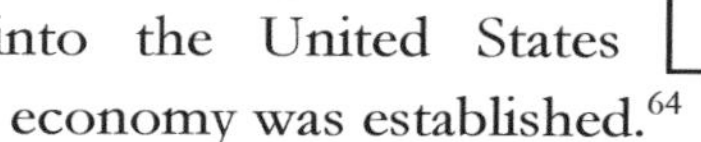

Entrepreneurial Lesson 8
Securities Exchange Act

The big ticket for entrepreneurs is to grant stock options to the best performers at an enterprise. Usually this helps retain key employees, who are entrusted with spreading the entrepreneur's vision around the world. As long as there is profitability, the options will increase in value over the long haul. Employees are known to switch companies just for an improved chance of becoming rich off the new company's stock options.

The Securities Exchange Act prohibits insider trading, but the inside people most in position to profit from a growing company are the high performing employees. To keep them from being runaways, entrepreneurs have been known to pre-date and post-date options in order to maximize an employee's loyalties. The Act is intended to prevent this kind of white collar crime.

The real way around fraud is the straight and narrow path—manage the company to consistently grow in real terms. Then no fixing of the books is needed to make the employees stick around long enough to become rich.

The final major piece of legislation passed during the "First New Deal" was the Securities Exchange Act (SEA) of 1934, a response to the overwhelming opinion in the United States that greedy Wall Street brokers and manipulators were the primary cause of the Depression. This comprehensive legislation, and related statutes, provided significant regulation to the financial markets for the first time.[65]

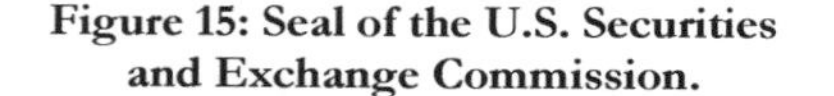

Figure 15: Seal of the U.S. Securities and Exchange Commission.

While the Glass-Steagall Act focused on the original issuance of securities, this law sought to regulate the secondary market for securities. These transactions between individuals, usually not related to the primary issuer, were often accomplished by brokers or dealers, the very individuals vilified by the public. The Securities and Exchange Commission was created to enforce securities law in the United States. As we saw with Roy Evans' unfortunate incident with Wall Street during 1936 and 1937, the law did not prevent all malfeasance in financial dealings.[66]

Figure 16: President Franklin Roosevelt Signing the Social Security Act of 1935.

The period during the hibernation between the collapse of the American Austin Car Company and the creation of the American Bantam Car Company in 1936, saw unprecedented and sweeping change in the American economy. However, despite this massive legislative juggernaut, the American public was not seeing enough results and was moving even further to the left of the American political spectrum in demanding an even greater Federal government response to the Depression. With his reelection campaign of 1936 fast approaching, Franklin Roosevelt was more than willing to accommodate these feelings and portray his candidacy as a choice between the "forgotten man," versus the greedy capitalists of Wall Street and business, and spawned the "Second New Deal."[67]

Social Security insurance was first adopted in Europe in the late nineteenth century, but the United States hesitated to implement this type of program. The stock market crash, however, and the subsequent Depression wiped out the retirement savings of millions of Americans. Then ubiquitous unemployment coupled with the swing of the American electorate to the political left made the ground fertile to enact a Social Security law. It was passed on August 14, 1935.[68]

Under the provisions of the legislation, for the first time the United States Federal government sought to assist the elderly. The purposes of the Act were to alleviate the deprivations of old age, poverty and unemployment, and a payroll tax was instituted to pay for the "trust fund." While the debate on the merits and flaws of the program, now almost eighty years old, still rage on today, the Act undoubtedly altered the relationship of the American worker, business people, and the elderly to the national government.[69]

Entrepreneurial Lesson 9
Works Progress Administration

The largest enterprise in the world is the United States government. It is virtually impossible to avoid doing business with the government. It employs the most people, owns the most real estate, spends the most money. One way entrepreneurs can take advantage of government spending is by attracting research grants in their fields. Whether it is wise to do so needs to be weighed against the government's power to control the innovations that are the result of the grants. Another interaction is selling to the government, making the United States a principal or sole customer. Whole industries arise and fall with the stroke of a government pen. Buyer and seller beware.

Two of the greater economic changes that occurred during the second New Deal were the massive public spending of the Works Progress Administration (WPA) and the rise of industrial unionism germinated by section 7(a) of the NIRA and its more important successor, the National Labor Relations Act (NLRA) of 1935. The WPA succeeded the Public Works Administration, and was authorized by the Emergency Relief Appropriations Act of 1935. The initial budget of $1.4 billion represented almost 6.7 percent of United States Gross Domestic Product in 1935, and the agency would eventually spend $13.4 billion, before being disbanded in 1943.[70]

Figure 17: Typical Works Progress Administration Sign.

The initial impact of the WPA on economic activity was positive. The massive infusion of Federal spending created employment through the building of roads and numerous public buildings around the country, including schools, theatres, and recreation centers. The WPA, in an unprecedented way, supported projects in the arts, drama, media and literacy. At its peak WPA spending provided employment for three million people. As with many New Deal programs, there were problems in implementation and administration; however, the WPA left a lasting physical legacy in the United States.[71]

The greatest change to business in the United States during the second half of the 1930s was the rise of industrial unionism, which occurred with unusual rapidity during late 1936 and early 1937, but the seeds of that flowering were sown for many decades prior to the Depression. Unionism in America can trace its ancestry at least to the 1840s and the mill girls in the textile city of Lowell, Massachusetts, who formed the first female labor union in the United States under Sarah Bagley. These pioneering efforts were far ahead of their time, and the union movement did not take hold in this country until after the Civil War ended in 1865, the foremost of which was craft unionism as represented by the American Federation of Labor (AFL). This form of worker representation would hold sway in the North American giant's labor movement until the 1930s.

Figure 18: Seal of the NLRB Created to Enforce Provisions of the NLRA.

The twin challenges of prosperity in the 1920s, and Depression in the 1930s, had seriously eroded union ranks by 1935, but the first ray of light for the proletariat was encapsulated in Section 7(a) of the NIRA. This section guaranteed the rights of employees to form unions and banned the "yellow dog contract" (an agreement between the employer and employee that the employee will not join a labor union as a condition of employment)[72] and specifically stated:

Entrepreneurial Lesson 10
National Labor Relations Act

The first principle of martial arts is to avoid combat of any kind. An entrepreneur has to have a similar attitude toward the employees who realized the founding vision. Avoid conflict. Pay generously and create big incentives. Treat all people with equanimity and kindness. The best way to avoid labor union strife is to never give employees the urge to organize. Impossible? Many high technology companies have operated without trade unionism becoming necessary to aid the fair treatment of employees.

...employees shall have the right to organize and bargain collectively through representatives of their own choosing, and shall be free from the interference restraint, or coercion of employers of labor, or their agents, in the designation of such representatives or in self-organization or in other concerted activities for the purpose of collective bargaining or other mutual aid or protection; [and] (2) that no employee and no one seeking employment shall be required as a condition of employment to join any company union or to refrain from joining, organizing, or assisting a labor organization of his own choosing ...[73]

However, employers can find clever ways to work around a law and in the case of section 7(a) the formation of "company unions," basically an organization controlled by the firm, along with time-honored intimidation tactics such as bullying and firing of "union agitators" impeded progress. These actions, combined with internal squabbling within the movement itself, slowed growth in membership between 1933 and 1936. The NLRA, also known as the Wagner Act, after its chief sponsor, Senator Robert Wagner, was passed on July 5, 1935. This bill corrected the flaws in section 7(a) and provided a more level playing field for unions.[74]

The Wagner Act limited the retaliatory actions employers could take against individuals who engaged in union activity, including forming a union, collective bargaining and striking. The law altered the relationship between employer and employee by protecting workers who engaged in unionism. The law defined employees as a class unto themselves, instead of the individual's relationship with the employer, which effectively allowed employees to organize as their own entity, i.e. a union. The legislation also stipulated that only one bargaining unit could represent a group of employees, promoted collective bargaining, and held employers to a duty to bargain with the duly selected representatives of the employees.[75]

Figure 19: Workers In February 1936 Celebrate Their Victory in the Good Year Tire & Rubber Company. Used with Permission from Akron Beacon Journal

The NLRA also invoked bans upon a number of unfair labor practices enacted by employers. They made it illegal to interfere with efforts to unionize and participate in union activities; to intimidate and discriminate against employees

Entrepreneurial Lesson 11
The New Deal

Although a shaky, flimsy old house of cards in need of colossal repairs, the New Deal is still ongoing. Conservatives have groused for eighty years about oversized government, while liberals are fighting hard to keep the New Deal programs alive. If the New Deal is so awful, why have no Republican presidents done anything to change its programs, reduce them, moderate them or make them less gangly and awful?

The possible answer lies in the reliance all citizens of the United States have for it to stay alive. From arch and staunch conservatives to undocumented immigrants, big government is the nation's and most of the world's largest benefactor. New Deal programs were established to bail the United States out of the Great Depression. Conservative, liberal or immigrant, big government was there to buy its way out of the cratered economy.

Who would not want to lose their Social Security benefits, which is their own money? Who does not want insured bank deposits, which is their own money? All of this seems to be humans doing the worrying that they fear the government is failing to do. Although it could be said that the government of the United States is too big to fail, many of the New Deal initiatives are still in place. Today industries are dominated by their unions; for example, the movie business, and major sports. In 2008, Chrysler, the owner of the Jeep, was bailed out by way of a New Deal method—government in business with business.

The upshot is that while the New Deal did not prevent the Great Recession of 2007-2008, its premises kept the United States an ongoing concern. As of this writing, the stock markets are at all-time highs. This all seems to point to the strengths of the New Deal, not its weaknesses.

who were involved in labor organization; to punish workers who filed charges or testified against an employer in court; and to refuse to bargain collectively with employees' representatives. The National Labor Relations Board (NLRB) was created to oversee organizing activities and enforce the other provisions of the law.[76]

By late 1935 the seeds sown by the Wagner Act saw germination when work disruptions began in the rubber industry on November 5, 1935. The United Rubber Workers engaged in a sit-down strike at the Goodyear Tire and Rubber Company over an attempted reduction in wages. This action was quickly resolved when the Ohio manufacturer softened its demands, but tensions remained high during the Christmas season, and would explode once again early in 1936.[77]

The Akron tire manufacturer again instituted a wage reduction in late January 1936, and when layoffs were announced shortly thereafter, another sit-down strike commenced on February 14th. The workers used the occupation of the plants, and long picket lines, to eliminate the use of "scabs," or replacement workers, a long-standing tactic of employers to break strikes. Management responded with firing notices and the labor action quickly escalated.[78]

Tensions mounted on both sides during February and March, violence was narrowly averted, and the strike was settled on March 21, 1936. While neither side was able to bargain for all it wanted, the agreement was a huge victory for the union, as they had forced the company to deal with them. With this catalyst in place the United Auto Workers gained ground in the auto industry (though not without difficulty) and in the steel industry, with less difficulty. The relationship between industrial worker and the employer was altered forever.[79]

Franklin Roosevelt won reelection in 1936 in the greatest Electoral College victory in American history, 508 – 6, over Republican Alf Landon. The President, emboldened by his victory, and the increase in the Democratic majorities in both houses of Congress, immediately made the biggest mistake of his political career, when he attempted to alter the makeup of the United States Supreme Court, known as the "court packing plan." The Chief Executive viewed the justices as an impediment to his programs, as the Court had struck down a number of New Deal laws.[80]

The public and political backlash from what was seen by many as an unconstitutional power grab would effectively limit Roosevelt's legislative effectiveness during his second term. While there were amendments to existing laws, as well as activity in many of the newly created New Deal agencies during the latter part of the 1930s, the only major domestic legislation passed during Roosevelt's second term was the Fair Labor Standards Act of 1938. This law established the minimum wage, guaranteed time and a half for overtime in certain occupations and outlawed most forms of child labor.[81]

When the economy entered a second slump in 1937 – 1938, due to pared back federal spending, the institution of the Social Security payroll tax and other factors, the energy of the New Deal dissipated. With the rise of Adolf Hitler in Europe, German annexation of the Rhineland in 1936, Austria in 1938 and all of Czechoslovakia in 1939, along with the Japanese invasion of China in 1937 destabilizing the Pacific region, the threat of world war grew exponentially as the decade waned, and the time for focusing on domestic issues drew to a close.

Figure 20: Adolf Hitler announcing the annexation of Austria in Vienna on March 15, 1938. Attribution: Bundesarchiv, Bild 183-1987-0922-500 / CC-BY-SA

With the rise in international tensions during his second term (chapter 3) Roosevelt increasingly turned his attention to preparing the United States for war. It was an increase in military spending that would eventually lead to a rendezvous with destiny for a tiny automaker building small cars in a non-descript city in Western, Pennsylvania.

Questions for Educators

How does the macroeconomic environment influence projects?

Discuss the impact of changing regulations on projects.

In what ways does government regulation / action create projects?

How does government regulation / action impact an ongoing project?

How can a project manager "plan" for government regulation / action?

Chapter 3: The Stakeholder: The United States Army

The review of leadership and corporate culture, as well as the macroeconomic and political environment, constitutes two fundamental areas a project manager must understand to bring an endeavor to a successful completion. A third critical component that requires attention at an endeavor's onset relates to understanding the needs of the stakeholders, and in particular, key stakeholders. The Project Management Body of Knowledge (PMBOK), published by the Project Management Institute, defines project stakeholders as: "an individual, group, or organization who may affect, be affected by, or perceive itself to be affected by a decision, activity, or outcome of a project."[82]

Entrepreneurial Lesson 12
Value of Understanding Foreign Affairs in a Global Economy

Like water markets expand to fill whatever space to which they have access. A player in the global economy builds dams and flood-control reservoirs. By understanding the foreign culture, one learns when to release the flow and when to cut it back. Since the earthquake and tsunami, Japan has re-examined its nuclear power industry, thus affecting foreign enterprises that service them.

Technology enables enterprises to have a virtual global presence. Fundamentals influence how one blends virtual with real structures in foreign countries. How do the overseas employees live? Is the country chosen for its climate? Its natural resources? Low wages? Is it a likely outsourcing gambit? Is it peaceful?

These fundamentals are always influenced, regulated or controlled by politics. National and personal interests might snag the entrepreneur in constantly changing plans and rules, and even inspire thoughts to abandon territories that do not work out. Foreign countries are prone to nationalize large businesses right out from underneath the visiting enterprises that built them. Be aware. Understand the foreign culture.

Within a project some stakeholders are referred to as "active" or "key" stakeholders that can possess decision making authority during execution of the project."[83] While there were numerous stakeholders vis-à-vis the Jeep prototype project, the "big kid on the block" was the United States Army. The woeful domestic economy, and rapid changes in internal affairs in the United States during the 1930s, played a role in the readiness of the Army for war. However, the precipitating events that provided the impetus for the military to modernize and initiate a project to develop a vehicle to move troops and small payloads to replace the cart and mule was the need to respond to international events.

This chapter comprises an overview of the international situation during the interwar period, in particular the 1930s, as well as a stakeholder analysis of the United States army. Cognizance of international affairs may appear unnecessary to many project managers; however, reviewing the events of nations can directly impact many projects, especially in today's global economy.

In addition, knowledge of how the key stakeholder, the United States Army, was so woefully unprepared for mechanized warfare in 1940 holds cautionary lessons for today.

The nations of Europe blundered their way into a cataclysmic war in the summer of 1914. The aging leaders of these states, operating from a 19th century mindset, thought a short war was in the offing. "It will be over by Christmas" was one mantra, but instead, they were embroiled in a conflagration of unprecedented proportions, due to new technology meeting outdated strategy and tactics. By the time of the signing of the armistice in November 1918, the war had claimed twenty-five million casualties and billions of dollars. This tremendous price in blood and treasure left many with a firm desire to avoid another global war at all costs.[84]

Figure 21: British Troops in World War I Trench—Battle of the Somme, 1916.

The United States had initially profited greatly from the European conflict by selling armaments to the Allies. America, since the founding of the Republic, had studiously avoided being embroiled in foreign conflict, following a policy of isolation from Europe set down by George Washington in his farewell address in 1796. When Woodrow Wilson brought the country into the war, he did so based on lofty progressive ideals encapsulated in the phrase, "the war to end all wars." When the fighting ended, and the American public counted their sacrifice, a large segment of the citizenry didn't believe United States involvement was worth the cost. In addition, to add insult to injury, many in America believed the European countries assisted did not appreciate their efforts. This reenergized the isolationism movement in the United States, which would play a critical role in the readiness of the United States Army in 1940.[85]

Figure 22: President George Washington.

When the major belligerent powers met in Versailles, France in 1919 to draw up a peace treaty, the aims and goals of the victors were not in alignment. France, the country which had suffered the most during the war, desired to punish and blame Germany for the conflict, exact as much payment from their defeated foe as possible, weaken their former combatant both economically and militarily, and restore their premier position on the continent. Britain wanted to restore the "balance of power" that, at least in the minds of English leaders, existed prior to 1914, and protect their empire. Wilson's aims were more idealistic, as postulated in his famous "Fourteen Points" speech delivered to Congress on January 8, 1918. What resulted was a compromise that satisfied no one. It did not leave Germany in a long-term weakened state. Moreover, the "unfairness" of the treaty would become the cause de jure in Germany that essentially fertilized the ground for the Nazi Party's rise to power in the early 1930s. French General Ferdinand Foch postulated after the signing that, "This is not a peace. It is an armistice for twenty years." His prophetic words were off by only a few months.[86]

While Wilson worked to resolve the immediate issues at the conference, his major aim was loftier, and that was the establishment of a League of Nations based upon the last element of the Fourteen Points:

> A general association of nations must be formed under specific covenants for the purpose of affording mutual guarantees of political independence and territorial integrity to great and small states alike.[87]

Figure 23: Signing of the Treaty of Versailles, June 28, 1919.

Wilson was awarded the Nobel Peace Prize in 1919 for his work to create this institution; however, his tireless efforts during the summer of 1919 to have the treaty confirmed by the United States Senate ended when he suffered a debilitating stroke. That left him unable to support the accord's ratification effort and the pact met an ignominious defeat in the United States Congress' upper house in 1920, reflecting the first waves of a reinvigorated isolationism. America never joined the League of Nations, seriously hampering that organization's effectiveness.[88]

Entrepreneurial Lesson 13
Conflict Resolution

When there is unresolved conflict, war is the uncompromising answer. More people have died in war in the name of God than have been saved by their religions. Conflict resolution comes from balanced compromise with all sides honoring each other's independence. Negotiators must prevent conflict resolution from breaking down into further conflict, because war is the dumbest thing that humans do. On the other hand, equitable compromise and cooperation are the toughest things for us to achieve.

"There's your side. There's my side. And then—there's the truth."

World War I significantly changed the economic dynamic in world trade. Throughout the 19th century a hegemonic Great Britain, bolstered by its early industrialization, large overseas Empire, and lack of another country threatening its status, acted as the stabilizing force in the global economy. However, the costs of World War I seriously damaged Britain's economy. The United States, in contrast, by sitting out most of the war, and profiting from it, was suddenly placed in the position of a major world economic power. However, the American public, and many of its leaders, were not ready to embrace that role. When Warren Harding was elected to the Presidency in 1920 on the slogan, "a return to normalcy," the cementing of a policy of trying to "turn back the clock" in both domestic and foreign policy was firmly entrenched.[89]

Figure 24: Signatories to the Kellogg-Briand Pact at the United States White House.

The United States had a history of maintaining a weak military other than in times of conflict. The nation followed this course once again after World War I, rapidly demobilizing after the conflict. This tradition, along with two major threads which weaved their way throughout the 1920s, one domestically, one internationally, eroded the level of preparedness of the United States military, even before the devastating years of the 1930s. The first thread was three successive Republican Administrations which believed in very limited Federal spending. President Calvin "Silent Cal" Coolidge epitomized this thinking and pursued a minimalist interventionist government policy. He encapsulated his understanding of the nation's destiny as, "the chief business of the American people is business."[90]

The second thread was the emergence of a strong desire for "peace" among the nations of the world. While this was a lofty goal, it was primarily the result of the fact that during the 1920s there did not exist a powerful nation which threatened to, much less start, a major conflict. This "peace movement" saw its expression in a number of treaties including the Washington Naval Treaty of 1922, which limited the number of capital ships of the signatories; the Locarno Treaty signed in 1926, which attempted to secure the post-war territorial arrangements, as well as restore relations with Germany; and the most ambitious of them all, the Kellogg-Briand Pact of 1928 (or Pact of Paris, officially General Treaty for Renunciation of War as an Instrument of National Policy), where the participating nations promised not to use war to solve their foreign problems. However, economic events were soon to overtake the international idealism of the 1920s, and bring the world to war once again in 1939.[91]

The economic crash detailed from a United States perspective in chapter 2 was global in scale, and the actions of America, as well as other nations in combating the economic dislocation led to increasing international tensions, and finally, to the outbreak of fighting in Europe at the end of the 1930s. The United States' decision to impose prohibitive tariffs on imports in 1930 (chapter 2) to boost domestic production, was quickly followed by other nations' pursuit of the same policy.

Figure 25: Edouard Daladier, Premier of France with French Delegation to the London Economic Conference, June 1933.

In 1931, the international banking system teetered on collapse and when England left the gold standard to devalue the pound, world markets were shaken. U.S. President Herbert Hoover's decision to suspend German reparations payments in 1932 was the stopgap that kept the global economy from failing completely. However, with the United States unwilling to assume a leadership role in the world economy and international relations, a vacuum was left that hyper-nationalism filled. When world leaders met in the summer of 1933 at the London Conference to try to craft a comprehensive response for economic recovery, newly-elected United States President Franklin Roosevelt signaled that America's intent was to go it alone. The conference broke up soon after America's chief executive's beliefs were made known. For the remainder of the decade nations worked independently to revive their economies.[92]

Entrepreneurial Lesson 14
Assuming a Leadership Role

To paraphrase the Dalai Lama—one finds love through service to others. The great masters of world history are merely servants to those who are led by them. True leadership is selfless and empowering to all. Leadership comes with hard decisions to make, highly independent and heavily opinionated teams to build, and finding an equitable means of sharing wealth. Entrepreneurs have blind faith in the efficacy of their visions, so much so that they will do everything that has to be done by themselves until the team is assembled.

The worldwide economic instability led to political instability across the globe as the 1930s progressed. Bolshevism triumphed in the Russian civil war fought immediately after World War I. From the early 1920s through the 1930s, the Soviet Union remained an international pariah even though the country was admitted to the League of Nations in 1934. An economically backward agricultural nation in 1914, communist leader Vladimir Lenin's successor, brutal dictator Joseph Stalin, led his country on a difficult forced path to industrialization, starting in the late 1920s and lasting through the 1930s.[93]

Figure 26: The Burning of the German Reichstag on February 27, 1933 was a catalyst to help Adolf Hitler consolidate his power after his appointment as Chancellor of Germany on January 30, 1933.

Fascism had taken hold in Italy in 1922 under Benito Mussolini, and was strengthened by the economic chaos of the next decade. However, the greatest national change precipitated by the economic chaos of the 1930s occurred in Germany when Adolf Hitler, the head of the Nationalist Socialists Workers or Nazi Party, was named Chancellor of that nation in 1933. The new head of government worked quickly to replace the Weimar Republic with a totalitarian regime.

Dedicated entirely to German national interests, and a policy of territorial expansion, even at the risk of war, the rise to power of the Austrian artist, and veteran of four years in the trenches during World War I, was to have dire world consequences. Lastly, in the Far East, a militaristic Japan had invaded Manchuria in 1931, to little effective response by the League of Nations or western world governments. By the middle of the decade that nation was committed to a policy of aggressive regional expansion to create the Greater Eastern Co-Prosperity Sphere under that ancient island's leadership.[94]

The second crisis to shake the world order occurred in 1935 when Italy invaded Ethiopia in its first attempt to recreate the glory of the long dead Roman Empire. The League of Nations response, which Japan had left in 1933, after censure over its adventurism in Manchuria, was so ineffective the organization became irrelevant for the rest of its existence. The western reaction to this and future provocations, led by Britain and France, both severely weakened politically, economically and militarily, but still perceived by themselves and others as dominant world powers, was a policy of "appeasement." This doctrine was based on the belief that Germany, Italy and Japan had some legitimate grievances and that avoidance of another world war by mollifying these issues was the path to continued world peace.[95]

Appeasement has garnered historical disdain; however, in the context of the 1930s the policy appeared reasonable. The western powers' miscalculation was to perceive that their opponents' aims were based upon rational national self-interest with limited scope, and in the case of Italy and Japan this was on the whole correct. Therefore, Italy might have a reasonable case to make vis-à-vis its historic role in Africa, and its second class status as a colonial power in need of markets for its goods, to invade Ethiopia to add it to its sphere of influence. While this argument may appear morally and ethically wrong, in the world of international power, morality and ethics are not always the top priority. Japan, in need of raw materials and markets, was also given the benefit of the doubt to some degree, and she took advantage of western immobilization to attack China in 1937.[96]

However, appeasement was to meet with total failure when applied to Nazi Germany. Hitler's aim, as described in his autobiography, *Mein Kampf* (My Struggle), was nothing less than total continental European domination, especially in Eastern Europe and the Soviet Union, to produce Lebensraum (living space) for the German people. Therefore, starting in 1936, Hitler proceeded to create one international crisis after another in the quest for European territorial hegemony, believing that weak and morally corrupt western nations would not oppose him.[97]

At first Hitler's gambles paid off as he occupied the Rhineland in 1936 in direct violation of the Versailles Treaty and also publicly announced a program of German rearmament, again in open defiance of the agreement ending World War I. Western leaders were reluctant to oppose Hitler for a number of reasons, including their correct belief that their nation's citizens were not prepared for another war, and the fact that due to the depression these nations were militarily weak. While Britain and France began their own rearmament programs in the late 1930s (as well as the United States) they perceived their military strength as deficient to Germany's, at least into the middle of 1939.[98]

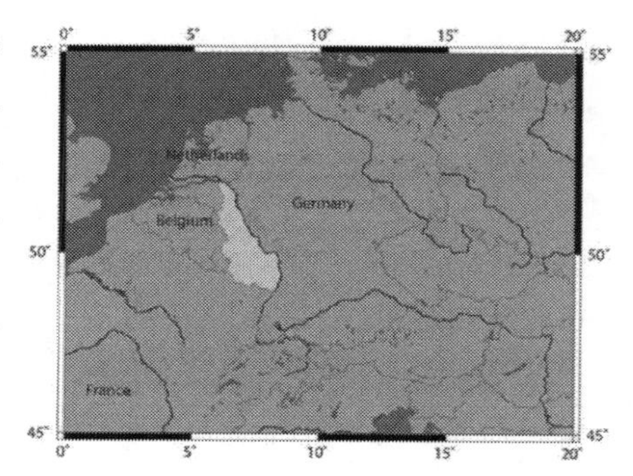

Figure 27: Location of the Rhineland circa 1936 when Hitler annexed it in violation of the Treaty of Versailles.

The policy of appeasement could entertain that Germany had some rightful argument in relation to the Rhineland, and its desire for Anschluss with Austria (completed in 1938), and for annexing the German speaking Sudetenland of Czechoslovakia, which was done under the auspices of the 1938 Munich agreement. However, when Hitler annexed the rest of Czechoslovakia in March 1939, Britain and France had reached the end of their patience and what the policy of appeasement would allow. As the summer of 1939 wore on it became apparent that Poland was next on Hitler's list, and the two former World War I allies issued public statements that war would result if Polish sovereignty was violated.[99]

Figure 28: German Soldiers Passing the Arc de Triomphe in Paris on June 14, 1940 after the fall of France. Attribution: Bundesarchiv, Bild 101I-126-0347-09A / Gutjahr / CC-BY-SA

The war that England, France and the United States were unprepared for erupted on September 1, 1939 when Germany invaded its eastern neighbor, which came just weeks after a shocked world learned that Hitler and Stalin had signed a non-aggression pact, which later events would reveal, included a secret codicil that partitioned the Polish state between them. Britain and France declared war on September 3, 1939, but were in no position to assist the Poles, who were defeated by the end of the month. While the new German tactics of mobile warfare were on display, the swift defeat was minimized as due to the weakness of the Polish army. The conflict then entered a phase known now as the "phony war" in which neither side made any moves militarily, but during which time Hitler prepared his forces for an invasion of France.[100]

The denouement to the "peace movement" in the 1920s, and economic dislocation in the 1930s, came swiftly in the spring and early summer of 1940. Germany invaded Denmark and Norway in April and the British and French response was weak and uncoordinated. Then, on May 10, 1940, Hitler unleashed his panzers against the Low Countries of the Netherlands and Belgium and then moved rapidly into France. Within weeks the British Expeditionary Force (BEF) was expelled from the continent and the French army, on paper considered the most powerful in the world, was defeated by the end of June.[101]

These events shocked the American public and a Congress that had only recently begun to release funds for

Entrepreneurial Lesson 15
Reacting to Rapidly Changing Events

Big things have small beginnings. It takes less time to turn a small vessel around than a large one. Entrepreneurs are ever searching for advantages over the competition. Small enterprises earn respect and become big (or bigger) by adjusting quickly to and taking advantage of swiftly changing circum-stances.

From the Stone Age to the new age, breakneck changes in the world are driven by technology. The victor is the one that can maintain itself in the perfect storm. The Arab Spring of 2011 demonstrates the powerful influences of technology in the political cauldrons of the Middle East. It shows the speed at which a communication, idea—or ideal—can go viral and how it can accelerate change.

rearmament. The defeat of France, and new funds for the military, led to an initial burst of activity to modernize the United States' armed forces, actions that would lead the Army to the doorstep of a bankrupt small car company in Butler, Pennsylvania

In retrospect it would appear that the West's, including the United States', complete lack of preparation for war in 1939 – 1940 had to result from gross negligence and/or incompetence on the part of their leadership. However, when reviewed in the context of the two decades following World War I, the fact that the United States army still relied on the cart and mule to move troops and small payloads in 1940 is understandable, if regrettable. Despite increasing world tensions in the second half of the 1930s, the American army in 1939 was still undermanned and ill-equipped from its low point in 1933. This was primarily due to public apathy during the peace period, parsimonious Presidents and Congress' during the 1920s, a lack of funds during the economically depressed 1930s, and ignorance on the part of the public, and by extension, its representatives in Congress and the Presidency, on the needs of a peacetime national defense.[102]

The origins of the Army's deterioration began immediately following World War I. The nation, adhering to its tradition of no standing armies in peacetime, fell into an all too familiar pattern after demobilization as outlined in *Chief of Staff: Prewar Plans and Preparations*:

Figure 29: The United States' M1 Combat Car light tank used by the Cavalry in the late 1930s was no match for Hitler's Panzers.

1) Prior to a war insufficient military expenditures, based on the public's prewar conviction that war could not come to America;
2) Discovery that war could come after all;
3) A belated rush for arms, men, ships, and planes to overcome the nation's demonstrated military weakness;
4) Advance of the producing and training program, attended by misunderstandings, delays and costly outlay, but gradual creation of a large and powerful army;
5) Mounting success in the field and eventual victory;
6) Immediately thereafter, rapid demobilization and dissolution of the Army as a powerful fighting force; and,
7) Sharp reduction of appropriations sought by the military establishment, dictated by concern over high cost and for a time by the revived hope that, again, war would not come to America.[103]

America fell right into this paradigm after World War I, fueled by historic precedent, and aided by the public's perception of a seemingly wasted sacrifice during World War I, that was also unappreciated by the United States' European allies. This was no more evident than when Warren Harding won the American presidency on his previously referenced promise of a "return to normalcy." While the 1920 National Defense Act authorized a peacetime Army strength of 280,000 enlisted men, that figure was never attained during the interwar years.[104]

Figure 30: Harking back to George Washington's Farewell Address a No Foreign Entanglements anti-war protest sign.

Harding and his extremely tight-fisted successor, Coolidge, would, along with a compliant Congress, significantly underfund the War Department during the decade of "peace." In 1929 newly inaugurated President Hoover ordered a review of the War Department's needs, but the stock market crash of the fall of that year (chapter 2), and subsequent Great Depression, effectively ended any opportunity to address the military's continued slide into decay and disrepair. The United States Army reached its lowest preparedness point in 1933, right when events were birthing the leader (Hitler), and causes (German remilitarization and territorial expansion) that would eventually lead to the outbreak of war in 1939.[105]

The over-arching policy of a military force dedicated solely to defensive actions, combined with scant funding through the middle of the 1930s, seriously hampered the Army's ability to bring on line new equipment, especially any which appeared to enhance offensive operations. While inadequate and poorly trained personnel were the norm during this period, obsolete and ill-repaired equipment was equally standard operating procedure.[106]

This lack of motivation to bring newer military hardware on line was rooted in the belief in the public's mind, and especially in Congress, that consumption of the overwhelming amount of surplus leftover from World War I was necessary before investing in modern arms. This policy had two fatal flaws: 1) over time this stock would become obsolete as technology rapidly advanced during the period, and 2) aging equipment needs ever-increasing maintenance, making it ostensibly more expensive than new purchases. By the low point in 1933 the active strength of the United States Army ranked 17th in the world.[107]

Figure 31: British Prime Minister Neville Chamberlain holding the Munich Agreement upon his return from that city on September 30, 1938. The agreement would hold for only six months when Hitler annexed the remainder of Czechoslovakia.

While the world was moving inexorably toward war as the 1930s progressed, the United States military continued to work under the handicap of the "decade of peace," which had spawned a small, but politically powerful "pacifist" movement, that when combined with America's traditionally strong isolationism faction, created strong political opposition to anything "military." Additionally, the decade of depression starved the War Department of funds. During the middle of the decade the Roosevelt Administration and Congress made some minor adjustments in military spending, in particular authorizing some naval ship building and munitions manufacture under the guise of making work for the unemployed. However, political opposition to these moves ended any use of relief funds for "weapons of war" in 1937.[108]

While America's future enemies were building modern, mobile armies, the United States was falling further and further behind during Roosevelt's first two terms. In 1936 a directive was issued that halted expenditures on research and development (R & D) for "unessential equipment" when "the Army needs large quantities of excellent equipment already developed." Caught between a rock and a hard place of investing in equipment that would produce improved weaponry in the future, or the bird in the hand of obtaining men and material that would provide an immediate betterment of a force, but possessing obsolete and failing equipment, the Army made the difficult decision to deemphasize research and development. The priorities for what little funds went into R & D were biased toward defense and the Army Air Corps as follows:

1) Detection of the approach of hostile aircraft;
2) Development of fire-control equipment for antiaircraft artillery and aircraft cannons;
3) Rapid methods of aerial mapping and map reproduction;
4) Development of anti-mechanized weapons;
5) Development of aircraft and their propulsion; and,
6) Improvement of air navigation equipment.[109]

Four years later a different set of priorities would lead directly to the American Bantam Car Company factory door at Butler, when the Blitzkrieg of 1940 demonstrably showed the need for a small mobile vehicle.

Entrepreneurial Lesson 16
Changing Priorities

The nature of priorities is that they dynamically change all the time. The entrepreneur arises in the morning. There is a to-do-list half a mile long, but it is highly likely that nothing on the list will get handled today. The military personnel at Pearl Harbor were enjoying a balmy Sunday, until their priorities and those of the whole country drastically changed.

The entrepreneur changes priorities as they present themselves. In a small enterprise, it might be impossible to delegate team members to handle them. In large enterprises, the entrepreneur rides herd on those to whom the priorities have been delegated. In managing the rushing flow of changing priorities, it is not how much entrepreneurs do for themselves, but how much they have done for them.

In 1938 the realization that Germany represented a serious threat to world peace became apparent in the aftermath of the Munich agreement. In October of that year a conference was held at the White House where increased military spending was discussed at the highest levels of government.[110]

However, throwing money at the problem could not make up for the one deficiency that funds can't overcome: time. In 1939, outgoing Chief of Staff General Malin Craig warned,

> "...the sums appropriated this year will not be full transformed into military power for two years. Persons who state they see no threat to the peace of the United States would hesitate to make that forecast through a two-year period..."[111]

In the early 1930s the United States had the time, but not the money or incentive to modernize its military; however, by 1939 the money was beginning to flow, but time had run out.

The period between the fall of Poland and the beginning of the Blitzkrieg in Western Europe saw incremental movement in the direction for American military modernization and rearmament. However, even with the outbreak of war in Europe, the strong isolationist and pacifist sentiments in the United States made a full blown effort politically difficult. This was especially true in the Presidential election year of 1940, with Chief Executive Roosevelt eyeing an unprecedented third term. Though America's 33rd President increasingly desired to assist the Allies, especially after the fall of France in June 1940, he was hamstrung by his own re-election effort that emphasized he was keeping America out of the war. The various Neutrality Acts passed between 1935 and 1939 also hampered American assistance to England, the only country fighting Nazi Germany in 1940.[112]

The low state of preparedness of the United States armed forces was apparent in maneuvers conducted during the summer of 1940. The National Guard division strengths listed on paper as 22,000 were actually at half strength; many divisions did not have newer mortars or antitank guns, and only 25% of its quota of rifles, some of the "cannons" were just iron pipes, "tanks" were simulated using trucks, and "bombers" were just light observation planes.[113]

Figure 32: Soldiers of the United States First Army Prepare to Fire Large Artillery Piece During Summer Maneuvers in 1940. Used with permission from Town of De Kalb, New York Historian's Office.

While these deficiencies were obvious to the casual observer, professional judgment was even harsher, noting problems with:

1) Tank and plane formations as well as equipment;

2) Challenges in defense against modern weapons; and,

3) Low marks in experience, discipline, leadership, supply, communications reconnaissance, liaison, and sanitation.[114]

One American witness commented, "Just visited the maneuvers and thought they were lousy. The troops appeared deficient in fundamentals of minor tactics, could not maintain contact with hostile forces, permitted gaps in the line, etc. Combat intelligence very poor." More ominous still was the view from overseas. In particular, came the Soviet assessment, the country which was to find out in 1941 that their military was no match for German arms. Mirroring General Craig's own assessment, the USSR opined that America's military was in a low state of training. They observed, prophetically, that, "the potential capacity of American industry is tremendous, but it is much more difficult to teach men to use arms in battle."[115]

The sudden and shocking Axis victory in May–June 1940 did open up an opportunity for increased appropriations to the United States military. The overwhelming display of mobility and mechanization led to issuance of directives on August 20, 1940 that greatly altered research priorities from the 1936 orders as follows:

1) Modification of antiaircraft guns and fire control for use against ground targets:
2) Development of tanks or armored vehicles for use as observation posts;
3) Further development of reconnaissance vehicles;
4) Development of personnel carriers;
5) Equipment for landing operations, including boats for installation on Army transports;
6) Antitank shoulder rifle; and,
7) Communications system for co-ordination of air support for ground units.[116]

Item number 3 provided official confirmation that the project to procure the truck ¼ ton 4 X 4 light begun in June 1940 was a key need for the future, and a small band of intrepid automobile experts in Butler, Pennsylvania were already working on a solution.

Questions for Educators

Why is it important to understand the history of stakeholders?

Discuss the relevance of understanding the state of stakeholders.

How important is it to identify and clearly understand the needs of the key stakeholder?

What lessons are important to gain from the United States Army experiences in the 1920s and 1930s vis-à-vis the ability to maintain preparedness in the face of obstacles?

Chapter 4: Project Genesis

Projects typically materialize from the realization that a need or needs have gone unmet and eventually enough organizational forces align to give birth to an endeavor to meet the necessity at hand. The effort that led to the creation of the first Jeep followed this pattern. Due to technological advancements during the period between the world wars it became apparent that an all-terrain vehicle for reconnaissance, and to move troops and small payloads to replace the cart and mule as well as the motorcycle with sidecar, was desired. However, the ½ ton truck, which represented the lightest truck in the United States Army arsenal at the time, was not up to the task. The tank had broken the stalemate of the Western Front in 1918, but rapid advances in mobility, especially by the Germans, pushed the envelope on vehicle technology and led to the need for a ¼ ton in the Army's fleet.

Figure 33: The Mule—Primary Transport for Troops and Small Payloads the U.S. Army was Looking to Replace with A Small Vehicle.

The critical problem that confronted American military leaders after World War I was increased mobility. However, a lack of funds had hamstrung the armed services in all areas of research and development, especially during the 1930s and that included vehicle experimentation. The need was obvious to replace animal based transportation which was too slow, cumbersome and vulnerable. The motorcycle with sidecar was dangerous to operate, and performed poorly in cross-country conditions. A light, highly mobile car that operated effectively in all conditions was required.[117]

During the 1930s, the Infantry, despite a lack of funds, and in response to urgency on the part of the American public and its leaders that war was coming, expended the most effort of any service branch to solve the issue from their perspective. The Infantry Board, the committee tasked with developing and testing equipment for foot soldiers, had worked on the issue for many years. The Chief of Infantry summarized the issue in a July 26, 1938 memo from that office to the Adjutant General.[118]

> In the opinion of the Chief of Infantry the lack of a suitable automotive carrier for the heavier Infantry weapons and their ammunition on the battlefield is the greatest deficiency in Infantry equipment today. Infantry weapons requiring transportation are the machine gun and mortars. The transportation provided at present consists of animal drawn carts in those regiments in which the combat trains are animal drawn, and 1 ½ ton trucks, supplemented by hand carts, in those regiments which are completely motorized. The Caliber .50 Machine Gun with its transportation is to be replaced by the 37 mm Antitank Gun with prime mover … the type of mover included in the estimates for fiscal year 1940 is the four-wheel, four-wheel drive, ½ ton truck chassis with pick-up body.

With the exception of the prime mover for the antitank gun, the present methods of transporting the heavier Infantry weapons with their ammunition show little improvement over the methods employed during the World War. They will not permit the weapons to advance as rapidly as, and to remain in close support of, the rifle elements due to the following limitations:

Attempts were made during the World War to use a mule cart but the vulnerability of the mule and leader, the size of the target presented, and the slow rate of progress across country, made this method entirely impractical under battle conditions. This resulted in the weapons having to be man-carried during forward displacements. It is reasonable to assume that similar conditions will exist in the next war if reliance is placed upon the mule cart as a weapons carrier.

The 1 ½ ton truck now used in motorized regiments is unsatisfactory for road movements, and it may be that these vehicles can be used in early stages of development for offensive action. However, it seems certain that trucks of this size, due to their weight, conspicuous silhouette and limited cross-country ability, will be impractical in cross-country movements to assembly areas and subsequent movements to initial and to successive attack positions. To provide some means of transporting the weapons from the point where it is necessary to detruck to the forward positions, hand carts were adopted in lieu of a satisfactory automotive vehicle for the purpose. The use of hand carts entails the same disadvantages as the use of mule carts. While the carts themselves are light (90 pounds), the loads placed on the carts average between 250 to 300 pounds and to move these carts over rough ground at least two men are required to pull and, dependent upon the nature of the terrain, additional men must push. The rate of movement over long distances is not much more than a mile an hour. Progress necessarily is slow, and the men present a conspicuous target. While the use of hand carts may be practical in the advance to initial positions, man-carrying the weapons will be required in moving to successive attack positions.

Figure 34: 1932 American Austin Roadster—Possibly the Model or a Similar Model Purchased by the Infantry for Testing in 1932. Source: sportscarmarket.comgure

Man-carrying these heavier Infantry weapons is a very slow, arduous procedure and is impractical except for short distances due to the weights involved. The average weight of the material that the members of the various gun crews must carry is 30 pounds in the Caliber .30 Machine Gun and the 60 mm Mortar squads; and 44 pounds in the 81 mm Mortar squad. Practical loads for the ammunition carriers of the various weapon squads are 42 pounds (2 boxes of 250 rounds each) in the Caliber .30 Machine Gun squad; 36 pounds (10 rounds in apron) in the 60 mm Mortar squad; 49 – 56 pounds (either 7 light shells at 7 pounds or 4 heavy shells at 14 pounds) in the 81 mm Mortar squad. Due to the type of material, the loads are necessarily unwieldy and cumbersome, and when man-carried, progress is slow and very fatiguing to the men.[119]

The Infantry's needs centered on weapons carrying; however, other branches had a need for a small vehicle, notably the Cavalry for reconnaissance patrol. The search was on for a solution to this frustrating problem.

1932: The Austin

In 1932 the Infantry Board requested procurement of an Austin roadster with oversized tires for testing at Fort Benning, Georgia, noting the problems with the motorcycle with sidecar. That group had heard reports that the British Army had used the car extensively with good results for "reconnaissance and messenger service." The Quartermaster General's office, while acknowledging the desirability of testing the Austin, replied that funds were not available as, "the Army Appropriations Act did not authorize the purchase of any automobiles for the Regular Army during the present fiscal year." However, soon thereafter, the War Department found the funding in the Quartermaster's budget to purchase "one or two Austin's of the reconnaissance truck type, carrying two passengers and having a pick-up body."[120]

Figure 35: 1930s era US Military Motorcycle with Sidecar Which Was Unsatisfactory for Modern Mobile Cavalry Uses. Used with permission from Auburn University Libraries Special Collections – Everett Leavins Papers.

One Austin was eventually purchased for $268.75 and sent to Fort Benning for testing. The Roadster did not meet Army requirements; however, this interest in Austin products served as an initial performance indicator for small vehicles. In addition, some of the parts from this car found their way from the Fort Benning salvage (junk) yard and into a key step in the process of solving the small vehicle mobility issue, the Howie Machine-Gun Carrier.[121]

1935: The Calvary—A Light Cross-Country Car

Another vexing issue facing the Army besides moving Infantry weapons was finding a vehicle that could act in a reconnaissance role. Those considering the matter realized a vehicle with a low silhouette, which could carry a small crew of one to two soldiers along with their weapons and ammunition, and was able to go where the horse could and return safely, was critical for information gathering in a future conflict.[122]

While various discussions and informal efforts were undoubtedly undertaken, the most likely first "official" recognition of the need vis-à-vis the reconnaissance role was documented in an article by First Lieutenant (later Colonel) Homer G. Hamilton published in the May / June 1935 Cavalry Journal. Colonel Hamilton joined the Army in June 1925 and served with the Cavalry for twelve years until he was transferred to the Ordnance Department. In 1935 he was stationed at Civilian Conservation Corps (C.C.C.) district headquarters at Fort Des Moines, and it was at this time he designed a number of items for light manufacturing, including a motor vehicle he thought was suitable for army use.[123] He described the origin of the vehicle as follows:

> At that time (1935) I had had a good bit of experience with the Cavalry. At one time I had been assigned to headquarters troop of the 113th Cavalry. I had the Intelligence section of headquarters platoon. Their duties, in part, we would conduct reconnoitering missions and scouting and patrolling generally. The Cavalry had been given experimentally a very heavy car called a scout car, to use for scouting and patrolling. We found through experience and by "we", I mean the Cavalry, that that car was too heavy, too bulky to meet the Cavalry requirements. So I conceived the idea that the vehicle that would be best suited to Cavalry use should have certain characteristics. It should be a cross-country vehicle.
>
> The principal objection to the scout car that had been issued, it was so heavy it could operate only on fairly hard surfaced roads. It would bog down as soon as you would get on a secondary road or off the road on ordinary terrain. So by cross-country, I had in mind the vehicle should be able to go almost anyplace that mounted Cavalry could go. That is side roads, unimproved roads or cross-country.[124]

Entrepreneurial Lesson 17
Value of Research and Development

Entrepreneurs constantly plan for the future. The survival of the enterprise is always at stake. Research and Development in response to market feedback as well as mold-breaking inventive genius never leaves the budget. It has incalculable value and makes the difference between an advanced enterprise and a copycat.

It is easy to be a genius if the lab-coats are reverse-engineering or, worse, stealing some other company's ideas. Many of the greatest inventions were discovered by fortuitously happy accidents—the point at which fate makes coincidence look nonexistent. It is all there in front of us. We just have to find it or have it find us.

The other characteristics Lieutenant Hamilton envisioned in this vehicle included:

- low silhouette,
- extended cruising radius,

- light weight,
- communication either by signaling device or radio,

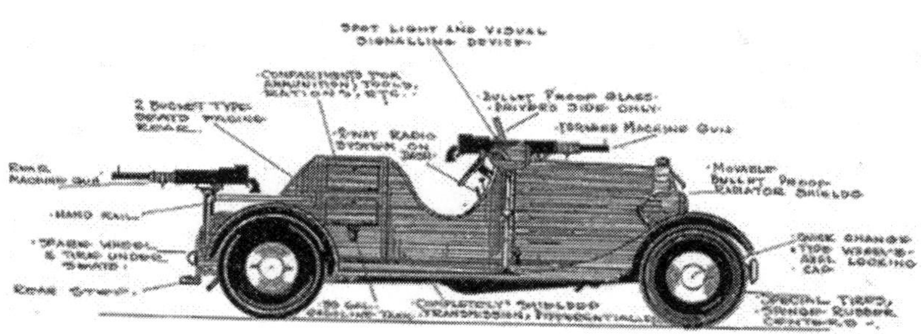

Figure 36: Lieutenant Hamilton's Light Cross-Country Car. Source: United States National Archives, College Park, Maryland

- equipped with a machine gun,
- sufficient undercarriage protection for operation across high center roads or ordinary obstacles that may be encountered,
- driver's side shatter-proof, bullet-proof windshield,
- radiator protected by a shield,
- passenger payload of one to four,
- fuel capacity to meet extended cruising radius,
- compartments for tools, rations, equipment and ammunition
- bucket type seats and,
- commercial chassis.[125]

Lieutenant Hamilton had certain specific uses in mind for this vehicle which he described as follows:

> In Cavalry there are three main characteristics, mobility, firing power and shot. As I told you a moment ago, in connection with scouting and patrolling, there are in general two types, reconnaissance patrol and a combat patrol. The mission of the reconnaissance patrol is to go out and secure your information about hostile forces. That information is of no value at all unless it gets back to the main body. Therefore, the combat patrol, rather than the reconnaissance patrol does not ordinarily offer combat, except as is necessary to insure their return.
>
> On the other hand, the combat patrol has as its mission making combat with the enemy and actually engaging in the firing. The use of this car, as I visualized it, was principally for reconnaissance. In other words, it was not to be heavily armored, but it was to have sufficient on vehicle armament to permit its return and it was intended to be sufficiently maneuverable to make contact with hostile forces and secure information.[126]

He envisioned using a commercial chassis from Ford, Chevrolet or Plymouth to build the vehicle upon, all of which had a wheelbase of 100 inches, much longer than the eventual 80-inch wheel base of the Bantam pilot model, and his vehicle did not have four-wheel drive. The Cavalry officer's primary audience for his article was his service arms leaders. He also knew from experience that in almost every post, camp or station there was an officer's club or officer's day room, where copies of all service publications, including Infantry Journal and Field Artillery Journal, were on hand for reading by leaders from those branches.[127] However, despite his efforts, support was limited. Lieutenant Hamilton's article was not sent through official channels for evaluation and he did not pursue a patent on his idea. In addition the Calvary officer did not approach a commercial manufacturer or the Quartermaster Corps (QMC) to interest them in building the vehicle.[128] Later, though, he was convinced that his car was the forerunner of the Jeep:

> Well, I certainly feel there are so many, many points of similarity, both in general appearance and in specifications and in specific statements of equipment and fittings, and knowing that this article was quite widely publicized throughout the services, that the similarities are way beyond the realm of just pure coincidence [...]
>
> I had hoped it (the article) would influence official opinion for the same reason that any, let us say, any manufacturer who produces a product advertises it in a magazine, he hopes to get people favorably impressed with his product and he hopes that the greatest number of people will see it and that their thinking will be influenced by what they have seen and read. So I feel reasonably certain that at least any of the service people who have been actually connected with the design and development, manufacture or any other phases pertinent to the Jeep, may have very conceivably have been influenced by this article [...]
>
> I could see perhaps one or two points of similarity might be a matter of some coincidence. But if you would take the drawing, its general appearance, specific appearance, the location of certain features, the textural matter and compare that with any Quartermaster drawings or specifications of the Jeep, you would find there was perhaps as much as eighty percent that was exactly similar.[129]

While the exact influence, if any, Colonel Hamilton's article had on the events of 1940 remain speculative, the piece does show that as early as 1935 individuals were conceiving of combining, as never before, features such as a short wheelbase, low silhouette, light weight, high mobility, compartments for ammunition, tools, rations, some firepower etc. into one vehicle.[130]

1937–1938: The Howie Machine-Gun Carrier

At the time Lieutenant Hamilton was focusing on the aspect of mobility and reconnaissance in a car, the Infantry was working on the issue of a small weapons carrier that would provide fast and close assistance to troops on the attack. The Infantry branch authorized a test in 1936 to formulate characteristics for such a vehicle:

- suitable chassis for Infantry cross-country cars and for trucks, reconnaissance, eight passenger,
- type of body which should be placed on the chassis for Infantry cross-country cars and for trucks, reconnaissance, eight-passenger and,
- fuel capacity for at least 300 miles, no armor, ½ ton or light touring car chassis, phaeton in body with folding top and windshield, cut down fenders, eliminate running board, provide for radio use.[131]

Figure 37: Front View of the Howie Machine Gun Carrier. Source: United States National

Three vehicles were tested against these characteristics: a Ford, a Marmon-Herrington truck and an International Harvester model. These tests did not lead to any further efforts to pursue these particular items for military use (other Marmon-Herrington products would later receive evaluation); however, the Infantry's dire need for a vehicle provided the impetus for the creation of the Howie Machine-Gun carrier.[132]

Captain Robert G. Howie led the team that built the vehicle named after him and completed the prototype in April 1937. His vehicle was a far cry from the eventual Jeep prototype, but proved a valuable evolutionary step. To maintain the low silhouette the builders had the soldiers lie in a prone position which differed significantly from the Bantam pilot model; however, the overall height of 33 and one quarter inches was only slightly lower than the first Jeep, the wheelbase was 75 inches--5 less than Bantam's creation--the weight of 1,000 pounds less than half of the standardized Jeep, and its top speed of 28 miles per hour a far cry from the 60 miles an hour of Bantam's work.[133] Captain Wendell G. Johnson wrote about the project that created the Howie vehicle in a 1937 Infantry Journal article, describing the problem as follows:

> Almost everybody agrees that truck-hauled machine guns give no closer support to attacking riflemen than do mule-towed guns, once they're in action and reduced to hand-hauling. Which is admitting that the front-line mobility of machine guns hasn't been accelerated materially during these lush years of military renovation. Trucks, in fact, because of their size are really worse off than mules, up where grazing fire persuades bay-windowed nomcoms to belly down like worms.
>
> So we still have pulling privates snaking guns along per TR 420-55 from one firing position to another—torment enough with the "thirties," and plain hell with the "fifties." And what is more serious, the muscle power of the best of them isn't up to the task. Whether creeping,

crawling, or bounding, machine-gunners can't lug their loads fast enough to get them where needed in time to hold a captured knoll or break up counterattacks. So there we are—right where we've been for years.

Entrepreneurial Lesson 18
Using What You Have

From mules in the Civil War to drones in the mountains of Pakistan today, U.S. warfare has been a matter of transporting weapons into firing position. A quip that was current in 1940 that Hitler had ordered 10,000 tanks, but don't bother delivering them, because he'd pick them up on his way through Detroit. He invaded Norway because he needed to protect his iron ore supply from Sweden that ran through Narvik. Stuck in the desert, Patton awaited an allotment of gasoline, so that his Shermans could proceed against Rommel's Panzers.

The first Jeep was made from off-the-shelf elements. What they did not have, they fashioned for themselves. The Entrepreneur makes do with the tools on hand. If there is something different needed, it has to be conceived, invented, designed, built, and implemented. The key is to maintain consistent delivery. Do the best you can do with the tools you have.

So we still have pulling privates snaking guns along per TR 420-55 from one firing position to another—torment enough with the "thirties," and plain hell with the "fifties." And what is more serious, the muscle power of the best of them isn't up to the task. Whether creeping, crawling, or bounding, machine-gunners can't lug their loads fast enough to get them where needed in time to hold a captured knoll or break up counterattacks. So there we are—right where we've been for years.

But not for many more, it is hoped. There is a growing clamor from the chorus of speeder-uppers decrying this immobility of supporting weapons on the battlefield, and advocating low-silhouette motorized carriers as the cure. Not baby tanks or tankettes as now used in several European armies, for such vehicles are too costly, too complicated for quantity production, and too conspicuous. What is wanted is merely a gasoline-propelled conveyance not much higher than a man crawling (or is it creeping?), that will be able to carry a one- or two-man crew, a grin, and plenty of ammunition, and scoot from one firing position to another at five to ten miles an hour.

Of course there are many who demand more, and propose a lot of trick characteristics and odd accessories for these scooters. Some would run them on wheels, others on tracks, and still others would make them convertible wheel-and-trackers—and thereby run their weight up into tons. One proponent would make this machine with a sharp nose of ponderous fangs to cut through wire entanglements. Another has it armored against .30-caliber AP, virtually a tank. There are backers of jack-of-all missions contraptions which would out-rube Goldberg.

Their Buck Rogerisms probably could be put on S.D. as lawn mowers and street sweepers in garrison, and might even carry retractable plows for use in company gardens.[134]

Captain Johnson then described the project that resulted in Captain Howie's carrier:

> The more practical-minded limit their proposals to a simple, lightweight, low-silhouette carrier with no complicating contrivances. This is exactly what we find the recently constructed Howie Machine-gun Carrier to be.
>
> The building of this vehicle was initiated by Brigadier General Walter C. Short while he was Assistant Commandant The Infantry School.
>
> Of course the Fort Benning salvage pile was put on tap.
>
> General Short specified that a vehicle be constructed for the sole purpose of transporting two men, a caliber-.30 machine gun, tripod, and ammunition. Other requirements were:

Figure 38: Side view of the Howie Machine Gun Carrier Powered by an Austin Bantam Engine, and using an Austin Radiator and Austin Steering Gear. Source: United States National Archives, College Park, Maryland

The gun not to be mounted for firing from the carrier.

The vehicle to be light enough for four men to lift into a 1-1/2-ton truck and across small obstacles.

To present as low a silhouette as possible—sacrificing ground clearance therefor, if necessary. Dimensions to be such that it could be carried in the 1-1/2-ton truck issued to machine-gun companies.

Speed no object—as low as 10 mph maximum.

Units to be commercially available as far as possible.
The job of designing and building the carrier was given to Captain Robert G. Howie, then an instructor in the Tank Section. The Infantry School. Another long-time tanker and expert

mechanic, Master Sergeant M. C. Wiley, was his partner in production. Assisting in the final assembly was Sergeant G. L. Rush, also of the Tank Section. Work began late in 1936 and ended in April of '37.

Here is part of Captain Howie's report on his fabrication:

It was decided to build a wheeled vehicle. . . . A track vehicle would greatly exceed the weight limitation. It was also decided that, in order to provide a low silhouette, the crew should be placed in the prone position. This should assist in determining the feasibility of this feature for future designs.

Several types of engines were considered... A light air cooled engine would be ideal. However [it] would require an additional cooling medium inasmuch as it [the carrier] would he run at low vehicle speed a great deal of the time.

The Austin Bantam engine . . . including . . . clutch and transmission, complete without radiator weighs 155 lbs. A new unit was purchased for the job.

The radiator used is the conventional Austin radiator, taken from salvage.

The propeller shaft, universal joints, and rear axle assembly were retrieved from salvage. The shaft was modified by shortening, and the rear axle assembly was reversed in order to provide for the reversal in drive.

In view of the nature of the vehicle, the engine was placed in the rear, the rear axle to form a jackshaft mounted amidships, a sprocket (11-tooth) fitted to the end of the shaft upon which to operate a standard Motorcycle chain to a motorcycle sprocket (21-tooth) on the rear wheels. This provided for an additional and necessary gear reduction of 2 to 1 . . . An additional wheel can be mounted on each jackshaft to be either driven or floated.

A salvaged Austin steering gear was used and was modified by shortening, mounting crosswise, and the installation of a crank [like a tiller] instead of a steering wheel.

Inasmuch as no springs were provided for the vehicle, and to take advantage of a standard commercial product, it was decided to use a 6.00 x 9 tractor tire with a ground-grip tread . . . A tractor-type cast-iron wheel was purchased. A [lighter] wheel which weights 16 to 20 pounds can be obtained.
Standard motorcycle brake drum assemblies were mounted on the rear wheels and operated mechanically through linkage to a conventional foot pedal.

Frame 1-1/2 x 1-1/2 x 3/16-inch channel steel … Aluminum alloy … is more expensive … and steel was used to reduce cost.

DIMENSIONS:
Height, overall (radiator cap) 33-1/4 inches
Width, overall 61-3/4 inches
Length, overall 124 inches
Tread 49-3/4 inches
Wheelbase 75 inches
[Ground] clearance 7-3/4 inches
Weight (less machine gun and equipment) 1,015 pounds
Speed (maximum) 28 mph
Climbing ability (with traction) 45 degrees
That, in word and figures, is the Howie carrier.[135]

As with all vehicles built or procured the Howie Carrier was rigorously tested and that process was described next:

> Now let's see what it had done in a few of the tests made by Lieutenant Charles R. Kutz and personnel of Company D, 29th Infantry.

Entrepreneurial Lesson 19
Evolutionary Product Development

Since 1980, the Toyota employee suggestion-box program has generated over 16,000,000 innovations incorporated into the design and manufacture of their vehicles. The nudges, tweaks, ideas and complaints come from the people who build them and buy them for themselves. Blips from recalls aside, most of their cars just run and run with little maintenance.

End-user product development through whatever suggestion-box system, physical or social media, is the heart of evolutionary product development. After decades of incremental changes and improvements, the brands do not resemble their original products, but they are the same products—only highly evolved. Think of the Toyota suggestion-box as the physical form of Twitter.

The [sic] found that although this puddle-jumper wouldn't jump puddles, it could run through then [sic] without balking or stalling. Its light weight and broad tires carried it skimming in high or second over the top of sand in which other vehicles would sink or wallow. It charged through light underbrush in a fashion that made even designed [sic] Howie's eye pop. Everywhere it had ample power to climb up or plow through, provided it could get traction. Where it was stopped, as by a ditch, the two men forming the crew usually could lift it out, over or through.

The two-man crew could dismount the gun from the carrier and set it up on the ground as rapidly as a three man crew could do it from a Matthew's Mount.
It was able to carry the 81-mm. mortar, its bipod, and 20 rounds of ammunition; likewise the .30 caliber machine gun and the 47-mm. gun. The 27-mm. gun also was easily towed by the carrier.
A pedestal was constructed on the front end of the carrier, and from it the caliber 0.30 machine gun fired with remarkably accurate results, both in stationary and moving fire. The slick feature

in firing from the carrier was the ability to fire a whole and from one chassis – detilade position, back up when simulated enemy fire came close, and pull up again into another firing position. Moreover, this was done in far less time that normally is required to go out of action from one ground position and setup again elsewhere.

Of all the admirable features of the Howie carrier, the one that was outstanding in the tests was its invisibility even on flat terrain with little vegetation to provide cover. Given a modicum of grass, weeds or ground furrows, this midget was easily concealed from even closer observation.

Here's what a machine gummer [sic] of the 29th Foot and [sic] said on seeing the carrier perform. "Jees, she's lower in the grass. You can't hardly see her even when she's going."

As would be expected, driving belly-buster without benefit of spine-rubber cushions has a tendency to trade tail troubles for tummy aches. But after a little practice one soon finds a reasonable degree of comfort by turning the body so as to rest on the side, rather than on the stomach. In this position the manipulation of the foot pedals aft, and of the gear shift lever and the tiller forward, is soon mastered. At least that is what an experienced automobile driver should find.

All in all, the testing people – and most of the observers who have chanced to see it – consider this unpretentious looking little cruiser a pretty swell job.[136]

Captain Johnson concluded that the vehicle had a future, but it was most likely not the answer to the vexing issue of creating "the" vehicle to solve the Army's light payload and personnel mobility issue.

Not that they rate it superior either as a road or cross-country vehicle. That couldn't be expected in an experimental machine, especially one that was designed largely to determine the feasibility of building such a vehicle.

And, naturally enough, containing plunder from salvage piles, they have found bugs in it. But what new product comes out of Flint or Detroit without a few bugs?

So it is not intended to hold up this carrier as the ideal in motor mounts. Perhaps it should be stronger, larger, faster, more suited to long moves, so as to eliminate the 1-1/2-ton truck. Or possibly it should be even smaller, lighter and slower. Maybe it should have an armor shield for frontal protection. Maybe.

Many, many questions remain to be answered in the difficult [sic] of determining how to move heavier-than-can-be-handily-handled Infantry weapons. Merely to pronounce "motor mounts" as the panacea isn't enough.

This machine and its modifications, other types of motor driven vehicles, truck-carried hand carts, all have to be tested to ascertain just what is wanted – and also what is practicable from a procurement viewpoint – for caliber .30 guns, for heavier guns and for mortars. Of course it would be ideal if a vehicle similar to this could be produced with characteristics that would fit it for general utility with all Infantry supporting weapons, both on the road and in action. But that is asking almost too much.

At any rate, just as the early tanks were a beginning in the field of armored fighting vehicles, so is the Howie Machine-Gun Carrier a start in the field of support-weapon carriers. And judging from its early achievements, a might good start too![137]

In a bit of historic irony it is noteworthy that the builders of the Howie Machine-Gun Carrier used salvaged Austin parts, most likely from the vehicle purchase in 1932, as well as installed a new American Bantam engine in the contraption.

Figure 39: M2 Light Tractor Cat Model—The Marmon-Herrington TA30 Was Most Likely Similar to this Model.

1938: Vehicle Testing

As 1938 dawned the Infantry was still wrestling with the issue of finding a lightweight weapons carrier, as described earlier in the July 26, 1938 memo from the Chief of Infantry to the Adjutant General that concluded, "the lack of a suitable automotive carrier for the heavier Infantry weapons and their ammunition on the battlefield is the greatest deficiency in Infantry equipment today."[138] This judgment was reached after significant effort was expended earlier in the year testing numerous vehicles to solve the problem; however, the Infantry, through this testing, believed they had found a solution. The intrepid staff at Fort Benning, where the Howie Carrier was built, was also busy evaluating an assortment of trucks, tractors and cars including:

- Cargo Carrier T-2
- Angleworm Tractor (Commercial)
- Silver King Tractor (Commercial)
- Marmon-Herrington Half-track Truck T-9
- Light Tractor T3E4 (Ordnance)
- Marmon-Herrington Tractor TA-20

- Marmon-Herrington Tractor TA-30
- G.M.C. 1-1/2 ton Truck 4 X 4
- Marmon-Herrington ½ ton truck 4 X 4
- Dodge ½ ton Truck 4 X 2
- Howie Carrier
- Marmon-Herrington Trailer (Ford)
- Quartermaster Trailers (4)
- Academic Department Cross-country Car139

Entrepreneurial Lesson 20
Evaluating Alternatives

What if? The Entrepreneur forever asks what if. Would products, productivity and profitability improve? In the 1930s, the U.S. Army did not have computer modeling to evaluate alternatives to mules and Howies. So prototypes had to be requested to determine if there were other ways to move certain loads of personnel and materials.

Now then, what if you have to make a prototype in 49 days, when it usually takes months? What if it is 1940, a war is raging and you have to act fast? You have no computers with which to model alternatives. The Entrepreneur is a pioneer, so even in 2014, those digital modeling techniques might not help. How does one reference something that never existed before? What if the survival of the company depended on this fulfillment?

At some point, the Entrepreneur bites the bullet, makes the leap of faith, and creates the alternative because there exists no other, well, *alternative.*

The conclusions reached from these tests as documented in a February 12, 1938 memo from the Office of the Infantry Board at Fort Benning to the Chief of Infantry were as follows:

> Careful analysis of the results of tests conducted to date show but three of the ten vehicles tested as possessing characteristics and showing performance which justify their consideration as possibly suitable for the purposes for which tested, i.e. the Marmon-Herrington tractor TA-30, the ordnance tractor T3E4, and the Marmon-Herrington truck ½ ton 4 X 4. Of these three vehicles the greater weight, cost and silhouette of the Ordnance tractor T3E4 and the fact that this is a specially built vehicle makes it undesirable for Infantry use as a cross-country carrier. The tests indicate, however, that this tractor may prove highly desirable in Infantry organizations in limited quantities as a trouble vehicle. Further tests along this line will be conducted. Of the two remaining vehicles the Marmon-Herrington truck ½ ton 4 X 4 outperforms the Marmon-Herrington tractor TA-30. While the performance of the TA-30 has fallen below the standard considered desirable for Infantry use as a cross-country carrier the Board desired to conduct further tests of the vehicle before definitely recommending rejection. In addition to its better performance the Marmon-Herrington truck ½ ton 4 X 4 has the added advantages of carrying a satisfactory pay load on the vehicle, equal performance when trailing an additional gross load of about 1000 pounds, a general type vehicle which can be procured commercially in large quantities and at a price about one-half the price of the tractor TA-30, simple in construction, easier and more economical to maintain and with considerably better strategic and tactical mobility.[140]

These tests, while unknown at the time, narrowed the field for the Infantry to a vehicle that was ½ ton, 4 X 4 and was possible to purchase commercially. The field would narrow in less than a month when a March 1, 1938 Infantry Board report was issued on the Howie Carrier which exposed its weaknesses:

> The vehicle has excellent mobility across dry terrain. It is unable to negotiate mud, loose sand or steep hills. Its low silhouette causes it to hang up on small obstacles such as stumps, logs, etc. It is light enough when lightly loaded to be readily lifted over small obstacles by its normal crew of two men. When one man is replaced by a load the vehicle cannot be man-handled by the driver alone. It is low in silhouette. It has great maneuverability. It is as sturdily constructed as is desirable in a carrier for cross-country use. It lacks strategic mobility. It is not commercially produced and it is not available in quantity production ...[141]

The Infantry Board had considered the Howie invention for two possible uses, as a weapons mount and/or as a cargo carrier and found that it was unsatisfactory for both. However, the report stated an eerie foreshadowing of many of the characteristics that would find their way into the bid specification for a solution a few years later that would constitute "a mean between the two vehicles in question," a quarter ton 4 X 4 truck.

> It is considered that the Howie Carrier basically presents many commendable ideas. However, if a specially designed vehicle of this general type were to be authorized for development for Infantry use certain modifications and improvements would be desirable. It is believed that when the necessary improvements are embodied in a unit of this type the result would closely resemble the chassis of the presently commercially available one-half ton truck.
>
> The Infantry Board is at present engaged in a test the purpose of which is to develop characteristics for a satisfactory cross-country carrier for Infantry. Because of its low silhouette its lightness and maneuverability the Howie Carrier is being continued in the test for purpose of comparison. The most suitable vehicle for the purpose sought yet observed by the Board is the Marmon-Herrington truck ½ ton 4 X 4. Unless some track laying vehicle subsequently furnished the Board out performs this vehicle it is quite likely that the Board will consider this vehicle as the point of departure for the development of a suitable four wheel drive tractor or truck for use as an Infantry cross-country carrier. The Howie Carrier which represents one extreme of a wheel cross-country vehicle will be used as a desirable standard in silhouette, lightness and maneuverability. Characteristics will probably be written contemplating for development purposes a mean between the two vehicles in question.

> The Infantry Board recommends no further immediate development of the Howie Carrier and that Captain R. G. Howie, Infantry, and Master Sergeant M. C. Wiley, Infantry School Detachment, be commended for their work in developing and building the Howie Carrier.[142]

However, the Infantry, through this testing process was forming a picture of the type of vehicle they would require as detailed in the July 26, 1938 memo.

> Since the World War the lack of a suitable carrier for the heavier Infantry weapons has been of paramount interest to the Infantry, and all means of transporting have been investigated or tested. Until recently, no vehicle has proved satisfactory, either due to the lack of cross-country ability or because of excessive weight and cost. Tests conducted by the Infantry Board in compliance with 1st endorsement, AGO, June 3, 1937 and reported upon in attached Infantry Reports Nos. 980 and 1014, have proved conclusively that the four-wheel, four-wheel drive commercial truck chassis, ½ ton, with pick-up body, is the most satisfactory vehicle of all types for the purpose of a weapons-and-ammunition carrier. This vehicle, a purely commercial type, has outperformed all vehicles including hand carts, power carts, commercial tractors and tanks. During the tests it has negotiated all types of terrain and terrain in which tanks have been stuck. It is capable of being man-handled in that, if temporarily bogged, men are able to lift and move one end to firmer soil. It is of low silhouette, possesses remarkable cross-country ability, has sufficient cargo capacity, and withal, is procurable commercially. It is adaptable for use as a carrier for the Caliber .30 Machine Gun, 81 mm Mortar, 60 mm Mortar, communications equipment, and as a prime mover for the 37 mm Antitank Gun. It is considered that this vehicle will fully meet Infantry requirements in a weapons-and-ammunition carrier better than any vehicle developed to date.

Figure 40: A 1/2 ton Marmon-Herrington 4 X 4.

> Adoption of this vehicle would eliminate the necessity for mule carts, hand carts, or 1 ½ ton trucks now used for special weapons. In the Caliber .30 and 81 mm animal-drawn machine-gun companies or mortar companies, it would replace two mules, two carts, and two hand carts per gun squad. In motorized regiments the automotive carrier would replace one 1 ½ ton truck and hand carts now prescribed for each machine-gun squad. From the economical point of view alone savings thus effected are well worthy of consideration.

In war, one weapons-and-ammunition carrier is required for each gun squad to carry all essential equipment and ammunition prescribed; in time of peace, one carrier per two gun squads is practical as the full war-time allowance of ammunition is not required for training purposes.

It is not contemplated that the automotive weapons carrier will eliminate entirely the necessity of man-carrying weapons and ammunition. The point will finally be reached somewhere near the front line where man-carrying becomes necessary irrespective of the type of carrier employed. However, the use of the automotive weapons carrier should permit weapons to be brought to the first cover in rear of the front line in the most expeditious manner and with the least fatigue to personnel. Due to its ability to cross-country more quickly and to negotiate rougher terrain, and because it presents a smaller target than a mule-drawn cart or a hand cart pulled and pushed by men, it is reasonable to assume that the automotive carrier can approach nearer the front line than either the mule-drawn or hand carts, thereby reducing the distance that the weapons must be man-carried.

Criticism of the four-wheel, four-wheel-drive vehicle has been presented by some on the grounds that such vehicles are not a commercial item and are not in general use in the automotive world. It is submitted that such vehicles are being used more frequently each year in commercial activities; Marmon-Herrington Company, GMC and Chrysler Corporation all produce 4 X 4 vehicles. Attention is also invited to the purchase by the War Department about two years ago of 39 extra light, 4 X 4 vehicles for experimental purposes at Fort Benning. At the time invitations for bids were issued the Marmon-Herrington Company only was making a truck of this kind. However, General Motors Corporation immediately undertook development of the type of vehicle desired and secured the bid. Demand by the War Department for 4 X 4 vehicles would unquestionably augment present commercial activities in production of that type of vehicle.

The Chief of Infantry recommends that a motor vehicle of characteristics equivalent in the tested Marmon-Herrington ½ ton, 4 X 4 truck, with the additional characteristics listed below, be adopted standard for Infantry use for the purpose of a weapons, ammunition and communications carrier, and as a prime mover for antitank guns:

- Be equipped with 7.50 X 15 Chevron type tires with non-puncture inner tubes, single front and rear.
- Have open cab with folding top.
- Have folding windshield.
- Heavy front bumper capable of pushing down saplings and brush.

- Have rear bumperettes.
- Have double windshield wiper.
- Have towing pintle.
- Have towing hooks at two front corners of frame.[143]

The Infantry had come to the conclusion that they needed the Marmon-Herrington ½ ton 4 X 4 truck; however, in reality their "perfect" vehicle would consist of a cross between the ½ ton truck and the Howie Machine-Gun carrier. While this solution met Infantry needs for a weapons carrier, it did not take into account Cavalry, Field Artillery or other branch's requirements. Yet the Infantry's testing had spelled out key requirements for the ultimate answer in a lightweight military vehicle: a weight of ½ ton or less, low silhouette, and four-wheel drive.

The German "Jeep"

While the United States Army moved cautiously into mechanized warfare the principle that competition drives innovation in business applied also to the military. Numerous wars have resulted from arms buildups based upon superior technology. A primary cause of World War I was a global contest to possess the strongest and most modern navy, and in the 1930s major powers were again competing to develop superiority in military capacity. Germany, under the Nazis, reignited the rivalry with an aggressive rearmament program which included research and development in light reconnaissance vehicles.

Hitler had made the development of the Volkswagen or "People's Car" a priority of his regime declaring that, "the automobile must become the means of transportation for the people" and he pushed for production of a car, "at a price which would make it affordable to the broad masses." With the dedication of the new Volkswagen plant on May 26, 1938 the Nazi leader had turned his vision into reality.[144]

Figure 41: German Kubelwagen on Eastern Front circa 1943. Attribution: Bundesarchiv, Bild 101I-022-2926-07 / Wolff/Altvater / CC-BY-SA

However, beginning in 1934, discussions were initiated to develop a military version of the vehicle designed to solve the same issues the United States Army was wrestling with in the late 1930s, i.e. develop a vehicle to transport troops and small payloads while also acting as a weapons carrier.[145]

The Germans worked slowly and the design of this vehicle took shape in early 1938 with a proposed weight of approximately 2,000 pounds which was significantly heavier than the 1,200 pounds the U.S. Army would require in a few short years. That weight was met by liberally using aluminum wherever possible. Developed during 1939 and 1940 the vehicle was named the Kubelwagen (Bucket Car) which originally was a generic name derived from the shape of all German Army vehicles; however, over time the term came to apply to the highly successful Kubelwagen built by Volkswagen, which became the sole military car for German forces in November 1941. The vehicle saw action and acquitted itself well in all theatres; however, in a testament to the superiority of the vehicle created by the Bantam team, it was eventually known as the "German Jeep."[146]

1938–1939: Bantam Strikes Out

Roy Evans and the team at the American Bantam Car Company struggled to sell vehicles in the commercial market. Evans, always the salesman, looked for other markets and he realized that the Army had a need for a small, light, mobile vehicle, just what his group in Butler was manufacturing. He would work to interest the Army in Bantam products with no success.

Figure 42: A 1937 American Bantam 1/4 Ton Pickup Truck.

In late 1937 the Army continued its cautious movement toward a small motorized vehicle authorizing the purchase of three truck chassis ¼ ton for testing. Early in 1938 procurement was authorized to secure the items, and through competitive bidding, the award went to the American Bantam Car Company. [147]

The overall objective of obtaining these units was "the development of a suitable self-propelled vehicle of the wheeled type, consisting insofar as practicable, of standard commercial units and parts and of the least possible weight and size for the purpose of transporting two (2) men, a caliber .30 machine gun, tripod and ammunition over c/c terrain as may be expected to lie between opposed Infantry and Infantry machine gun positions." The June 2, 1938 memo outlining the program also contained detailed specifications, marking one of the earliest lists of characteristics for a light reconnaissance vehicle.[148]

While American Bantam had made an inroad into the military market, their initial efforts turned out unfavorably. The Infantry reported in August that they "no longer require the development of a vehicle of the subject type for the purpose mentioned in the subject project, this project is hereby cancelled" and recommended incorporating the chassis into a "truck master's vehicle."[149] This decision most likely resulted from the fact that the Infantry had settled on the Marmon-Herrington ½ ton 4 X 4 for their needs.

The Cavalry conducted a detailed test of the chassis as follows:

> The vehicle was equipped with two seats in front and with a light "pick-up" type of wooden body. It was then issued to the Headquarters Troop, 2nd Cavalry, for test. This troop used it in lieu of a motorcycle to accompany the Scout Car Platoon and, at times, the Transportation Platoon during all garrison and field training conducted by the unit until the end of the test period. It accompanied the troop of the Cavalry School spring march during which the regiment operated over wet clay roads. It was also used on the reservation on several occasions to transport a caliber .50 machine gun, with ammunition and one man in addition to the driver.[150]

Unfortunately for Evans and Reuben O. Gill, the general manager of the company, who approved the sale of the units, these tests also went against American Bantam's product. The Cavalry Board concluded in November 1938, "that the subject vehicle is not suitable for any tactical use in Cavalry, either horse or mechanized" and that, "the Bantam chassis be considered unsuitable for any tactical uses in Cavalry either horse or mechanized."[151]

In addition, also during 1938 a Bantam ¼ ton 4X2 truck was furnished for testing by the Infantry against the remaining vehicles from the February 1938 evaluation: the Marmon-Herrington Tractor TA30, Light Ordnance Tractor T3E4, Marmon-Herrington ½ ton 4 X 4 truck as well as a new entrant, the General Motors 1-1/2 ton 4 X 4 truck. How Bantam was able to have their entrant considered remains unclear, but the truck in question represents the first ¼ ton item included in any of the tests.[152]

The Bantam vehicle furnished consisted of, "the standard Bantam chassis on which a ¼ ton body and open cab was mounted by the local Quartermaster. The vehicle is powered by a 4-cylinder, 4-cycle engine which develops 20 horsepower at 4000 revolutions per minute. The maximum torque developed is 31 foot-pounds at 2000 revolutions per minute." The report stated that the tests were conducted against the requirement, "that the vehicle visualized as an ideal cross-country carrier for Infantry was one of the small tractor type, of low silhouette, inconspicuous, without armor and capable of moving rapidly across country and on roads, as well as at the slow speeds approximating the march of foot troops."[153,154]

Once again, Bantam would fail, as the report concluded, "It was the unanimous opinion of all concerned with the test at its commencement that a vehicle of the above stated characteristics would be desirable. As the test progressed and as the capabilities and limitations of the vehicles under test began to be disclosed, opinion gradually changed until it became completely and unanimously crystalized in favor of the ½ ton truck as a cross-country vehicle" and the Marmon-Herrington ½ ton 4 X 4 truck was the clear favorite. The discussion section of the report went into great detail on advantages of the ½ ton 4 X 4 truck over the other vehicles examined and dismissed Bantam's entry at line 29 of a 30 line discussion, "the Bantam ¼ ton truck proved to be entirely unsuitable for use as a cross-country carrier and no requirement is known for Infantry use of this vehicle. This vehicle lacks adequate power, performance and capacity for use as a cross-country carrier," or in other words, Bantam was laughed off the field.[155]

Nearly a year would pass and with an executive change at American Bantam the Butler car manufacturer would make another effort to interest the Army in a small reconnaissance vehicle based on their product. Frank Fenn replaced Gill as President and General Manager in 1939. He immediately penned a detailed letter to Lieutenant Colonel Herbert J. Lawes (though Lawes was actually a Major) of the Holabird Quartermaster Depot (the focal point of all vehicle procurements of the Army) to reignite the Army's interest in his products.

Fenn began by acknowledging the chassis failure, as he wrote, "Some months ago this company made the error of selling three Bantam chassis chasses [sic] to the Quartermaster Corps for trial, which was a serious mistake inasmuch as these cars in no way came up to the government requirements – in fact they were the first series of cars manufactured by this company and had I been connected with the company at that time I would not have permitted the sale." Fenn then made his pitch, "Since then, however, our entire unit has been redesigned and our 1940 models will, in my opinion, provide anything and everything demanded for army use up to their carrying capacity."[156]

Fenn described the improvements, marking another milestone in the evolutionary development of the specifications that would emerge for the first Jeep prototype in June 1940, as follows:

- an improved three-bearing engine with 25% more horsepower;
- two-way springs and hydraulic shock absorbers;
- a frame and radius rod assembly in front greatly strengthened;
- can cover hills within a hundred mile radius of Butler at speeds of 45 to 60 miles per hour fully loaded with a level ground speed of 70 miles per hour;
- can shift through gears from a dead stop to 30 miles an hour in 30 seconds;
- new self-equalizing brakes stop the car in twice their own length from 30 miles an hour; and,
- no oil usage and gallonage consumed in ordinary work is from 40 to 50 miles per gallon.[157]

The American Bantam President and General Manager then stated his objective, "and the thing we are after, Colonel, is an opportunity to demonstrate these cars again at our expense" and he used the tried and true testimonial (an early example of the love troops would have for the Jeep) referencing a contact to buttress his case:

> During the Maneuvers at Manassas, Majors Eggers and Leetch used one of these cars for reconnaissance purposes and found them far more satisfactory than a motorcycle and sidecar. They could go anywhere the foregoing vehicle could go and many places where they could not because of their power. The use of these cars is in no way confined to highways. They followed marching troops everywhere, over any trail which the troops chanced to follow. The cars were extremely well liked with the result that Major Eggers has given me your name, together with several others in the War Department, in the Quartermaster Corps, because he is of the opinion that there is a definite place for our equipment in the service.[158]

Fenn closed his sales letter by again making his offer, "if it is possible to arrange demonstration of the new 1940 car anyplace which you may see fit, we will gladly take the necessary equipment to whichever spot may be designated, together with any instruments which may be required to prove out compression, mileage, etc." and humbly asked for a second chance, "I realize that it is pretty difficult to get a second trial on any product but we feel our present cars will be extremely useful and would like very much to conduct a second test for you. Thanking you for whatever consideration you may see fit to show us, I remain …"[159]

Lawes' December 12, 1939 response was succinct, "It is suggested that in the event favorable consideration is given to this request of the Bantam Car Company by higher authority that one or more of these vehicles be assigned to the Streamlined Divisions. These organizations undoubtedly could, and would give a more positive answer to the utility of this vehicle than any other in the Army."[160] Fenn's effort may have failed; however, rapidly changing events only months away would bring the military to Butler and would make the words of the long-forgotten Major Eggers, "that there is definitive place for our (American Bantam's) equipment in the service" as prophetic as any ever uttered.

1940: Evolution of a New Vehicle

1936–1939 saw numerous attempts by various using arms of the Army, especially the Infantry and Cavalry, to find a solution to the vexing problem of increased battlefield mobility. The Cavalry, as described by Colonel Hamilton in 1935, needed a reconnaissance car that could equal the best characteristics of the horse, while the Infantry required a weapons carrier for the heavier arms and their ammunition to replace the mule and cart. Development and testing during the latter half of the 1930s had shown an adequate vehicle did not exist between the motorcycle and sidecar and the ½ ton 4 X 4 truck. Infantry testing had shown that the latter vehicle was the most suitable foundation for their needs; however, they needed the best characteristics of the Howie Machine-Gun Carrier incorporated into any solution, and that did not exist. Other branches of the Army, the Field Artillery in particular, needed a vehicle, but were slower than the Infantry and Cavalry to investigate solutions.

As World War II commenced in September 1939, and carried on into 1940, all using arms of the United States Army were still without a vehicle that combined all the requirements and characteristics into one solution needed for so many different stakeholders. Without a doubt no one at the time, in the American military, or the automotive industry, would think the answer would come from, as 1940 dawned, the now bankrupt American Bantam Car Company.

1940: The Procurement Challenge

For many projects procurement represents a significant phase of work and usually presents numerous challenges and complications. Evans and his team were already at least familiar with Army purchasing bureaucracy through the failed chassis procurement. Fenn's letter to Lawes demonstrated that he knew that Camp Holabird was the motor transport center and the post assigned to coordinate the purchase of all vehicles for the Army. However, not surprisingly, the red tape of peacetime Quartermaster procurement was extensive, and adding to the challenges was the fact that the process was in a state of flux in 1940. Understanding this complexity provides context for action and events in June – July 1940 that culminated in the awarding of the contract to build the Jeep prototype to American Bantam.

The Quartermaster Corps was the primary group assigned to purchase items for the Army. During the interwar period this group suffered from the general degradation of capability described in chapter 3. However, the primary issues were within the purchasing process between conflicting objectives on the method for vehicle procurement compounded by the rules governing government purchasing. These factors not only led to the involvement of the American Bantam Car Company in the development of the requirements for the Jeep prototype, but also as to why they had to compete in a request for proposal to secure the contract.[161]

The overriding objective of Quartermaster vehicle purchasing after World War I was a quixotic quest for standardization of models. During the Great War over two hundred different varieties of vehicles had made it to France with the American Expeditionary Force, making the inventorying of spare parts and maintenance a nightmare. The Quartermaster Corps desperately wanted to avoid that scenario in the future. Starting in the late 1920s, and continuing during the 1930s, the Army's purchasing arm, though forbidden by law to purchase finished vehicles according to specific requirements, had instituted a program where they would build a "standard" vehicle by procuring commercially available parts.[162]

The standardization objective was in direct conflict with the views held by powerful forces in the Army and the automotive industry. These voices contended that the "standard" vehicle program was not practical, would entail unacceptable delays during wartime and would not improve maintenance to the extent the program's champions envisioned. Additionally, private manufacturers viewed the program as a direct threat to their ability to supply product to the Army. The overriding opinion was that the Army should not only avoid manufacturing and assembling vehicles, but that it should not even engage in automotive research and development, due to the rapidity of technological change in the industry.[163] These views were encapsulated in regulations promulgated in September 1939 which:

- limited the Army to models produced commercially by two or more competing companies,
- restricted the service to the use of commercially available trucks with few modifications,
- mandated the use of parts and assemblies from standard production from the automotive industry and,
- forbid the use of specially designed vehicles and a "standard fleet."[164]

These regulations limited the Army to five chassis sizes ½, 1 ½, 2 ½, 4 and 7 ½ ton models which made vehicle size the only standard item in truck procurement, and note that a ¼ ton size was not specified.[165]

While the Army wrestled with conflicting objectives for vehicle development the overarching rules pertaining to government purchasing also limited the Quartermaster Corps effectiveness in this area. These laws and regulations directed the awarding of contracts to the lowest responsible bidder, as well as forbade the Quartermaster from providing detailed requirements. Additionally, only general specifications such as carrying capacity, speed, or weight were allowed and nothing that could lead to standardization. These rules had the good intentions of guarding against favoritism, to allow the Army to benefit from competition between bidders on price, and released the service from keeping up-to-date with vehicle technology advancement. However, these rules directly conflicted with the Quartermaster's desire for standardization to alleviate maintenance and parts availability in the field.[166]

Further complicating matters were the unique characteristics involved with vehicle procurement, versus the innumerable other items the Quartermaster purchased. For example, it was possible to develop specifications for a uniform from one design because clothing manufacturers, in most cases, were able to produce similar products, if necessary. However, for motor vehicles, it was impossible to create matching models based upon another's design, as the tremendous amount of retooling and machinery changes in relation to the small amount of peacetime purchasing made this option cost ineffective. The economics, as well as the rules favoring the awarding of contracts to only the successful low price bidder, meant that only that concern could produce the desired vehicle effectively, which negated any chance for standardization.[167]

With the German victories in May – June 1940 the opportunity for change appeared in the procurement area as the Quartermaster sought authority to purchase vehicles through negotiated contract versus competitive bidding. This dynamic would allow for working directly with one manufacturer, significantly speeding up the process and enhancing standardization. Congress passed Public Law 703 on July 1, 1940, which allowed for negotiated contracts; however, the Army was slow to adapt the process. Therefore, in June – July 1940 American Bantam would encounter a muddled procurement process which led to numerous twists and turns for the Butler small car manufacturer.[168]

After the war, the director of the Military Planning Division would comment on the results of this confusing and conflicting situation as follows:

> It has been said too often that the Army started this war with the equipment which it had ended World War I. Actually, the situation was much worse. Many items which had been developed as the result of field experience in the mud and rain of northern France in 1917 and 1918 were "modified" in peacetime to be more suitable for the garrison life at Ft. Benning, Georgia, or Ft. Sam Houston, Texas. Even after the outbreak of the war, the importance of immediately improving existing equipment was not recognized by many … Furthermore, many of the items which are procured by the Quartermaster Corps are of commercial types. In peacetime research had to be carried out on Ordnance material because there were no commercial items available. On the other hand, it was felt by many that the Quartermaster Corps could and would accept standard commercial designs without difficulty. No single point of view has perhaps done the Army more harm than this one. There are extremely few commercial items which are suitable for military use. The demands which the Army places upon equipment are such that the use of commercial items results in lower efficiency, higher casualties, and incidentally, higher costs. The inadequacies of existing equipment and the dangers implicit in its use were brought out at once in the snow and mud of supposedly subtropical North Africa and in the early campaigns in the Aleutians.[169]

Fortunately for the Army, a "commercial design" for a ¼ ton truck 4 X 4 light, did not exist, which meant designing, building and delivering it from scratch, but was that possible in the muddled procurement rules and regulations in place in the summer of 1940?

While there were many issues impacting the Army procurement process throughout the interwar period, which impacted the building of the Jeep prototype, the actual procurement process was also not simple. Ideas for new developments originated from many sources including the using arms and services each of which maintained its own test board (as shown by separate tests by the Infantry and the Cavalry of the Bantam chassis), the engineering branch of the Quartermaster Corps, civilian inventors and direct solicitation by manufacturers (exemplified by Bantam's attempts to interest the Army in a small vehicle throughout the 1930s). In motor vehicle procurement the first action was the development of an overall definition of the desired military requirements which was the responsibility of the using arm (Cavalry, Infantry, Field Artillery, etc.) The General Staff would approve these specifications as the representative of the Secretary of War upon which the Quartermaster General was ordered to commence with the procurement.[170]

The Quartermaster Corps was responsible for general purpose vehicles, hauling of cargo, ammunition, personnel, or equipment, as the Ordnance department maintained jurisdiction over combat or fighting vehicles such as tanks or armored cars. The QMC divided its vehicles by administrative and tactical, with the former being used for interior lines use, while the latter were intended for field conditions and were distinguished by having four-wheel drive. The first Jeep prototype project was a tactical vehicle procurement.[171]

With General Staff approval, the project was reviewed and approved by the Quartermaster Technical Committee (QMTC) which had members from all using arms and services. For vehicles, the Motor Transport subcommittee would have jurisdiction over the procurement and report to the entire QMC Technical Committee. The QMTC was responsible for reconciling differing opinions over the specifications from the using arms (which, not surprisingly, occurred frequently). The QMTC would consolidate, and update the requirements, if necessary, which after approval went again to the General Staff, for the Secretary of War's sign-off.[172]

With general characteristics finalized, the Quartermaster Motor Transport Division, as mentioned, housed at Camp Holabird, Maryland, encapsulated the service branches' wish list into a detailed specification that included every military characteristic desired, which when approved by the Assistant Secretary of War, launched the purchase of the vehicle.[173]

Figure 43: A German Panzer Mark IV Ausf C. Attribution: Bundesarchiv, Bild 183-J08365 / CC-BY-SA

1940: The Challenge

As Hitler's panzers rolled into the Low Countries and Ardennes on May 10, 1940, two major issues confronted the United States military. First, the need for a lightweight, low silhouette, four-wheel drive vehicle to meet all the using arms mobility needs and, second, a complex procurement process in a state of flux that added increased bureaucracy and time to any purchases made. It was these challenges that the intrepid, never-say-die, American Bantam Car Company would once again take on, beginning in January 1940.

Questions for Educators

Discuss the importance of pioneering research.

Discuss the challenges of having a visionary idea, such as Lieutenant Hamilton's light cross-country car concept, accepted and acted upon?

How can an earlier "failed" project help another project succeed?

Discuss the challenges inherent in the procurement process.

Discuss the unique difficulties inherent in government procurement.

Chapter 5: Project Initiation—General Requirements

The success of a large project usually results from numerous individuals completing their assigned tasks at a high level over the course of the endeavor. Similar to the offense in United States football, if all eleven players complete their responsibilities properly on any given play positive yardage will result. However, if even one competitor fails in their assignment, no gain or even a loss will mark the outcome of their efforts. One of the key responsibilities of a project manager focuses on ensuring team members finish their work satisfactorily and according to the agreed-upon schedule. The project which resulted in the delivery of a small vehicle for use by the United States Army was marked by numerous individuals each contributing his unique talents to the project at the proper time.

February 1940–May 16, 1940—Butler, Pennsylvania and Washington D.C.

The first of these was Francis H. Fenn, President and Chairman of the Board of the American Bantam Car Company. Fenn was one of many seasoned automotive veterans who would work on the quarter ton effort. Bantam's top executive had cut his teeth as an official with the Hupp Motor Car Company, Pontiac, Willys-Overland and Ford before joining the struggling Butler firm in 1937 and taking over as the head of the organization in 1939, as mentioned in chapter 4, from Reuben O. Gill.[174]

Figure 44: Francis H. Fenn.

Before becoming a manager he obtained practical manufacturing and automotive experience during his stint at Ford as a managing and production student. In that capacity he had, "studied such matters as the preparation of bills of material, routing, efficiency reports, and the paper work that goes with production, in addition to the actual processing of components and the assembly of the final vehicle."[175] The ¼ ton project would have a highly knowledgeable and skilled leader heading the business side of the endeavor.

After assuming the role of President of the company, Fenn had attempted to reverse the military's rejection of the Bantam commercial car with no success (chapter 4). However, like a lover pursuing their beloved, Bantam's chief would not take no for an answer. Even though the Army had soundly rejected his firm's commercial offering through the Infantry's testing, those working at the Butler firm had concluded that, "we could produce a satisfactory vehicle for the Army but it would have to be a special vehicle."[176] He also knew that his company's small cars were not selling, that by the beginning of 1940 the firm was bankrupt, and that producing an automobile for the Army was the only option left to save the company.

The old adage states, "when the going gets tough, the tough get going" and at the beginning of 1940, Fenn initiated the series of events which would improbably lead to the creation of the first Jeep.

> Early in 1940 Major William H. Ward, Jr. now executive officer of Hunter Field at Savannah, Georgia contacted Assistant Secretary of War Lewis Johnson as a follow-through on correspondence which had taken placed [sic] between the American Bantam Car Company and the Army for some months ... and had a very lengthy discussion with him respecting the possibility of our producing a special car for the Army ... Major Ward was connected with the American Bantam Car Company as its general counsel and as a director of the company.
>
> Major Ward reported to me that the Assistant Secretary of War made it very plain to him that while the Army might be interested in a small, lightweight, high-powered vehicle, it would have to be comprised of certain definite military characteristics, such as four-wheel drive.
>
> That was in January or February 1940. Shortly after that time we employed Harry Payne. Harry Payne was originally employed by us to sell aviation parts. However, in going around the Munitions Building in Washington he reported to me that he had *aroused some interest in a lightweight, high-powered, very small, low-silhouette vehicle* (emphasis added).[177]

The journey of a large project mirrors in many respects the trek of a marathoner, and during the 26 miles and 385 yards, or 42.195 kilometers, of the race there are times when only dogged, determined, and persistent effort will keep the runner's legs moving. The almost super-human effort to weed through, and overcome, the Army's bureaucracy to have a project officially created to procure a ¼ ton reconnaissance vehicle would fall to Commander Charles "Harry" Payne. As with so many associated with the creation of the Bantam pilot model Payne was the right person, in the right place, at the right time, with the proper skills sets to successfully complete his role.

Payne was a serial entrepreneur, extreme extrovert and consummate salesman. He began over twenty years of preparation for his moment in the sun in 1940, immediately after the close of World War I, in which he served as a pioneering naval aviator, pilot 483.[178] The history of Payne's activities during the inter-war years reads like a shadowy Hollywood thriller. The product pitchman founded and/or participated in a plethora of businesses, including the Payne Export and Import Company during the 1920s. Under that moniker he personally sold forty-five to fifty planes, along with spare parts, to the Mexican government, as well as selling planes and a tractor to the Peruvian regime.[179]

Also during the 1920s Payne became the managing director of a firm called the Inter-Allied Aircraft Company. His work with this company would impress upon him the absolute necessity of a small lightweight vehicle that could traverse rough terrain at high speeds.[180] The mission of Inter-

Allied was to purchase surplus training aircraft, in particular the Avro, and change over the aircraft to a three-person passenger plane.[181] However, it was through the side business of training pilots that the Commander would become acquainted with the life-and-death need for an all-terrain small vehicle:

> Back in 1922 when I was managing director in the Inter-Allied Aircraft Company, we were selling wartime planes, and also instructing students at Roosevelt field. In those days aircraft motors were not very dependable. We had a lot of trouble with motor failure and in teaching men how to fly we had some very unfortunate experiences, a man cracking up – or students, rather – cracking up two or three miles away from the field, and as a result, a lot of these crashes would catch fire.
>
> Several men were burned up needlessly because the rescue party could not get to them due to the rough terrain of the country. We tried motor cycles and so forth, and they would bog down. Finally, due only to lack of money, -- and we were pretty well broke in those days—I developed a Ford chassis with an OX-5 engine and a wooden propeller. This would carry 2 men and fire extinguishers. This job weighed around 1200 or 1400 pounds stripped but the wheels and tires were so small that we had difficulty. However, it could be easily manhandled.
>
> This was a very rough rescue car and in 1924 and 1925 I contracted with the Mexican government for several planes, and I built another car which consisted of a Ford Chassis with a Ford engine, and put some over-sized airplane tires on it, two bucket seats, fire extinguishers, and on the right hand we had two jacks and a drum.
>
> To secure – to this drum we attached a cable so that when a plane crashed part of the fuselage could be connected with the wire cable, the rear end of the car jacked up and the wreckage separated so that we could rescue the men who were penned in. The front wheel of the car was anchored to a nearby tree or boulder as the case may be.

Entrepreneurial Lesson 21
Project Champion

"It's not what you know, it's who you know." —is a mistaken notion. What if who you know snubs you, because you have delivered a piece of trash?

All entrepreneurs are not like Steve Jobs, who was his own champion. Every project needs its earliest adopter, the one who disseminates it into the world. The adopter-champion is not necessarily the Entrepreneur, or a functioning member of the enterprise. The champion is the someone who loves the project and knows what to do with it to make it succeed.

Do not embarrass yourself by giving who you know a piece of trash project. After all, the champion knows what to do with what you know. Who you know will spread it upstream to all the people s/he knows. Here is how it really goes:

"It's not *only* what you know, it's *what* you give to who you know."

> About that time I also sold a lot of equipment to the Peruvian Government and built another one of the same type of cars which was used with great success. In those days, as I said before, we lost the lives of many men through fire, and there was no car suitable, and we did not have the money to go into heavy engineering and develop a car that was really needed. However, these cars were a lot better than anything we had, including the motorcycle.[182]

Payne would bounce around in numerous ventures from the mid-1920s on, including attempting to pioneer aviation and aircraft insurance as an agent of Payne and Richardson through National Liberty, founding the Aviation Business Bureau Incorporated involved with aviation consulting work and statistics, work on establishing aircraft factories and passenger work, barnstorming and endurance flights, creating the P & E Corporation working on aviation technical advising, and even selling juices for the Bruce's Juice Corporation.[183]

During the early part of 1939 Payne's endeavors brought him into contact with a Major Brownell of the Reconstruction Finance Committee, the agency which had loaned Roy Evans funds to keep Bantam in operation (chapter 1). Brownell introduced the serial entrepreneur to the aforementioned William Ward, American Bantam attorney, and Ward brought Payne to the attention of Frank Fenn.[184]

While Fenn was working on his military small car "Hail Mary pass" in late 1939 he also had another idea to keep the Butler car manufacturer in business. As Payne related, "there was a great demand – yes, there was a great demand about that time for subcontracting from a lot of aviation companies like Douglas, Boeing and so forth. They had men out looking for automotive factories that could build certain aviation parts."[185]

Payne, however, had not forgotten his experience with the small rescue car:

> In the early part of 1940 in my apartment one evening, there was Johnny Moore, who is now acting chief engineer of the Small Airplant Division, Colonel Kutz, who is now Brigadier General Kutz, and I think Commander Hagan of the Navy -- I am not sure but there were several others. We got beefing about the war and how soon we were going to get into it, and the question came up about the motorcycle, and how useless it was in cross-country work, especially in muddy weather. These men knew about what you might call my phobia that I had for a small light-weight car, and they suggested the Army might be interested.[186]

The American Bantam President decided in February 1940 to hire Payne to, "try and get them some aviation business because they were more or less at a standstill."[187] In 1940 the United States air arm was still part of the army (the United States Air Force was created in 1947 after World War II). Therefore, Payne's efforts to secure work for the Butler factory would lead him to the Munitions

Entrepreneurial Lesson 22
Persistence

One of the keys to entrepreneurial excellence is persistence. The Entrepreneur is consistently persistent and persistently consistent about it. Thorough. Doggedly determined. Sticks to the knitting. All the time.

Testing and re-testing products can lead to happy accidents, that is, unexpected gems that would not have presented themselves were it not for the Entrepreneur being persistent about looking at everything and checking it more than twice.

Goal achievement is a result of persistence in the cause of a project. Were it not for this trait, we would still be jungle animals living in caves without fire and wheels. Persistence is the heartbeat of success.

Building to, "start ringing door bells in the Army." He carried with him his experiences in the 1920s with the small rescue car.[188] Fate, karma, luck, call it what you will, had brought the one man who understood the basics of a small cross-country vehicle, and who was connected to the premier small car manufacturer in the United States at that time, into the building where one branch of the Army, the Infantry, desperately desired such a car.

Payne's initial forays into the labyrinth of the Army's bureaucracy met with little success:

> First, to the Planning Division and met a Colonel Young. He was on the first floor of the Munitions Building. I told him my idea for a small cars [sic]to take the place of the motorcycle. He said he had no authority and he started introducing me to army officers that he thought might be helpful, and I got nowhere in a grand hurry. He (Young) introduced me to some people in the Signal Corps and that was the wrong entrance. They said they had no authority. Finally, I met a dozen different officers probably, whose names I do not recall, and finally I met Lieutenant Colonel Hester, who was in the Quartermaster Department, and then assigned to the office of the Secretary of War. Colonel Hester was very sympathetic and knowing Army routine a lot better than I did, he suggested that I to [sic] go the chief of infantries office (headed by General George A. Lynch).
>
> Lieutenant Colonel Hester introduced me to W. C. Lee, who is the material officer in General Lynch's office, and at the time – the same time, I met Colonel Oseth and a Sergeant by the name of Thomas.[189]

Payne's journey had taken from February 1940 to mid-May 1940; however, his efforts had led him to the exact service arm he needed to find, the Infantry as well as the next key link in the truck 4 X 4 light journey, Colonel Ingomar M. Oseth.[190]

Colonel Oseth was stationed at Fort Benning during the late 1930s at the exact time the Infantry was conducting the tests to find a suitable light cross-country vehicle, the results of which had settled upon the ½ ton Marmon-Herrington 4 X 4 (chapter 4). In addition, his duties had required of him to develop special knowledge related to cross-country weapons carriers for troops:

In 1936 and 1937, I was on duty with the 24th Infantry at Fort Benning, Georgia. I had nothing personally or officially to do with the tests conducted at that time. I witnessed them as a spectator. And talked to the test officers, because I was interested. Later, I came into a position where my official duties required that I examine those reports.

I was detailed by the Chief of Infantry to the tank school in 1938 for the one-year course, the nine months course. From there, in June 1939, I went to Washington, to the Chief of Infantries' Office, where I was assigned to the Arms, Equipment and Finance Section, and charged with the development of motor vehicles and signal equipment. Those were my special – that was my special job.

The course itself covered all phases of motors, army motors, including tanks and motor vehicles, motor trucks. Mechanical construction, operation, everything that is necessary for an officer of the line, one of the using services, to know about, including maintenance, and things like that.

As part of that course, I was required to make a research and write a paper on this subject, "Characteristics, Field of Usefulness, and Present Trend of Motorized Cross-Country Carriers for Infantry Weapons and Battlefield Supply." I didn't compose that title myself. It was shoved at me.

I spent several months researching all the records that I could find, foreign publications, especially the Germans, who had German reports, some periodicals, in the German language, and so on, on the general subject of motor vehicles fit for, or suitable for military use. I studied the characteristics and the records of the performance of probably a hundred and fifty vehicles of different types at that time in preparation for this paper.[191]

Entrepreneurial Lesson 23
Identifying the Key Stakeholder

The Entrepreneur recognizes many tangent and unconnected stakeholders involved in a project. In a wager, a neutral party holds the bets and pays the winner. That does not make the stakeholder or the gamblers the key player, even if they are the actual players. They all count in the equation. They are either all key, or perhaps there is no such thing as a key stakeholder.

Interdependent then are the stakeholders. Perhaps that is the key. Such considerations make the Entrepreneur become sensitive to all of the threads that can affect success with a project. If the project is developed with the sword of war hanging overhead, then the key stakeholders are the citizens of the countries or warring factions involved. Maybe not tangent, but certainly not entirely neutral.

Active or passive, there are multiple stakeholders. The key ones are identified as they appear on the scene.

Additionally, during the time Oseth was at Fort Benning, as he stated, he had witnessed the vehicle tests and was familiar with the type of vehicles and the pros and cons of those means of transport:

> There was an Ordnance track-laying vehicle, as I recall it, built on the chassis of a light tank. There were two commercial track-laying vehicles. Full track, you might call that, full track vehicles. One by Marmon-Herrington, and I don't remember who made the other one. They were slightly different in size. There was a small car designed from spare parts found in the junk yard there by Major, or Captain Howie, which he was at that time, and Sergeant Wiley, made at Fort Benning, called the Howie-Wiley machine-gun carrier. That was in those tests.
>
> There was also tested a bantam commercial car. I believe, as I recall it, it had a pick-up body. I am not too certain about that. The Marmon-Herrington four wheel, four by four, half ton, came in while the tests were on, were in progress. It wasn't initially in there. One of those vehicles came to the Port Ordnance Officer at Fort Benning as a utility vehicle. It belonged to the Port Ordnance Officer, and he showed it to the Infantry Board, and it was entered into the test that way.
>
> I witnessed, I think – I know there was an ordinary farm tractor. Large wheel, large rear wheels and two wheels in front. One or more of those were tested at the same time. Also a quarter-ton four by two truck of another make. I observed many of the tests and the results of these tests. I did not see them all, naturally. I had other things to do.[192]

It was from these tests that a general set of military characteristics were coalescing for a lightweight infantry weapons carrier and the denizen of Fort Benning was intimately aware of what those requirements were, including the need for four-wheel drive for all battlefield and combat vehicles for the Infantry.[193]

May 17, 1940–June 6, 1940—Washington, D.C.

Oseth was posted to the Chief of Infantry office in Washington D.C in 1939 reporting directly to General Lynch. As part of his official duties, the expert on Infantry trucks was assigned to the Quartermaster Technical Committee and that group's subcommittee on motor transport. [194] That assignment placed him at a key meeting from May 17 – 20, 1940 at Camp Holabird during which the Army's lack of a suitable means for cross-country movement was discussed at length.[195]

> That three-day conference at Holabird was for the purpose of considering and revising military characteristics of all motor vehicles, military motor vehicles. And the two that the Infantry were mostly concerned with were the half-ton four by four, which hadn't developed as we wanted it to. It was much heavier and higher, had a higher silhouette. The other was the motorcycle, which was thoroughly unsatisfactory from the modern viewpoint. It had no cross-

> country ability. We had been trying to get a motor tricycle which has two driven wheels and had much better cross-country ability. Those two projects, among others were discussed at great length for three days there at Holabird.[196]

The conclusions reached by the attendees at this gathering was that there was no hope of reducing the weight of the half-ton, or the silhouette, of the half-ton 4 X 4 within the foreseeable future, and that the motor tricycle was years away with no prospect of getting it.[197] It was also decided that both the Bantam truck and Howie Carrier were unsatisfactory as they, "lacked cross-country ability and sturdiness, the Howie Carrier was deficient in speed, the Bantam was too frail having just about fallen apart with about five thousand miles on it and it got bogged down whenever it got in sand, or mud, or on an upgrade or into a shell hole, or ditch or anything of that nature, in fact both these contenders lacked all military characteristics."[198] When the conference ended on May 20, 1940 the United States Army had no vehicle to fit into its arsenal between the motorcycle and the ½ ton four by four and no plan on how to procure such a weapon. Then fate once again stepped in on the very day that all seemed lost:

> When I (Oseth) returned from the three-day session at Holabird, I had spoken of, as I recall it, it was in the afternoon of the third day, and the Chief Clerk in the office, Sergeant Thompson, told me there was a man there waiting to see me. I then met Mr. Payne, who was sitting in the window, behind my chair, as a matter of fact. That was the first time I met him. He was not introduced to me by anybody. He introduced himself to me.
>
> He was looking, he told me he was looking for Major Howie. Major Howie had been with me as a sort of technical advisor out at the three-day conference at Holabird. Mr. Payne told me he had told – that is, he had been told that Bob Howie could probably be found there. He came to ask me about it. I told him Howie was somewhere in Washington and probably would be in, but I didn't know when. Then the conversation developed between Mr. Payne and myself.
>
> I asked him what particular business he had with Howie. And he told me that he wanted to talk to him about the Howie-Wiley carrier, because he thought the War Department was out to take the vehicle up again. It had been tested and rejected before.
>
> I told him if that was all he wanted to see Howie about, he had been wasting his time, because I was the one making the decisions, subject to being overruled by the Chief of Infantry in respect to what type of vehicle the Infantry would have. And that the Howie-Wiley carrier was out. I then talked with him, and we had some considerable talk and argument on that.

> There was quite a lot of conversation after that, and in the course of that Mr. Payne proposed to me that we accept and test again, retest, the newer model of the bantam, which he claimed was a great improvement over the one we had tested previously, and found deficient. I informed him again that we had thoroughly tested the bantam and even though it might be slightly improved, it lacked the essential military characteristics that we had definitely adopted and decided upon, and that it would be a waste of time.[199]

The Army's leading vehicle expert then expressed to Payne what he believed was needed in a small lightweight vehicle for Infantry use.

> I told Mr. Payne, in substance, this, after we had definitely dismissed these other two vehicles, if you will take your bantam and put a front wheel drive, a front wheel driven front axle on it so as to make a four by four, strip the body down to the bare essentials and put power enough in there to keep those wheels turning, we will be willing to talk business with you, because that is what we are looking for. Mr. Payne said it was almost impossible, that there was none in the world that would make axles like that, that there wasn't one in existence, and he didn't know anyone who could make it. That just about terminated that particular conversation for the day.[200]

Payne was discouraged, but was not about to give up. What exactly transpired from May 20, 1940 – June 2, 1940 when Oseth submitted a draft of a memo laying out for the first time the general specifications for a ¼ ton four by four truck remains unclear. Payne recollected that he had developed the specifications with another individual in General Lynch's office, Colonel W. C. Lee, and that he had provided the requirements to Lee. However, Oseth remembered that he, given his extensive knowledge of Infantry vehicles and the needs of that service arm in that area, had presented what was needed to Payne. Given Payne's gift for self-promotion, as well as his lack of expertise, along with Oseth's character as an officer testifying under oath, the account the Colonel offered represents what most likely transpired.

> Colonel Lee's desk and mine were placed side by side and without any spacing between them, so that I could reach over and touch his shoulder any time. Our offices are very small. We were crowded in there.
>
> There were no conferences, official conferences, that is, other than possible desultory conversations around the hall between Mr. Payne and Colonel Lee regarding that project or any motor transport project, between the time I first met Mr. Payne (May 20th) and the time when I submitted in rough form to Colonel Lee, the draft of the letter of June 6, 1940. Now

> I have no knowledge as to what conversations Mr. Payne may have had with Colonel Lee or anyone else outside the office.
>
> I was the representative of the Chief of Infantry authorized to speak for them and confer about matters of that kind. Mr. Payne addressed himself to me when he had anything to confer about.[201]

The "letter of June 6, 1940" referenced by Colonel Oseth represents the first official document produced in the project that led to the creation of the first Jeep. It contained a general list of characteristics of a vehicle that would fill the Infantry's needs between the motorcycle and sidecar and the ½ ton truck. The Infantry officer steadily maintained he had provided the specifications included in that memo to Payne and that he had drafted the document.

> Mr. Payne testified at page 370 of the record that in giving specifications to Colonel Lee, he told him that the car would have to have a short wheel base between 78 and 80 or 81 inches; that it should be narrow gauge, between 47 and 48 inches; that the silhouette was of great importance; it should have 36 inch silhouette was of great importance; it should have 36 inch silhouette to the cowl; that the overall length should be around 126 inches; the ground clearance, 8 ½ inches at the lowest point which is the differential. That the car should have a four-wheel drive and that it should have a weight of between 1,200 and 1,300 pounds.
>
> (Those are) the characteristics of the one-quarter, 4 X 4, to which I at that time gave the designation, tentative designation, liaison and reconnaissance car as I recall it. I gave those to Mr. Payne myself. I told him what we wanted. He didn't tell us what the characteristics would be.
>
> The specific dimensions, wheel base, clearance, things of that kind, did not enter into the question at all. They were details which were determined upon by the Quartermaster General people later on. They were given not given at that stage by Mr. Payne or myself or anybody else.
>
> The characteristics which were given by me to Mr. Payne and later to Colonel Lee was weight not to exceed 1,000 pounds. Silhouette not to exceed 36 inches. Capacity at least two men with a machine gun and 1,000 rounds of ammunition. Drive, an all four, four-wheel drive; road ability and grade ability equal, at least equal to that of other standard vehicles of the same type.

> Those were the characteristics I communicated to Mr. Payne and asked him if he could produce such a vehicle. Those were the characteristics I later communicated to Colonel Lee, in order to get his approval and support, and still later to General Lynch.[202]

While Colonel Oseth was the driving force behind developing the general specifications for the quarter ton truck, he did credit Colonel Lee with having an interest in light Infantry vehicles and he worked to gain Lee's support for the ¼ ton project.

> Colonel Lee had been for a couple of weeks previous to this carrying around a file of papers describing a Swiss motor car, very light Swiss motor car, called the Bentz car. The file had been sent to him by his friend and mine, Barney Legge, Major Legge, Military Attaché, Switzerland. I had previously examined the specifications of this Bentz car and had decided against it because, for the same reason we decided against the Howie-Wiley Carrier. It didn't have the drive on more than two of the wheels. So when I presented this matter to Colonel Lee, he was intensely interested already in light transportation for the infantry. I remembered I said:
>
> "Colonel, this is right down your alley with your Bentz car project, only it is much better." Then there was some discussion. I think Mr. Payne was there when that conversation took place. I am sure he was. From that time on, Colonel Lee was, if anything more, of an enthusiastic supporter of it that [sic] I was. He followed it, supported me in every possible way and took a sufficient personal interest. So he accompanied me to some of these technical meetings where the characteristics of the jeep were discussed.[203]

The stage was set between Oseth, Payne and Lee to draft a memo officially documenting the general requirements for a quarter ton vehicle for the infantry:

> At the time of the conversation with Colonel Lee, when I won him over by telling him it was right down the alley with his Bentz car, I was at that time engaged in drafting this letter (the June 6, 1940 memo) to the Adjutant General. The procedure when a new development was to be initiated was for the Using Service, the Chief of the Using Service branch write a formal letter to The Adjutant General, stating there is a requirement for that equipment and giving the main military characteristics, not in their final form, but the main military characteristics. That is what I did. That was my duty in the office. That was what I did.[204]

To settle the matter Oseth summarized the events of May 20, 1940 – June 6, 1940 when the memo was finalized and sent to the Adjutant General. He emphatically reiterated that the general specifications originated with him in conversations with Payne and that General Lynch and Colonel Lee were not involved, other than Colonel Lee's cursory interest through his Bentz car project.

> General Lynch came into this thing about the 29th or 30th of June (probable misstatement by Oseth, should be May), after Mr. Payne and I had worked out all these characteristics between us, as I have testified before. It is entirely possible, in fact quite probable that General Lynch thought the thing originated when we presented that finished or semi-finished product to him. I am not sure that Colonel Lee wasn't under the impression the first time I called it to his attention that was the origin, the very beginning of this thing, which was definitely not. There had been days and days of consideration and planning before then that neither Col. Lee nor General Lynch knew about personally.[205]
>
> As I testified yesterday, the function of Mr. Payne and the American Bantam Car Company was to tell us whether they could give us what we wanted. We told them I personally gave to Mr. Payne and to Mr. Finn [sic], who occasionally came in with Mr. Payne, the military characteristics that we wanted. The plan, the vehicle in general outline as was designed – I hate to use the first personal pronoun so much – it was designed in my own brain initially. And Mr. Payne and The American Bantam Company were informed what that picture was. They informed what that picture was. They informed me whether they could produce it or not.[206]

Entrepreneurial Lesson 24
Gathering Support

The Entrepreneur gets buy-in for an idea by making it seem like it came from other people. Members of a team will support their own ideas over input from anyone else.

How does the Entrepreneur plant an idea into the team's mindset so that it gathers the kind of support from the group that brings it to life? Part of it is knowing or sensing how others think or react to stimuli. The most effective techniques are somewhat logical, but somewhat magical, as well. Another part of the technique is to seek advice. People love to freely give their own opinions.

If you want to gather support, make it look like you are supporting those from whom you are gathering it. Treat others as you would want them to treat you. A spiritual teacher once said never ask a question the answer to which you do not already know.

After two weeks of intense discussion Colonel Oseth began preparing the memo around the first of June 1940 following office protocol as follows:

> The system there in the office was anything that has to be worded very carefully, the officer drafting it draws it up in pencil, lead pencil (Oseth). Then it is submitted. After he is satisfied with it, for the time being, it is given to the stenographer, the typist, to make a rough draft. Then the rough draft is the one that forms the subject of conference around, any further

> conferences among personnel. That was probably the one shown to General Lynch by Colonel Lee, the rough draft, the first typed draft of that draft.[207]
>
> They approved it (Lynch and Lee). They both approved it as soon as I had the thing drafted. It was after two or three days discussed around the office, and discussed, I think between, perhaps referred to the Quartermaster people, matters of that kind. The thing was typed in final form for the executive signature. He (Lynch) habitually signed papers issuing from the Chief of Infantry's office.[208]

By June 6, 1940 all conferences were completed and the memo finalized for signature. The document was forwarded to the Chief of Cavalry to begin to gain support from other using arms for this vehicle. In the communication the need for greater mobility was stressed, that current offerings were too heavy and possessed too high a silhouette for a close combat vehicle, and once again, pointed out that the motorcycle with sidecar was also unsuitable for this purpose.[209]

The Chief of Infantry then articulated the first organized requirements for the vehicle as follows:

- Minimum height: 36 inches;
- Maximum weight, without pay load: 750 – 1,000 pounds;
- Adequate cross-country ability and grade ability equal to that of standard cargo vehicle;
- Caliber .30 machine gun mount either integral with the body of the vehicle or detachable;
- Capacity: a crew of at least two men, one machine gun with accessories, and three thousand rounds of ammunition or equivalent weight;
- Armored face shield for driver;
- Four-wheel drive (except where tricycles are considered);
- Ground clearance: maximum possible consistent with desired silhouette.[210]

The memo also indicated that a frame and body designed for amphibious operations was desirable if it did not unduly delay procurement of the vehicle and the obtainment of "a sufficient number of vehicles conforming to the above characteristics, to equip an infantry regiment (rifle) with such vehicles in lieu of standard command and reconnaissance trucks for company units with 6 additional for the Infantry Board (or a total of 40) for extended field test in comparison with the present standard vehicles."[211]

Oseth had thrown in the requirement for an "armored face shield for driver" for a specific purpose. It was not only to protect soldiers, but to attempt to keep the Quartermaster Corps from taking over the project, due to a bad experience with obtaining a vehicle based upon the 1938 tests which had identified the Marmon-Herrington half ton 4 X 4 as suitable for Infantry weapons carrier purposes (chapter 4).

> I put in there a requirement for face armor. It was, I will admit, sort of a lawyer's trick, because that automatically would take it out of the hands of the Quartermaster General with whom we had been having trouble in development of the motor vehicle and made it an ordnance vehicle. The peculiar rule in effect at that time was if a vehicle had armor, laid a track, was a track-laid vehicle, had some other thing like that on it, the Chief of Ordnance was responsible for its development, if it was of the general purpose type, truck carrying on truck, passenger cars, so on, the Quartermaster had it. I didn't want the Quartermaster General to get a hold of this thing because of this difficulty of putting it out of bid and then getting something we didn't want.[212]

The Infantry Colonel had also included in the memo a last recommendation that, "Since the desired type of vehicle is a special one, and since experience has shown the impracticability of securing development of the proper type of vehicle from among present commercial types, it is recommended that the requirements for competitive bidding be waived to the extent necessary to bring about procurement of the best possible design."[213] He described his reasoning as follows:

> Well, we had some sad experiences with the Quartermaster people on this motor procurement matter because in the case of the Marmon-Herrington half ton, 4 X 4, the law was interpreted by the Quartermaster required they call for bids, and the contract for the vehicle was let to the best bidder. That resulted in the case of the half ton in an unsuitable vehicle. The Quartermaster people, I think Colonel Van Deusen hold told me shortly before that, it may have been Colonel Laws [sic], I am not sure, they had told me they were considering, or had gotten authority form the Secretary of War, I am not sure which it was, to waive the requirements for bids, competitive bidding, in certain special cases, if requested by the Using Arms. That was the purpose of putting that in there.[214]

Therefore, due to Oseth's "lawyer's trick" it would fall to the Ordnance Technical Committee to determine the next steps in the development of the truck 4 X 4 light. Oseth summed up the significance of his June 6, 1940 memo vis-à-vis the specifications laid out:

> Individually, singly, there was nothing new in any of these characteristics. They had never been combined in one vehicle before. That was the only new thing about this vehicle, combining those characteristics in a vehicle that was light enough, small enough for infantry battle-field use.[215]

In one memo Oseth had combined years of research, testing and effort surrounding a light truck for military use into one coherent list of general specifications. In doing so he initiated a series of events over the course of the summer and fall of 1940 that would result in the building of one of the most iconic vehicles created in military and automotive history, the Jeep.

Questions for Educators

Discuss the various options to develop high-level product requirements.

What are the key items to capture in high-level product requirements?

Why is it important to solicit and secure support for a project early in the endeavor?

Discuss the importance of identifying potential issues early on, such as Colonel Oseth's problems with the Quartermaster Corps procurement process, and the value of dealing with them as soon as possible.

Chapter 6: Project Initiation—Specific Requirements

> **Entrepreneurial Lesson 25**
> **Evolving Requirements**
>
> Ever designed anything that never changed in medias res? Ever written, rewritten and rewritten a report, a thesis, a book, a poem?
>
> In the middle of writing or designing something, the specifications can change constantly and drastically. Often the most fabulous ideas come as a result of committing in Direction A, only to end up ultimately at Point Z. Time management works in a similar manner. During the day, priorities shift and evolve moment by moment.
>
> As the slogan goes, the idea seems to be to just do it. Plan it, let it evolve, and if it does a better job when it is done than the original concept, so be it.

The majority of professionally managed projects originate from a business necessity. When an authorized effort to fulfill that need forms, the assignment of a project manager to guide the work usually results. One of the first responsibilities of the newly selected leader centers around guiding the gathering of the specific requirements for the endeavor, typically handled, if possible, by a business analyst guided by the project manager. In the project-case presented here, however, at this stage the ¼ ton truck 4 x 4 light had a key stakeholder (the Infantry), but no one guiding the project other than Colonel Oseth.

Throughout June 1940, through a series of actions coordinated by the Ordnance Technical Committee, to which Oseth had deliberately steered the project, the procurement would by the end of the month rest squarely in the hands of the very agency Oseth had attempted to avoid, the Quartermaster General. The challenge of developing a detailed set of specifications from which an automotive manufacturer could build a vehicle would rest squarely with that agency of the United States Army.

June 7, 1940-June 18, 1940—Ordnance Technical Committee, Washington, D. C.

Chapter 4 detailed the Cavalry's interest in a small lightweight reconnaissance vehicle as articulated by Lieutenant Hamilton in his 1935 Cavalry Journal article. Oseth's gambit to begin gathering support for the project by transmitting the June 6, 1940 memo through that using arm, paid immediate dividends as the Chief of Calvary responded quickly, writing to the Adjutant General on June 8, 1940, endorsing the endeavor as follows:

> The Chief of Calvary is interested in the possibility of using a light, cheap car for command and reconnaissance purposes in the cavalry. He therefore concurs in the recommendations of the Chief of Infantry in the basic communication and recommends that he be kept informed of the development and that twenty cars, when manufactured, be made available to him for test.[216]

However, the Adjutant General was not about to break protocol and exclude the official purchasing department of the Army from the project. He forwarded, on June 14, 1940, the Infantry's general specification memo to the Quartermaster General and Chief of Ordnance seeking "comment and recommendation."[217]

During that eight day period Payne was actively promoting Bantam's interest, as Fenn recalled:

> He (Payne) telephoned me and asked me if we could produce such a car. I told Payne that I thought we could. A few days later (early June 1940) he wrote me and asked me to send him all correspondence between our company and the Army, which I did.
>
> Approximately fifteen days after that (most likely June 17 or 18, 1940) he called me and said he was bringing to the American Bantam Car Company plant a technical committee of several officers. At that time he did not name the members of the technical committee.[218]

The exact nature of Payne's efforts after he received all correspondence from Fenn remains unclear; however, he must have read in those records of Bantam's efforts with the Quartermaster General during the late 1930s to interest the Army in their products. Bantam's D.C. player likely spoke with representatives of that department, as the Administrative division of the QMC forwarded the Adjutant General's request for comment and recommendation (on the same day the request was received, June 14, 1940), to the Commanding Officer of Camp Holabird stating the following:

> In view of the fact that the vehicle is required for command-reconnaissance purposes as well as for combat purposes, it is considered that the chassis development be a responsibility of the Quartermaster Corps. Comment is required as to the practicability of securing a commercial vehicle with all-wheel drive conversion, meeting the vehicles characteristics set up in the basic communication. *The light passenger car of the American Bantam Company is suggested as a possible solution of the problem (emphasis added).*[219]

American Bantam's long odyssey to interest the Army in their vehicles was now a reality as the Army's chief procuring arm, just six months after that same department had condescendingly brushed off their products, now recommended them![220] By June 15, 1940 the War Department General Staff, Supply Division was now in the loop and acting under the authority of the Secretary of War, Brigadier General R. C. Moore, Assistant Chief of Staff who issued orders, labeled "IMMEDIATE ACTION," to the Adjutant General, Quartermaster General, Chief of Ordnance, Chief of Cavalry and Chief of Infantry as follows:

1) In view of the fact that the Chief of Ordnance is being directed, in a separate communication, to give further consideration to the Howie Experimental Weapons Carrier, the attached copy of a letter to this office, regarding the proposed military characteristics of a vehicle for Infantry use (Oseth's June 6, 1940 memo), is forwarded for appropriate action and recommendation through the Ordnance Technical Committee.

2) In this connection it is desired that consideration be given to the possible use of the American Bantam car manufactured by the American Bantam Company, Butler, PA.

3) It is further desired that the subcommittee appointed to investigate this matter, include, in addition to those members of the Ordnance Technical Committee you wish to designate, a representative of each of the following arms and services:

4) Chief of Infantry (Lt. Col. Lee)
Chief of Cavalry (Maj. Tompkins)
The Quartermaster General (such representatives as he may wish to designate)

5) You are authorized to request travel orders for such members of the Ordnance subcommittee as may be necessary to conduct a thorough investigation into this matter, and to confer with officials of the automobile industry in the development of a vehicle possessing the desired characteristics.

6) Your recommendations are desired at the earliest practicable date.[221]

To add weight to these orders, Moore had forwarded the memo to the Adjutant General and that individual, George A. Miller, also on June 15, 1940, sent the exact same orders to the Chief of Ordnance and the Quartermaster General under his authority to act on behalf of the Secretary of War. Oseth had placed the Army's key munitions expert squarely in the sights of top brass regarding the development of a light infantry vehicle. With "immediate action" being called for from the highest levels, the Ordnance Chief quickly called for a meeting of his technical committee on June 17, 1940.[222]

The project had gained attention and momentum and Bantam was right in the middle of the action! The fate of Butler's small car manufacturer rested with the Ordnance Technical Committee. However, the successor to American Austin had an ally in that group, the Infantry's representative, Colonel Lee, the same individual Oseth had interested in the project during his interactions with Payne in late May, early June 1940.

The Subcommittee of the Ordnance Technical Committee met on the subject of the development of a light infantry vehicle on June 17, 1940. Whatever the exact discussions were remain lost to history; however, the meeting went decidedly in favor of Bantam's interests as the official minutes recorded:

2. DISCUSSION:

1) From a consideration of the above references (Oseth's June 6, 1940 memo and the Adjutant General's June 15, 1940 orders [mirroring Moore's directives]), the Subcommittee concludes that two types of vehicles are under consideration:

a. The Light Command and Reconnaissance Car.
b. The Howie Weapons Carrier.

2) The Light Command and Reconnaissance Car represents a new type of vehicle, the proposed military characteristics of which are stated by the Chief of Infantry in reference b. (June 6, 1940 memo) The Subcommittee feels that these military characteristics are satisfactory, in general, but will give them further study at the conference to be held at the American Bantam Company's plant.

3) The letter of instructions from the Adjutant General to the Chief of Ordnance (reference c.) [June 15, 1940 orders] refers to par. 1 to instructions to the Chief of Ordnance to further consideration of the Howie Weapons Carrier. The Howie Carrier was considered by the Infantry Board (reference a. [1938 report detailed in chapter 4] in 1938. In this reference the Chief of Infantry recommended that no further development be made of the Howie Cart.

4) In view of the instructions which have been received (O.O. 451/10001, reference c.) it will be necessary to give further consideration to the Howie Weapons Carrier at this time. This vehicle is closely related to the Light Command and Reconnaissance Vehicle discussed above.

5) In order to obtain full and prompt information concerning the design of both types of vehicles, the Subcommittee will visit the plant of the American Bantam Company, Butler, Pennsylvania, on Wednesday, June 19, 1940. The Subcommittee desires that Major Howie be present at the plant in order that the design of the Howie Weapons Carrier can be considered at the same time.

3. RECOMMENDATIONS:

1) That the Subcommittee visit the American Bantam Company for conference with the officials and engineers of that Company in regard to the military characteristics and design of:
   a. The Light Command and Reconnaissance Car.
   b. The Howie Weapons Carrier.

2) That after this visit military characteristics be drawn up for both vehicles, and further recommendations made as to the future development of both vehicles.[223]

These minutes were sent that very day to the Adjutant General who quickly replied on June 18, 1940 that, "the recommendations contained in Paragraph 3, attached Subcommittee Report of the Ordnance Technical Committee, dated June 17, 1940, subject: 'Light Infantry Vehicles – Development Of,' are approved. It was likely that Fenn received Payne's telephone call concerning the subcommittee's visit either on June 17th or 18th, giving him very little time to prepare. However, the Army was coming to Butler and Bantam would have one opportunity to prove they could get the job done."[224]

June 19, 1940-June 20, 1940—Butler, Pennsylvania

While Evans, Fenn and Payne formed the executive team for the project, American Bantam, despite its bankrupt status, had available a small cadre of "hands on" automotive talent that would comprise the individuals who would actually build the prototype. With the Army heading to Butler it was time to bring into the project the first of these individuals, Harold Crist, the Butler automotive manufacturer's factory manager (chapter 1).

Crist served Bantam in that capacity from 1937 – May 1, 1942. Before that, his work in the automobile industry dated from the same year World War I began, 1914, and in a twenty-five year career (up to 1940) his primary work was as a draftsman, as well as supervision, design work and as a machinist, i.e. he had extensive knowledge of cars from the ground up.[225] Crist's knowledge and experience would come in handy, as Payne put it, to prove, "the theory of the short-wheel base, narrow gauge, lightness, and in fact that it (Bantam chassis) could be made into a four-wheel drive" and that, "Bantam knew how to engineer a small car." [226]

In the annals of Jeep history the Army's visit to the Bantam plant represents an indispensable milestone in the creation of that vehicle as it eventually developed over the course of 1940. Frank Fenn provided a detailed description of exactly what transpired during those two critical days:

On June 19 Mr. George Thompson, the treasurer of the company, and myself, met this group at the Pittsburgh Airport and brought them to the plant. The committee consisted of Major Howie, Armored Forces, Colonel Lee, Infantry, Major Tompkins, Cavalry, Lieutenant Colonel Atwood, Ordnance, Mr. Robert Brown, civilian engineer, Quartermaster Corps, and Mr. Beasley, civilian engineer, Ordnance.

When they arrived at Butler they were introduced to various members of our organization, among them Mr. Crist, the factory manager, Mr. McMillan, purchasing agent, Mr. Croll, secretary, and after a general discussion we got in Mr. Tompkins car and my car and accompanied by two standard Bantam roadsters went to the county fairgrounds.

Figure 45: The Bantam Chassis with 4,500 pounds of sandbags—June 19, 1940. Photo taken in Shipping Department at the American Bantam Company Plant. Source: United States National Archives, College Park, Maryland

When we reached the county fairgrounds we first ran the roadsters around the race track at high speed. Then we took them to the inside of the racetrack, which, like all county fair racetracks, most of them anyway, is full of rubbish and high grass and mud and muck, and the various members of the committee drove the cars at high speed. They performed quite satisfactorily.

Then we took them down to the far end of the racetrack, which was already steeply banked, went outside and drove them up the steep embankment on the outside of the track. The cars came up to the fence but couldn't go any further because of the fence.

Then they had some discussions (at the fairgrounds). I mean by that the Army committee group broke up, some of them talked with Mr. Thompson, some with Mr. Crist, and some myself. We came back to the plant and took a trip through the factory.

After taking a trip through the factory we then took a standard Bantam chassis and loaded it with 4500 pounds of sandbags. The chassis did not collapse in any way. A picture of it was taken. And then Mr. Crist and Mr. Beasley and Mr. Brown began to talk about our production facilities, and again they walked through the plant. After, I would say, 45 minutes of that procedure, we then went up to the offices and went into my office and had a general discussion regarding the proposed car that the Army had in mind.

I did not see any papers or any documents or specifications or anything else in the possession of any member of the committee during that discussion. Down at the factory we had more or less decided that it would be necessary for us to add 5 inches to the wheelbase of the car and we made it very clear that in our opinion only a few components of the standard Bantam could be used. Those points were emphasized during the conference in my office.

Colonel Atwood, Colonel Lee, Major Tompkins, Major Howie and Mr. Brown outlined what they expected of this car. They said they wanted a small silhouette because it would be used for reconnaissance purposes, and that it would be necessary to drive it up close to enemy positions, probably park it behind low bushes, something of that sort, and the men would get out, take a look around, get out and run, if necessary.

They stressed the desirability of outstanding performance and great power because the car would have to go anywhere. Colonel Tompkins made it clear that as far as cavalry was concerned they wanted an extremely tight radius and expressed the opinion that perhaps we would have to build four-wheel steering jobs also.

We discussed whether any parts of the present Bantam car could be used in the construction of that car. I told them that in my opinion certain body parts, such as the cowl could be used, that the transmission could be used, with small changes, that a great portion of the sheet metal, such as fenders, might be used, the hood, that is, it was possible, if we were successful in keeping the weight low, that we might use standard Bantam axles.

It was definitely understood that it would have to have a four-wheel drive (eliminating Bantam axles). I (Fenn) called Fred Hall, of the Spicer Manufacturing Company, who were the manufacturers of our regular axles, and told him that we're in a huddle with the Army regarding the production of a special vehicle that must have a four-wheel drive, and asked him if they had any four-wheel drive experience.

Mr. Hall told me that they had thoroughly explored the four-wheel drive field, and that they, with very little difficulty, provided the proper universal joints for the front axle could be obtained, which they thought could be obtained from Bendix-Weiss or Zephyr, that they could produce the axle.

I told him that time was of the essence and that we would like to talk to him about it immediately and Mr. Hall agreed to come, to arrive at Butler the next day. After calling Mr. Hall we took an ordinary yellow scrap pad, such as this gentleman is using (indicating) and Mr.

Beasley and Mr. Brown made a sketch which incorporated their ideas of what this car should likely be like and look like.[227]

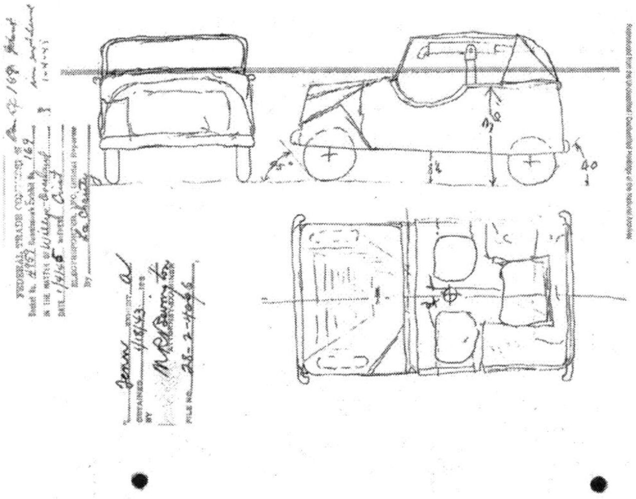

The Army and the Butler team had covered a great deal of general ground in just one day. They had identified what would become the key component of the ¼ ton truck 4 X 4 light, the front axle. During that same day the committee and Bantam officials had also delved into the engineering details of the vehicle taking shape as Fenn described:

Figure 46: The Beasley-Brown Drawing—June 19, 1940. This is the very first sketch ever made of a Jeep-type vehicle. Source: United States National Archives, College Park, Maryland

> Well, I believe you might call it one time because, after all, the whole day was spent in discussing characteristics of the proposed car and the possibility of using any Bantam components, and also using their (Bantam) "know-how" in constructing the proposed vehicle.
>
> Now, there are certain well-established procedures that have been followed in the construction of these light vehicles over a period of years. They naturally wanted to know what our frame construction was. We showed it to them. We pointed out to them the fact that we could not use the present frame. In fact, we stated very promptly that that type of frame would not be sufficiently strong to do the job they wanted.
>
> We discussed transmissions, with the possible change of the second speed and one of the shafts, would be entirely satisfactory. We discussed our axles. It so happened that we had a safety factor of about 150 percent in those axles as far as the commercial Bantam was concerned. There was considerable conjecture as to whether those axles would stand the gaff or not. On the first day we were inclined to believe they might, because of the safety factor involved, take care of the heavier engine.
>
> We discussed our own power plant and we rejected it. We discussed other power plants and I made the statement to Mr. Brown and to the other members of the committee that we weren't concerned about a power plant because there were three or four other engines on the market which we could obtain in reasonable quantities until this entire thing had been entirely worked out that would suit the job.

> I made it very plain to Mr. Brown and Mr. Beasley, and to the other members of the committee, that the Bantam Car Company, while it had a complete engine plant, could not attempt to build a special engine unless the quantities involved ran to 25 to 35 thousand, the cost of tooling would make the cost of the car entirely prohibitive.
>
> We discussed body construction and we outlined this, that by widening our roadster cowl we could use it, and that by using our flooring pan and making some adjustments in that, we could use it. At that time members of the committee raised no question as to the type of fenders and we said we thought we, without a question we could use our own fenders.
>
> They explained the standard headlights were used but in addition to standard headlights, blackout lights were used. They also explained about taillights, how the taillight they used was a special taillight, that light, because of possible attacks and strafing from the air, could only show so many feet to the rear, and that the blackout lights could only show so many feet from the front.
>
> We had an idea that we could use our regular 16 by 5 inch tire but they explained that in their opinion the car would have to have more flotation than a 5-inch car (probably meant tire) would provide. On top of that they insisted that the tire be of a standard size which they were using in other vehicles, because they were interested in standardization and could not have a lot of 5-inch tires standing around the place which were useless on any other vehicle.[228]

The definitive outline of a vehicle was forming in the minds of Army officials and the representatives of the American Bantam Car Company. For the majority of the committee their work was completed the first day as Fenn remembered:

> Colonel Atwood, who seemed to have charge of the group, suggested that they all return to Washington with the exception of Mr. Brown and Major Howie and that Mr. Brown and Major Howie and ourselves continue to canvass the situation so that Mr. Brown might bring back with him more conclusive data after conferring with Mr. Hall of Spicer.
>
> The second day Mr. Fred Hall arrived. We told him what we had in mind. By "We", I mean Mr. Brown with a few remarks by Major Howie who was not particularly active that day. Also Mr. Crist and myself. We told Mr. Hall very frankly that in the opinion of everyone the Bantam engine was out, although we were going to explore it and see whether it could possibly be used. But we did express the opinion to Mr. Hall that the Bantam axles could be used. Mr. Hall said that he thought they might if the horsepower and the torque and size of the engine did not exceed a certain size.

> We talked about costs. Mr. Hall explained to us that it would be necessary to produce the pilot model actions out of nothing but bare stock and that they would simply have to be organized out in the tool room. We discussed constant velocity joints and Mr. Hall recommended the Bendix-Weiss job. We discussed our transmission, and Mr. Hall agreed with the position that the American Bantam Company had taken the day before that it would be necessary to modify the transmission to a small extent.
>
> We discussed whether Mr. Hall could produce transfer cases and whether such a transfer case could be attached to our present transmission, which Mr. Hall agreed to be done. We made up certain figures as to the cost, the probable cost of the axles. Mr. Hall, with what meager information we had, was compelled to do quite a little guessing, and so stated. However, we did get some figures which Mr. Brown took back with him to Holabird. We started to type those figures about 5:30 in the afternoon and the minute the figures were typed Mr. Crist took Mr. Hall and Major Howie and Mr. Brown to Pittsburgh.
>
> Mr. Brown left us, taking back certain information and drawings which Mr. Crist gave him, which dealt essentially with the commercial Bantam car and left with the understanding that we were to immediately go to work and do our best to get together information and specifications which would be forwarded on to Mr. Brown and that jointly we would develop this unit, using the best knowledge of what the Army wanted and our best knowledge of what we could manufacture.[229]

The Ordnance Technical Subcommittee on light infantry vehicles upon their return to Washington now had in their possession a more detailed idea of what the ¼ ton truck 4 X 4 light might consist of; however, detailed specifications were still not developed that a car manufacturer could build from. That document would result from twelve days of frantic effort centered on the very department the Infantry had wanted to avoid, the Office of the Quartermaster General.

June 21, 1940 – July 2, 1940 – Washington D. C. and Camp Holabird, Maryland

The subcommittee on the development of light infantry vehicles met two days after returning from Butler (June 22, 1940) and developed a detailed directive for the next steps of the project as follows:

- The subcommittee and the officials and engineers of the American Bantam Company discussed the possibilities and limitations of the Bantam chassis for use as the basis of the light vehicles under construction;

- A brief operating test was conducted with several of the Bantam 2-wheeled drive cars on roads and cross-country. Some of this operation was hilly country including grades estimated at 10%. These 2 wheeled drive vehicles performed well with loads of one or two men. The gross load was approximately 1500 pounds;

- A stripped down chassis weight 600 lbs. was statistically loaded with 4500 lbs. of sand without damage to the chassis;

- Discussion of engineering details resulted in tentative decision to require the following:

  - A driving front axle with a 2-speed transfer case including provisions for de-clutching the drive to the front axle. The tread of the axle to be the same, front and rear. Tires 5.50-16 with bullet sealing tubes;

  - Body of rectangular construction to enclose the wheels, in lieu of mud guards, with bumpers front and rear. All bumpers to be provided with means for attaching tow ropes. Angles of approach and departure at least 45° and 40° respectively. A folding windshield to provide for maximum height of vehicle not to exceed 36 inches. The top to consist of a single bow at the rear and a quickly removable strip of canvass attached to the rear of the body and top of the windshield. Three bucket type seats, two forward and one centrally located in the rear part of the body;
  - Provision for mounting a cal..30 Light Machine Gun on a telescoping pedestal located between the two forward bucket seats and provision for the transportation of 3000 rounds of cal..30 machine gun ammunition;

  - Amphibious characteristics to be included if this is practicable;

  - The following miscellaneous items:

    - Mount the radiator on its side to reduce silhouette and add a water pump;

    - Increase engine power at least 10%

    - Increase fuel capacity to 8 gallons and an auxiliary fuel filter;

    - Increase the capacity of electrical units and use shunt wound generator with voltage regulator;

- Provide a radiator guard;
- Provide blackout lighting system;
- Oil bath cleaner;
- Hydraulic Brakes;
- Full floating axles; and,
- Skid shoe under transfer case[230]

The memo then outlined the "draft military characteristics for the Light Reconnaissance and Command Car are stated as follows" (similar with some additions to the June 6, 1940 initial requirements):

- Weight without payload: Not to exceed 1200 lbs;
- Height: Not to exceed 36 inches;
- Four-wheel drive chassis: Wheel base approximately 75"
- Angles of approach and departure 45° and 40° respectively;
- Driver must be able to see the road at a distance of not more than 10 ft. ahead of the front of the car;
- Armament: One Cal..30 Light Machine Gun on telescoping pedestal and 3000 rounds of machine gun ammunition;
- Crew: 3 Men including the driver; and,
- Performance:
  - Sustained low speed of 3 m.p.h. and maximum speed of not less than 50 m.p.h. on level hard-surfaced road.

- Two speed transfer case with provision for de-clutching the drive to front axle for good road operation
- Maximum practicable ground clearance, but not less than 8 ½"; and
- Cross-country performance and grade ability comparable to that of standard multi-wheeled cargo vehicles.[231]

The final recommendations for the committee would form the outline for the procurement as follows:

- That the military characteristics stated in paragraph 2 above be approved;

- That 70 Light Reconnaissance and Command Cars be procured for service test by Infantry, Field Artillery and Cavalry. 40 cars for Infantry – 20 for Cavalry and 10 for Field Artillery;

- That since this vehicle is a commercial wheeled type without armor protection, the Quartermaster General be charged with its development and procurement;

- That this light vehicle development be limited to the Light Reconnaissance and Command Car type, in general accordance with the military characteristics stated in paragraph 2; and,

- That if this vehicle is found satisfactory, consideration be given to its use in place of the motorcycle with sidecar and the tricycle type of vehicle.[232]

It was the directive to officially transfer the project to the Quartermaster General that brought into the effort the next individual who would act as defacto project manager, Colonel Edwin S. Van Deusen. A 1917 graduate of Syracuse University with an AB degree in chemistry, minor in mineralogy, and some engineering courses, he joined the Army right after graduation during the mobilization for World War I.[233]

Van Deusen was detailed to the Quartermaster Corps in 1920 and served as a commanding officer of operating companies, shops, instructor at the motor transport school, commander of supply depots, and command of the overhaul and spare parts depot at Sandy Hook, New Jersey. He also was a senior instructor at the Quartermaster motor transport school; chief of engineering branch at Holabird Quartermaster Depot; from 1937 – 1940 he attended various Army schools; and from 1939 to 1940 performed planning work pertaining to motor transport matters in the Office of the Quartermaster General.[234]

During the 1930s the Quartermaster Corps monitored developments in the field of light combat vehicles as Van Deusen recalled:

> We kept abreast of all developments, both domestically and in the foreign fields (of light combat vehicles). Our mission was not particularly with relation to combat vehicles. That was the responsibility of the Ordnance Department. We were aware of certain developments that had been undertaken by the Ordnance Department and we also later—in the later thirties, when we knew about certain developments that had been undertaken at Fort Benning which involved the use of wheel vehicles—also studied the light type of wheel vehicle.
> In the late thirties we had tested at Holabird, had worked with a bantam, an American bantam, commercial chassis, in developing the capabilities, possibilities of that chassis for use with a project paralleling that inaugurated by Major Howie at Fort Benning in connection with what is known as the Howie carrier.
>
> The Bantam commercial car, as tested at Holabird, proved itself totally incapable as performing or having the stamina required for military service. It was underpowered and was structurally weak for military application. We had a development project on a vehicle in the half-ton class. I think in 1936, the records will show that we procured a group of half-ton four by fours from the Marmon-Herrington Company to fulfill a request from the Infantry for a light-weight weapons carrier type of vehicle. Those vehicles were all wheel drives, and were quite satisfactory.
>
> Previously, the half-ton four by four was very acceptable to the Infantry as produced and tested in the design of the Marmon-Herrington Company. At that time we were entirely following the competitive rule in Procurement under the provisions of revised statute 3709, and other limiting legislative acts, and were not able, under the general policy of procuring motor vehicles, to specify or model or details of construction. The Infantry was so well pleased with the half-ton four by four, as built by the Marmon-Herrington Company, that we were requested to procure larger quantities of a similar type vehicle.
>
> However, the competitive angle of that procurement resulted in the procurement from another manufacturer of a vehicle of the same general type and classification answering generally to the characteristics which were not acceptable, however, to the Infantry. It was a heavier vehicle. It was a much higher silhouette, and, generally not as satisfactory.[235]

Van Deusen was well aware of the Army's efforts to develop a light vehicle during the 1930s and in 1940 his duties would place him squarely in the path of the ¼ ton 4 X 4 light procurement. He was present at the pivotal Quartermaster Corps Technical Subcommittee meetings on Motor Transport held from May 17 – 20, 1940, the very same conference Colonel Oseth attended. The procurement officer vividly remembered the Infantry's position:

> The need for lighter vehicles was stressed by the Infantry representative, some replacement for the motor cycle and sidecar. We discussed tricycles, which were also involved. The matter was left in abeyance at that time for further investigation of what could be done with the dissatisfaction, expressed by the Infantry, of the half-ton four by four as being produced at that time. We knew we would have to go into some form of investigation regarding the other type of vehicle they wanted.
>
> They (the Infantry) wanted definitely to go back to that type of vehicle (Marmon-Herrington half-ton four by four truck) in a lighter model. They were not satisfied with the truck that was being produced in the half-ton class.[236]

The beginning of Van Deusen's involvement with the ¼ ton truck 4 X 4 light occurred right around the time Colonel Oseth was drafting the critical June 6, 1940 memo, and that connection was the ever-present Charles Payne.

> When, and under what circumstances did you meet Charles H. Payne? Either the last week in May, or the first week in June 1940. I was in the Office of the Motor Transport Service. Col. Johnson was out. I was in charge of the office. I was notified that a gentleman must see the Chief of the Service immediately on a matter of great importance. Mr. Payne was admitted to the office, and I talked with him at my first meeting.
>
> He represented himself as being connected with a high executive position, the American Bantam Car Company of Butler, Pennsylvania. And his expressed purpose of the visit was to sell bantam cars to the government, feeling that would be something which the American Bantam Car Company could do.
>
> In the original discussion with Mr. Payne, it was pointed out to him that we were using an entire four-wheel drive, that the bantam design of commercial chassis was not suitable for our purpose.
>
> I told him (Payne) we were unable to act. Our hands were tied so far as any action toward procuring is concerned. I suggested that requirement for any vehicle of that class would have to be presented to us by the using arms and services. And I also suggested that he might be able to develop some requirement for a vehicle such as the Bantam people were producing by

further discussion with the officers of the Chief of Infantry, who were primarily interested in such a type of vehicle.[237]

Payne may have taken his advice, or was already working with the Infantry, as previously documented. Nevertheless, within a week after the June 19 – 20, 1940 Butler conference, the responsibility for the development of specifications to procure a lightweight vehicle for the United States Army would fall squarely on Colonel Van Deusen and the Quartermaster Corps.

Entrepreneurial Lesson 26
Conflicting Objectives

"Everything and its opposite has an opposite opposite both." "There's your story, there's my story, and then there's the Truth." And the rallying cry, "Remember the cookie!"

A baker dreams of a cookie s/he thinks will sell like hot cakes, well, cookies actually. S/he wakes up and starts concocting the ingredients and bakes a dozen. For research, twelve different people taste the new cookie.

There are twelve different opinions, as if not one but a dozen new recipes had been invented. A consensus needs to be more than a majority opinion. It needs to be a rallying cry.

If the key stakeholders are saying "what if we" instead of "but if I", then terms of agreements can come about, with all the compromises and patience needed to overcome all the various interests being blended into the right recipe.

Remember the cookie.

Immediately on the return of the Quartermaster Corps, with a representative from Butler (June 21, 1940), we were advised that the project would be transferred to the Quartermaster Corps. I immediately gave a directive to the engineering group at Holabird to start the drafting of specifications based on the general characteristics appearing as part of the committee report of the Butler meeting.

The formal transfer, I believe, occurred about the 27th or 28th of June, 1940, by formal endorsement. But immediately following the committee meeting, we had already started the mechanics of the engineering work that would be required.

For several days I participated directly in the work which was performed in respect to the writing of the specifications. In fact, the specifications were written by our engineers, one of the engineers in my office. I had brought this engineer over to Washington to write these specifications in our office to expedite the publication of them and to permit conferences with the representatives of the using arms and services who were located in Washington, and would thereby be more readily accessible in connection with the writing of those specifications.

Mr. Robert F. Brown was the engineer in charge of the drafting of the specifications and at various times, sometimes alone, singly, sometimes jointly. Then I believe Lt. Col. Lee, Major Oseth, Capt. Tompkins, or Major Tompkins, Capt. Claybrook. They were the principal officers who conferred with us.

> Under Mr. Brown's supervision, George Engler prepared the body drawing which was issued as part of the specifications who was an engineer at Holabird, one of our engineers. The body drawing was prepared at Holabird in accordance with certain agreements that had been reached as result of the Butler conference, certain agreements among the army personnel.[238]

Van Deusen's small team, Brown, Engler and one Mr. Dowd had two primary documents to create, the aforementioned detailed specifications and a body drawing which later became specification ES-No. 475 and QM Drawing 08370-Z. A tremendous amount of seat-of-the-pants engineering work went into the development of these two critical requirements documents.

> There was no ¼ ton 4 X 4 truck available at the time. However, after date of their return from Butler and the return of the specifications, since we had one or two Bantam chassis at Holabird, which had been subject to previous testing and since the general characteristics developed at the Butler conference fitted somewhat generally on to a chassis of that size. At Holabird we did make up in a wood body in general as described, as a result of the Butler conferences. And also demonstrated for representatives of the using services who went to Holabird, in that period, performance of that time of a vehicle as represented by the two-wheel drive Bantam chassis. It was hardly a ¼ ton truck. It was a cobbled up sample of what could be made at the time to approximate that type of a vehicle, less the all-wheel drive feature and limited power to that available in the Bantam engine.[239]

The Quartermaster Corps was determined to not repeat the mistakes that had led to the ½ ton truck debacle by including the using arms at the ground floor of the specifications development as Colonel Oseth recalled:

> The first thing that happened after this project was referred back to the Quartermaster General was that Colonel Van Deusen called a meeting of the technical, Quartermaster technical committee on motor transport. He had just succeeded Colonel Johnson as chairman of that Committee. At that meeting we received the report, went over the reports that came back from the Ordnance Department and adopted certain changes that had been suggested, approved certain changes that had been suggested by the Ordnance technical committee.
>
> And as I recall it, one or two further slight modifications that were suggested by the Quartermaster representative, of which Colonel Van Deusen was one, were approved. Then there were two or three meetings of a small committee. The infantry and cavalry were the only

two branches interested. The others showed no interest in the thing so the committee meetings were very small. I suppose there were two or three of those meeting in Washington, here, to come to a definite understanding, going a little further, I mean proceeding from the point that this letter (June 6, 1940 memo) brought us to.

Entrepreneurial Lesson 27
Thinking On Your Feet

Possibly the easiest person to identify who has to think on one's feet is an athlete. A quarterback is given three plays to run at the same time—the play being called, and two modules to switch to before the ball is snapped. Based on the defensive setup, the player calls an audible signal to confirm the original play or one of the modules. After the ball is snapped, because things are collapsing all around the quarterback and around the field, it might turn out that the actual play is an uncalled improvisation.

The Entrepreneur is a coach and quarterback, one or more steps ahead of everyone else. As the comic book and TV show put it, "Able to leap tall buildings in a single bound." If you can think on your feet, handle moment to moment interruptions and changes, you are going to make a good leader.

Then the next step was that the chairman of the committee and the representatives from Holabird, stated they wanted the committee to go to Holabird and consider on the ground a body type and size and dimensions and all that sort of thing, in connection with the Bantam chassis that they had at the depot, the Quartermaster depot there at Holabird. So a few days afterwards, Colonel Lee and myself and Major Tompkins' office went out there to Holabird and they had this Bantam chassis setup on the concrete floor. They had sketched in chalk on the floor the outlines of what they conceived the body would look like under these characteristics. They had put the front wheels up on a four by four in order to compensate for the difference in height between a normal axle and the power-driven axle that was to go in there. We went over the sketch on the floor and all those various things were changed on the suggestion of various members of the committee.

Then after we agreed on that step, the Quartermaster technicians up there, the engineers, said they would go ahead and make a mock-up which is a wooden model, a cardboard practically, model of the body so we could come out and look at the thing. It was two or three days later they said they would have that thing ready. At the end of that period we went back there. At that time I don't think Colonel Lee accompanied me, although I am not too sure about that. I still don't remember if Mr. Payne was there that particular one. They had this Bantam chassis with this wallboard mockup body on it. There wasn't anything to that body. It was just a rectangular, low body, hollowed out a little, making a little cut there to enable the driver and assistant driver to get in and out without catching a heel in the thing. It was also necessary to put wheel wells or houses, whatever you call them in the body itself, in order to get room enough in the vehicle for any useful purpose. In other words, instead of putting a fender, a

> mud guard on the outside of the wheel, the mud guard was incorporated right in the body of the vehicle.
>
> They had that wallboard mock-up there and we went over it, suggested changes. Their object was to find out whether the using services represented by myself and Tompkins were satisfied with it, and we finally approved the thing as it was. The next step was to make a wooden body of sufficient strength so we could get in it to sit in it. And as I recall it, that was the first trip out there when we looked at the final effort and tried to take this vehicle up a steep test ramp they had out there, about I don't know what, it must have been about thirty degrees, I guess, or better, the slope of the thing. We loaded both the driver and assistant driver, and I sat in the back of this thing. It got half way up the hill and wouldn't go any further.[240]

After all the effort expended to develop a working model of the ¼ ton truck 4 X 4 light the initial test was a failure and Colonel Oseth was ready to declare defeat, to, once again, Charles Payne, who saved the day.

> As I understood it, although I am not sure about that, the original Bantam engine, the four-cylinder, water-cooled engine was in there at that time. As the representative of the majority stockholder, the infantry, I announced I was afraid the thing was washed up, the whole project was washed up, because it didn't have the power. Mr. Payne was there at that time, I remember now, because he spoke up and said, "Don't worry about that. We have already got a larger engine lined up that we can put in there." And so he saved the project from being shipwrecked on that particular rock.
>
> That was in general the procedure, a constant series of visits, by myself and Major Tompkins to Holabird to confer with the engineers, Mr. Brown, being Robert Brown, and Captain Engler and Major Skip Johnson – I don't know his first name – and Colonel Laws [sic] out there at Holabird. Step by step the specifications were being developed by them, and as they came to something which they thought might conflict with our views, on the thing, they asked us to come out and conferred with us personally on it. I personally, on behalf of the Chief of Infantry Ok'd such parts of the specifications as they were submitted to me. That is the specification part, not the characteristics. It was more detailed specifications they were working on.[241]

In terms of current information technology software development, the Quartermaster Corps conducted a classic iterative requirements analysis / development. The engineers followed a structured step-by-step methodology that took what was a concept and brought it to life. By actively including the key stakeholders in the process the QMC ensured that the requirements (specifications) eventually drawn up matched what the stakeholders wanted. In addition, the engineers had included Bantam in the process through both Frank Fenn and Harold Crist.

The Bantam President remembered his role at this time as follows:

> I talked to Mr. Brown over the telephone regarding many of the details and many of the conclusions which we had arrived at at Butler (chapter 5), and he suggested that I come to Holabird and discuss it with him. I went to Holabird and discussed them with Mr. Brown.
>
> At approximately June the 28th … what was the subject matter of the discussion that took place between you and Mr. Brown on that occasion? Placing a minimum cubic displacement on the engine of 85 inches; the use of the Studebaker axle, our transmission and a Spicer transfer case; a discussion on the size of the wheels and the tires and the consequent necessity for having a minimum of 85 cubic inches. I stated to Mr. Brown that we were convinced that the power plant must have a cubic inch displacement of at least 85 inches. Mr. Brown agreed. I stated that as a result of work by Spicer and ourselves we were convinced that, due to the service which they expected of this car, it would be unwise to use or axle, and it would be wise to use a Studebaker axle, although a large sum of money would be involved in tooling. Mr. Brown agreed.
>
> I stated that Zephyr joints were available or that Bendix-Weiss joints were available in limited quantities but they were the best on the market as we thought and recommended, and recommended that joint. I don't remember if Mr. Brown agreed to that or not. I stated that we could use certain of our body parts, such as the cowl, the windshield, brackets, and so on, and Mr. Brown accepted that statement. I stated that it would be necessary for us to revamp any commercial engine then in production that we used in order to get sufficient oil capacity to take care of the sharp angles at which the vehicle would have to operate. Mr. Brown agreed. And I discussed cost of tooling and told him that in my opinion that the extent of tooling would run in the neighborhood of $25,000 and Mr. Brown agreed.
>
> We discussed the flotation of the vehicle, and I took the position that I thought our 5-inch tire would do. Mr. Brown on the other hand reiterated the position of the Army that they would have to use a tire then in production and being used on other vehicles, and I acquiesced. At that time I said it might effect [sic] the size of the engine we would have to use, but there would be no considerable increase in cost. I discussed the facts that we would undoubtedly ask York-Hoover to build the first bodies because they would have to be handmade and we wouldn't attempt to tool our body plant for pilot models. Mr. Brown said he thought it was a good idea, and we discussed such other possibilities as the use of the panel hooks, spare tire,

and items of that sort. We took the position that no spare tire was needed. Mr. Brown said that would have to be a matter to be decided later, and would appear in the specification under which we would ultimately build.[242]

Crist conferred with Brown by telephone and also visited Holabird on July 1, 1940. The Bantam factory manager discussed primarily the body and axles along with other items and took prints with him to the in-person meeting.[243]

The Army finalized a detailed specification on July 2, 1940. A chalk outline on the floor, a cardboard mock-up, and a wooden mock-up that was thoroughly reviewed by all interested parties resulted in Quartermaster Corps drawing of the vehicle numbered QM 08370-Z. Numerous meetings, consultations and informal discussion resulted in an eleven page specification given the number ES-No. 475 detailed in the table below.

Table 1: ¼ Ton Truck 4 X 4 Light – Specification ES – No. 475

Army Requirement
A. Applicable Specifications
A-1. The following current specifications and drawings in effect on date of Invitation to Bids, shall form a part of this specification.
A-2. Responsibility for obtaining copies of the latest revisions of Specifications and Drawings listed under A-1 rests with prospective bidders.
B. General
B-1. Quartermaster Corps Specifications ES – No. 459 applies.
C. Service Requirements
C-1. General – see above
C-2. Abilities. The truck, fully equipped and loaded, shall demonstrate the following speeds:
C-2a. A level road maximum speed of not less than fifty(50) miles per hour, at a corresponding engine speed that shall not exceed the peak horsepower speed.
C-2b. A level road minimum speed of not more than three (3) miles per hour, at engine maximum torque speed.
C-3. Cruising range – The truck, fully equipped and loaded, shall be capable of making an average day's run of one hundred fifty (150) miles, at an average speed of thirty-five (35) miles per hour, on good roads over average rolling terrain, on one initial filling of the gasoline tank and without requiring the addition of oil.
C-4. Traction devices – Tire chains will be required for use on the driving wheel tires, and the truck construction shall permit the satisfactory installation and use of the tire chains.
D. Specifications

D-1.	Chassis. The chassis shall be of sturdy construction capable of withstanding the strains of the service.
D-1a.	Weights and loads – The weight of the truck, fully equipped and serviced (less only the payload), shall not exceed 1275 pounds (amended to 1300 pounds) and every effort, consistent with the best recognized engineering practices, shall be made to minimize weight. The truck shall have a nineteen hundred (1900) pound gross weight allowance to provide at least a six hundred twenty-five (625) pound payload carrying capacity.
D-1b.	Dimensions – The wheelbase shall be the minimum practicable, not more than eighty (80) inches. Ground clearance under the axles eight and one-half (8 ½) inches, clearance under transmission, transfer case skid shoe, gas tank, battery and propeller shaft brake clearances shall be sufficient to permit operations over unimproved roads and cross country terrain the clearance under the lowest unit to be at least nine and one-half (9 ½) inches. Angle of approach not less than forty-five degrees, angle of departure not less than 40 degrees. Overall height not to exceed 40 inches. Radiator shell, engine hood, cowl and front fenders and headlight mounting permit a driver of average height, 68 inches, to properly see road at a distance of not more than ten feet.
D-2.	Frame—The chassis frame shall support the maximum gross loads imposed under the most severe operating conditions.
D-3.	Power unit—The power unit shall consist of an engine, clutch and transmission embodied in a unit power plant.
D-4.	Engine—shall be internal combustion, four-stroke cycle type, no less than 4 cylinders, piston displacement not less than 85 cubic inches, fuel knock rating not more than 68 octane number, cylinder heads not made of aluminum, crankshaft counter balanced, supported by at least 3 main bearings.
D-4a.	Governor – if install, set to manufacturer limit, but not hinder engine operation at speeds of 55 miles per hour
D-5.	Cooling system – shall be of the type using a circulating pump.
D-6.	Lubricating system – Manufacturer's standard – oil filter detailed requirements, chassis lubricating system high pressure type.
D-7.	Ignition system – Complete battery and generator ignition system, 6 volt potential.
D-8.	Fuel System – 1 gasoline tank, 10 gallon capacity, flexible fuel line.
D-9.	Exhaust system – substantial leak-proof, amply proportioned, securely mounted.
D-10.	Clutch – torque capacity at least equal to maximum engine torque.
D-11.	Transmission – no less than 3 forward, 1 reverse speeds, can provide 4 speeds.
D-12.	Transfer case – 2 speed type having a high range ratio of 1.0 and low range reduction of approximately 2.0 to 1.0 if 3 speed, gear ratio 1.0 – 1.0 for 4 speed.
D-13.	Propeller shaft – rugged construction and positively lubricated, universal joints latest design, length to manufacturer specifications.
D-14.	Axles – single reduction type, identical tread front and rear, front axle full floating type.

D-15.	Springs – strength adequate to sustain the gross speed loads, without evidence of overload or permanent set.
D-16.	Shock absorbers – Hydraulic, double acting, of adequate capacity on both axles, side frame mounting, brackets not to protrude below axle housing.
D-17.	Bogie – does not apply.
D-18.	Wheels and tires
D-18a.	Wheels – pressed steel ventilated disc or steel spoke type interchangeable on axle hubs.
D-18b.	Tires – balloon type, size 5.50-16 4 ply with mud and snow tread design.
D-18c.	Inner tubes – heavy duty type, bullet sealing type.
D-18d.	All wheels, tires and tubes same size.
D-19.	Brakes – safely control fully equipped and loaded truck under all operating conditions.
D-19a.	Service brakes – hydraulic application type, brakes and drums on all wheels, sufficiently control and hold fully equipped vehicle on 50 percent grade, complete stop at deceleration equivalent to a stop within 30 feet from speed of 20 miles per hour on dry, hard, approximately level road, free from loose material. No evidence of excessive fading.
D-19b.	Parking brake – hand lever operated mounted at rear end of transfer case main (top) shaft.
D-20.	Electrical equipment – chassis equipped with complete electrical starting and lighting system, 6 volt potential.
D-21.	Chassis equipment – complete including enumerated articles
D-21a.	Engine hood – water proof, readily removable, easy access.
D-21b.	Instrument panel – speedometer, recording odometer, fuel gauge, ammeter, engine heat indicator, direct reading oil pressure gauge. Carburetor choke control, ignition lock, hand throttle control, spark control (when provided) located convenient reach of operator.
D-21c.	Tool equipment – Type I, Q.M. Specification ES – No 422, 4 chains required.
D-21d.	Accessory equipment – at least rear view mirror, windshield wiper, locks, electric horn
D-21e.	Lighting equipment – best commercial grade, 2 head lamps, 1 combination service tail and service stop, license plate, "black-out" tail lamp, sketch of all lamp mountings, all lamps moisture, dust and rust proof, standard and "black-out" switch best commercial grade, I.C.C. regulation reflectors.
D-22.	Controlling mechanism – steering mechanism withstand strains of cross country operation.
D-23.	Operating mechanism – all controls within convenient operator reach, clutch, brake and accelerator pedals spaced so operated properly without interference, accelerator pedal located to the right of brake pedal.
D-24.	Name, caution and shifting plates – name plate with specified information, caution plate with maximum road speeds, shifting plate with specified information, plates etched with black background.
D-25.	Body – conform to specification Q.M. 08370-Z.
D-26.	Special operating equipment – rear pintle, brush guard, towing hooks.

D-27.	Painting – key components clean and dry before primer, polished finish conform to requirements specified, surface primed, surface coated and finish painted, at least 2 coats of synthetic enamel meeting Quartermaster specifications.
D-28.	Marking – War Department Registration Numbers stenciled in block letters and figures 4 inches in height in white synthetic enamel, on each side of the engine hood.
E.	Test Requirements – preliminary tests at manufacturer's plant under government supervision.
F.	Questionnaire – A summary of Bantam's questionnaire presented in chapter 7.[244]

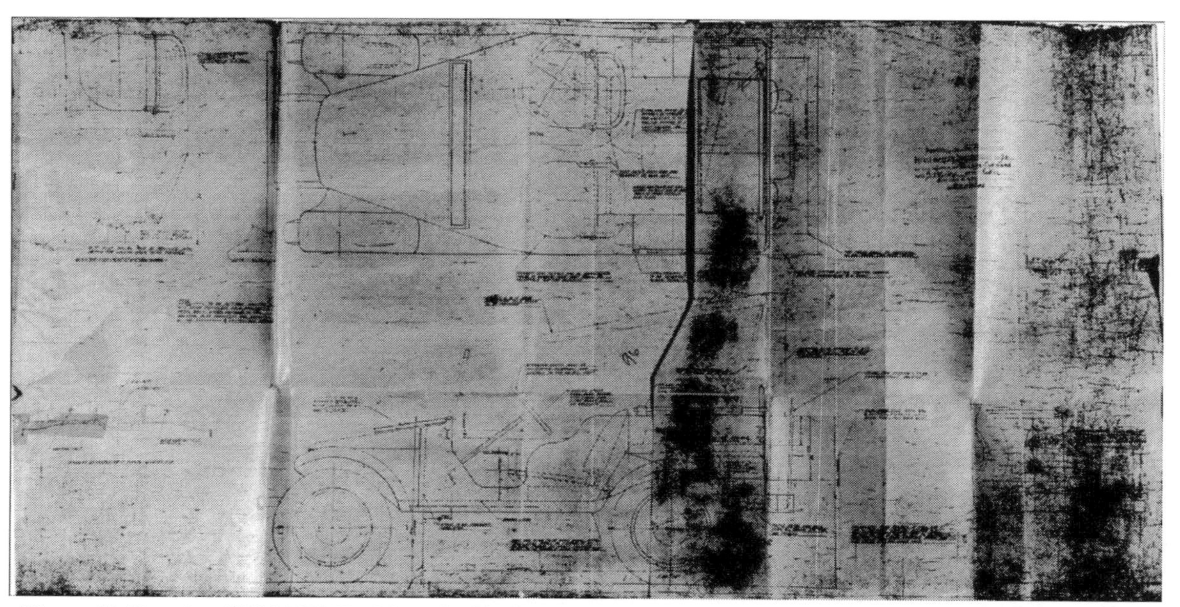

Figure 47: Drawing QM 08370-Z – Note the Similarities to the Beasley–Brown Drawing Made at Butler on June 19, 1940. Source: United States National Archives, College Park, Maryland

In twelve hectic days at the end of June and into the beginning of July 1940 the Quartermaster Corps had put on paper the specifications of a vehicle many in the Army had desired since the end of World War I, and had achieved signoff on the requirements from the key using arms, the Infantry and Cavalry.

As Colonel Oseth succinctly observed, this incredible process done in such a short timeframe represented, "a very fine piece of coordination."[245] The next phase of the project would entail answering the question, "What process would the Army follow to find a manufacturer who could build the vehicle to specifications?"

Questions for Educators

What are some of the challenges to obtaining specific requirements?

Why is it important to include stakeholders in the specific requirements gathering, especially in reviewing drafts?

What lessons from the Jeep requirements gathering are applicable to today's projects?

Discuss the pros and cons of how "specific" the specific requirements should be.

How does one determine when "enough" requirements have been gathered?

Chapter 7: Project Initiation—Bid

The procurement of products and services for a project represents a critical area for a project manager to administer. The Project Management Institute recognizes the importance of buying items for an endeavor by including procurement as one of the ten knowledge areas in the Project Management Body of Knowledge (PMBOK). The plethora of rules and regulations that usually accompany purchasing often represent some of the most difficult challenges a project leader will encounter over the course of the effort (chapter 4).

The Quartermaster General and prospective bidders would have two critical challenges to overcome in finding a way to obtain the vehicle described in specification ES-No. 475 and QM Drawing 08370-Z; the first, navigating the usual litany of "red tape" that goes along with government procurement, the second, a military establishment caught squarely in the middle of attempting to reorganize its purchasing process from a peacetime paradigm to a wartime footing (see chapter 4). The acquiring of a light vehicle for military use would fall right into the sweet spot of both challenges and the burden to overcome them to win the contract would fall squarely on the shoulders of Frank Fenn.

Washington, D. C. —July 3, 1940–July 11, 1940

The Quartermaster Corps under the leadership of Colonel Van Deusen had created a detailed specification and drawing for the proposed car the Infantry and Calvary desired. As stated in chapter 5, the purchasing leader mentioned that the official transfer of the project to QMC auspices occurred on June 27, 1940. The orders accomplishing this action emanated from the highest level, the Chief of Staff. The memorandum officially recognizing and organizing the project was in fact, in today's project management vernacular, a project charter. This document summarized the work through the end of June 1940 and would guide this endeavor through its completion:

Figure 48: George C. Marshall—Chief of Staff, U.S. Army, 1 September 1939-18 November 1945

> June 27, 1940 – MEMORANDUM FOR THE CHIEF OF STAFF: Subject: Military Characteristics for Light Reconnaissance and Command Car.
>
> The problem presented

Entrepreneurial Lesson 28
Project Sponsor

In the enterprise, the Entrepreneur is usually the sponsor of projects, without whose approval the projects cannot proceed. When the enterprise is a vendor to a multi-faceted group of external organizations, the approving sponsor becomes the executive most impacted by the results of the project being birthed.

If there are a lot of divergent conflicting objectives from within individual units of the group, the sponsor needs to orchestrate and conduct the project through its managers. The project sponsor wields the power of a catalyst. The goal develops in the group, and comes to the sponsor for approval, then returns to the former for execution.

Much of its success lies in how the concept for a project is presented by its managers for approval by the sponsor. It takes a lot of thinking on one's feet.

To determine advisability of developing and procuring a Light Reconnaissance and Command Car.

Facts bearing upon the problem:
In letter, dated June 6, 1940, (copy attached, Tab A), the Chief of Infantry recommends development of a light vehicle to be used for reconnaissance and other purposes in the Infantry battalion. He states that the present standard command and reconnaissance car (1/2 ton) is unsuitable for this purpose because of its weight and relatively high silhouette. Military characteristics for a type of vehicle desired are submitted in his letter.

In a conference with the Chief of Infantry (Lt. Col. Lee), a representative of the American Bantam Company expressed the belief that a vehicle could be developed by his company which would meet the needs of the Infantry. In accordance with verbal directive of the Chief of Staff to give immediate consideration to the possible military use of the Bantam Car, the above letter from the Chief of Infantry was referred to the Chief of Ordnance for action by the Ordnance Technical Committee (Tab B). This action was concurred in by the Quartermaster General in order that both the Bantam car and the Howie Weapons Carrier, an Ordnance development item, could be considered by one technical committee in the final determination of military characteristics of a vehicle to meet the requirements of the Chief of Infantry.

The results of study by a subcommittee of the Ordnance Technical Committee are contained in the attached subcommittee report dated June 22, 1940 (Tab C). The subcommittee concludes that in its present state of development the Howie Weapons Carrier is unsuitable for the purpose proposed by the Chief of Infantry; that after conference with the American Bantam Company it is believed a suitable light vehicle can be developed.
Based on the military characteristics proposed by the Chief of Infantry in his letter of June 6, 1940, and on technical considerations brought out in conference with representatives of the American Bantam Car Company, the subcommittee submits revised military characteristics (par. 2a, page 3 of Tab C). The subcommittee recommends:

That the revised military characteristics for a Light Reconnaissance and Command Car be approved.

That 70 Light Reconnaissance and Command Cars be procured for service test by Infantry, Field Artillery, and Cavalry (40 for Infantry – 20 for Cavalry – and 10 for Field Artillery).

That the Quartermaster General be charged with the development and procurement of this vehicle.

That light vehicle development be limited to the Light Reconnaissance and Command Car type, in general accordance with the military characteristics submitted by the subcommittee.

That if this vehicle is found satisfactory, consideration be given to its use in place of the motorcycle with sidecar and the tricycle type of vehicle.

The above recommendations are concurred in by the Quartermaster General, Chief of Field Artillery, Chief of Infantry and Chief of Cavalry, through representation on the subcommittee of the Ordnance Technical Committee.

The Chief of Infantry (Lt. Col. Lee) informally requests that a quantity of these vehicles be procured immediately in order to give them an extended service test during the August maneuvers. The Chief of Ordnance (Lt. Col. Atwood) informally advices [sic] that officials of the American Bantam Company stated the 70 vehicles desired for service test could be manufactured within eight weeks at a cost of approximately $165,000; that is thereafter this type of vehicle could be supplied at a cost of less than $600 each.

G-4 believes that if a satisfactory vehicle can be developed which will meet the needs of the Infantry, as stated in letter from the Chief of Infantry, dated June 6, 1940 (Tab A), and provide a possible solution to the present unsatisfactory situation with regard to the motorcycle, the expenditure of $165,000 for this purpose is warranted.

The Quartermaster General (Lt. Col. Johnson), Chief of Infantry (Lt. Col. Lee), Chief of Field Artillery (Lt. Col. Beasley) and Chief of Cavalry (Maj. Tompkins) concur in action recommended below.

Action recommended

That the military characteristics for a Light Reconnaissance and Command Car proposed by the subcommittee of the Ordnance Technical Committee in Tab C be approved.

The Secretary of War directs: —

That the attached correspondence, with inclosures [sic], be forwarded to the Quartermaster General (through the Chief of Ordnance) by Immediate Action indorsements [sic] substantially as follows:

Attention is invited to the attached subcommittee report of the Ordnance Technical Committee, dated June 22, 1940, subject: Light Infantry and Cavalry Vehicles – Development of. The Military Characteristics of a Light Reconnaissance and Command car, as recommended in paragraph 2e of this report, are approved. The Quartermaster General is charged with the development and procurement of this vehicle.

As recommended in paragraph 3b of the attached subcommittee report, it is desired that the Quartermaster General immediately initiate development and procurement of seventy (70) Light Reconnaissance and Command Cars in accordance with the approved military characteristics. The expenditure of not to exceed $175,000 from funds allotted the Quartermaster General is authorized for this purpose. When procured, these vehicles will be given an extended service test by the Infantry, Field Artillery and Cavalry; the number of vehicles to be supplied each of these arms for this test to be in accordance with the recommendations contained in paragraph 3b of the attached report. If possible, it is desired that these vehicles be procured in time to be employed in the maneuvers scheduled to be held late this summer.

These vehicles will be tested under the supervision of the Infantry, Field Artillery and Cavalry Boards. The recommendation of these Boards will be coordinated by the Quartermaster Technical Committee, after which final recommendations will be submitted to this office by the Quartermaster General. In the conduct of this test, it is desired that consideration be given to the use of this vehicle in place of the motorcycle with sidecar and the tricycle type of vehicle.

That the Chiefs of Infantry, Field Artillery and Cavalry be furnished copies of Action a.[246]

Project management practice stresses that obtaining top executive support for an effort constitutes a critical component toward successfully meeting the endeavor's objectives. This memo formally endorsed the Light Reconnaissance and Command Car effort from the highest level in the Army, the Chief of Staff. This document additionally laid out the parameters of today's triple constraint model as follows: time (by August maneuvers); budget ($175,000), resources (Quartermaster General, Infantry, Cavalry and Field Artillery) and quality (the requirement of an extensive service test).

Colonel Oseth, representing the key stakeholder, the Infantry, realized this directive changed the priority of the project, "After the project was referred to the Quartermaster General's office, it had very powerful support of General Marshall, the Chief of Staff, and his office. I merely mention that because it was a fact that he had set aside $170,000, as I recall it, from some fund, towards this project."[247] In 1940, like today, money talks.

The question confronting the Quartermaster General was what process to employ to procure the seventy vehicles, a competitive bid procedure, or a negotiated contract with one vendor. After the Butler conference Fenn was under the impression the latter method was the preferred choice, "Mr. Brown left us with the understanding that the two companies (Bantam and Spicer) were to collaborate in the production of this vehicle and as soon as we could arrive at a price we would submit it. There was nothing said about any possibility of anyone else being in the picture." [248]

> However, Van Deusen was operating under a different set of constraints:
> Our procurement policy since 1933 and up until the time we actually were able to break away from the competitive method of procurement depended on the use of manufacturers' proprietary designs, which resulted from their own independent engineering efforts; that is, in motor transport. There was a different policy that has been followed by the Ordnance Department with tanks or with artillery and small arms and ammunition items. We adopted, as a standard, the proprietary design of a manufacturer. We never detailed in our transport vehicles all the factors in the vehicle.[249]
>
> Not very well (ability to procure identical vehicles from different vendors) under the system we were operating under at that time (1940), which was the competitive type of procurement, and, under the policy which I mentioned yesterday, expressed in G. O. 9, War Department, 1933, which forces us to take complete vehicles as such from the producing industry, we would not have been assured of securing the identical vehicle from each of the three manufacturers. We were, as I explained yesterday, depending on the manufacturers for detailed engineering, and we adapted and accepted the proprietary engineering designs that independent manufacturers developed in so far as the vehicle was concerned as long as it met our characteristics and specifications.
>
> Colonel, what was the effective date of the Act of Congress commonly referred to as the Negotiable Contract Act? (allowing sole sourcing to a vendor without competitive bid) That was the Act of July 1, 1940. That Act was in force at that time, but we had been advised and instructed by the Assistant Secretary of War that the principles of that Act would not be applied to the procurement of motor vehicles which were an article of commercial manufacture.[250]

Therefore, despite Fenn's belief the Quartermaster was under direct order to proceed with the procurement of the Light Reconnaissance and Command Car through a competitive bid process. Specification ES – No. 475 was forwarded from Camp Holabird to QMC headquarters on July 3, 1940, one day after their finalization.[251] Officials in Washington, D.C. reviewed the requirements against the June 22, 1940 Ordnance Technical Subcommittee report and differences were noted. The assessing officer, a one Mr. Burgan, in a July 5, 1940 memo to the Chief of Motor Transport recommended approval of ES – No. 475 and reported that he had ironed out the discrepancies as follows:

> I discussed the apparent differences mentioned above with Mr. Brown, Holabird Quartermaster Depot, on July 2, 1940, and again this morning after checking the specifications, and the differences referred to either have been agreed to by conference at the last meeting at Holabird, or are the best compromise that is possible under the circumstances. For instance skid plate mentioned in D-1, but not specifically called for, and omission of definite grade ability requirements due to lack of data as to weight and the increased amount of power that can be obtained from the modified engine they propose to furnish.[252]

Entrepreneurial Lesson 29
When Handed a Lemon Make Lemonade

Receiving a lemon is a blessing in disguise because it forces an Entrepreneur to do the best with what is on hand. Making do can be liberating. It is awkward when comfortable, well-fed people understand that, in impoverished countries, perhaps the most well-adjusted are the poor. Their lemonade might not be sweet, but they make do.

The song goes, "Oh, I got plenty of nothing and nothing's plenty for me." What matters is that you do with what you have rather than doing what it takes to get what you want, when you might not really need it to fulfill your goals. Another saying: "I've been rich. I've been poor. Rich is better." Maybe. But remember the cookie. If the worst thing that can happen is that you make do with what you have, instead of ruining your life going after what you think you need, then, rich or poor, you can live with it.

The Adjutant General (also on July 5, 1940) signaled his support of the project endorsing the Chief of Staff's July 27, 1940 directive.[253] On July 9th, Payne, operating under the incorrect assumption of a negotiated contract process, sent a letter to the Quartermaster General detailing a sole source contract based upon ES – No. 475 and QM Drawing 08370-Z quoting a price of $2500.00 per vehicle for a total contract amount of $175,000 and promising delivery between August 20 – 30, 1940, in time for the August maneuvers, as directed by General Marshall.[254]

The Quartermaster; however, had inquired on that same day of the Infantry if delivery for the August maneuvers was feasible and that using arm had replied that by the summer was impracticable and recommended, "October 15, 1940 a satisfactory date for the completion of the delivery of the test lot to the troops."[255] On July 10, 1940 the die was cast for a competitive procurement as the purchasing arm of the Army requested the following of the Assistant Secretary of War:

1) Approval is requested for 10-day advertisement under Invitation for Bids to be issued by the Holabird Quartermaster Depot for the following:

   70 Trucks, Light Reconnaissance and Command Cars, ¼ ton, 4 X 4, for extended service test by the Infantry, Field Artillery and Cavalry, authorized by the Adjutant General in 4th Indorsement [sic] dated July 5, 1940: Files AG 451(6-15-40)M-D.

2) In view of the fact that delivery of these vehicles is required by the Infantry within ninety-five (95) days from this date, and considerable engineering development will be required by the successful bidder, the 10-day period for advertising is the maximum which can be used. Since preliminary development of this project has been accomplished with the collaboration of the American Bantam Car Company, Butler, Pa., this firm has offered to produce the vehicles under a negotiated contract at a price considered reasonable for such a development program, but this offer involves tooling costs and acceptance would place the firm at a decided advantage over competitors in possible future procurement of this type of vehicle.

3) It is believed advisable, therefore, to issue 10-day advertisement for the vehicles in order to permit any other qualified and interested potential producers to submit bids. A longer period is deemed unnecessary, since only one potential bidder besides the American Bantam Car Company is known to this office, and the quantity involved is small.[256]

Eight hundred and fifty (850) copies of the bid documents, under the moniker Invitation for Bids No. 398-41-9 were sent to Holabird for forwarding to "prospective bidders" on July 11, 1940. The proposal opening date was set at Monday, July 22, 1940. The package included a standard vendor questionnaire, specification ES-No. 475, QM Drawing 08370-Z and a number of QMC standards pertaining to vehicles.[257]

The papers were sent to one hundred and thirty-five members of the automotive industry following a, "policy of circularizing an entire cross-section of the industry in 1939 or previous to that time because of complaint that we had received from various manufacturers in the use of selective lists of manufacturers capable, in our (the QMC) opinion, of manufacturing certain types of vehicles."[258] The small car manufacturer from Butler would have to compete to win the opportunity to build the vehicle whose requirement they had contributed greatly to developing.

Butler, Pennsylvania—July 12, 1940–July 21, 1940

The rejection of their offer and the need to participate in a bidding process caught Fenn and Payne off guard. American Bantam in fact did not have an engineering department and would have to immediately create one to compete for the contract. That would bring into the project the next key individual to move the effort forward: automotive engineering veteran Karl K. Probst.

The Detroit engineering expert, at sixty and having thirty-seven years industry experience by 1940, would represent the seasoned veteran of the Bantam team. A mechanical engineering graduate of Ohio State University, he worked for a number of years for various companies, landing in Detroit by 1933. He established a consulting office in that city, and over the next seven years, would work with almost all the firms in the car business including Packard, Ford, Chrysler, and some for General Motors.[259]

As Probst recounted years later "1940 was a time to work and pay your bills, not consider jobs with no guaranteed salary," but was also a time when the Germans were mounting daily bombing raids against England. Fenn took the initiative and called Arthur Brandt, a General Motors employee (and former President of American Austin) working with the newly formed National Defense Advisory Committee (a body created to begin coordinating efforts between the government and industry for the nascent military buildup) which was headed by William Knudsen, the head of General Motors. Fenn's goal was to have Brandt convince Probst to come to Butler and work for free (with provision that if Bantam won the contract he would receive compensation) to design the vehicle for the bid.[260]

Brandt contacted Probst on Saturday, July 13, 1940 and the Detroit automotive designer was reluctant to drop everything to go to Butler, but told Brandt to have Fenn call him on Monday. Fenn contacted the engineer on Monday, July 15th and after some discussion Probst told the Bantam President to call him when he had the bid specification.[261] Brandt contacted Probst on Tuesday and he pulled out the big guns as the Detroit consultant recalled:

Figure 49: Karl K. Probst.

> I got a call from Art Brandt in Knudsen's office in Washington. Knudsen knew of my work; years before, I had presented my plans to him for a light weight GM car. Knudsen was deep in the Army Scout car project.
>
> When Art told him of my attitude, Bill said to tell me that this was important to the country, forget about the salary, to forget about my own office. "We think you can do this job faster than the big companies," Art told me referring to Bantam. "Financing will be available if you produce a vehicle to specs," Art advised me.
> "Well, if you put it like that," I replied, "I can't refuse Mr. Knudsen."[262]

Fenn called again on Wednesday, July 17th, after receiving the bid specification. The two executives engaged in a detailed discussion on the challenges inherent in what the Army proposed, but eventually Probst decided to leave for Butler that night. He stopped at Spicer Axle to discuss that critical component with Fred Hall and Robert Lewis, manager of the axle division and chief engineer of the railway and axle division, respectively.[263] Probst recalled:

> I discussed with them the requirements of this proposed vehicle. They showed me the four-wheel design, roughed out, using the Bantam axle, which were considerably lighter than were later selected. They had previously done work for Bantam on a vehicle of this type but of somewhat less horsepower, and the specifications which came through called for more horsepower; therefore, the axles and the other work which had been done by Spicer were not applicable, so it was necessary to get heavier axles and transfer cases. We discussed that and got them set and they were started at that interview, at the time I stopped, on Wednesday.[264]

Entrepreneurial Lesson 30
Working Under a Tight Deadline

For Entrepreneurs, time is always running out. Less than two minutes to go, no time outs left, four points behind, their ball on their own twenty, and they have to score to win the biggest prize of their lives. Not to mention it is human nature to use every second allotted to a project. Lead times only indicate how much or how little time there will be left at the end with which to pull off the delivery.

Now put them into a situation in which their country is faced with decimation and annihilation by war. Now give them forty-nine days to design, build and deliver a prototype to the Army. A nearly bankrupt small company little-known —not only back in 1940, but also today still virtually unknown—delivers the first Jeep with thirty minutes to spare.

Life is a two-minute warning.

The seasoned automotive designer arrived in Butler on Thursday, July 18th. Bantam's bid proposal was due on Monday, July 22nd.[265] Probst was introduced to Crist that morning. Probst conferred with the Bantam factory manager, who presented the Detroit engineer with tentative "specs" for the vehicle, and the former Studebaker employee helped Probst develop a vision for the vehicle.[266] They decided 50% of the chassis parts would need to come from already existing components changed to meet the needs of the new vehicle. After consulting the telephone book for possible parts suppliers, and the available blueprints for ideas, the designer began drafting the vehicle at 1:00 PM.[267] Probst worked throughout that day, slept, and then worked a full day on Friday July 19th to complete his work. A chassis parts list was completed over night and on the 20th estimated costs were calculated with the help of Crist. The bid forms were completed on Sunday by Fenn and Probst, and the two headed toward Baltimore for an evening meeting with Payne.[268]

Baltimore, Maryland—Late Evening—July 21, 1940

While reviewing the documents that night, Bantam's Washington D.C. representative initially only found some minor items to correct:

> Well, if I remember, he (Payne) thought the angle of approach we had shown – I believe he wanted that changed, and I believe the size of the gasoline tank in our specifications I believe were a little under. I can't remember exactly what changes we made that night. I think they were minor changes that would conform more to the specs than the ones we had drawn. They were minor changes affecting minor changes in the job and the thought we had not quite met the specs as originally issued and maybe we could do better on a few dimensions and we changed a few figures.[269]

The seasoned automotive expert, testifying in an official court case in 1945, failed to mention that Payne had found a major issue, as Probst explained in a later recollection:

> Going over the bid forms, he came to my weight figure of 1,850 pounds. He exploded, "Don't you fellows know you can't get accepted at that weight? They never expect you to make the weight in the specifications but you've got to bid it at the 1300 pound figure. We'll get it revised after we get the contract."[270]

Probst was flabbergasted at the idea of misrepresenting the weight, knowing full well that it was impossible to meet the 1,300 pound requirement. The designer figured the gig was up. However, Payne stated he would use a contact at Holabird to obtain new blank forms that night and would enlist the hotel manager's stenographer to retype the forms. She arrived at 3:30 AM, retyped all the forms (with a new weight of 1,273 pounds). She finished just in time for Fenn, Probst and Payne to make it to the QMC motor vehicle depot at 8:30 AM on Monday, July 22nd.[271]

Entrepreneurial Lesson 31
Ethical Choices

Ethics are complicated. That is, if a person possesses some and adheres to them. Truth is uncomplicated. Truth is always the truth. It just is what it is.

At what point does an Entrepreneur compromise ethics in order to tell the truth? On the final play of the game is it okay to purposely commit a penalty to allow the team to win the big prize, hoping that the referees do not see it or call it? Maybe the course of World War Two and subsequent history of the world would be different without the Bantam Jeep, in that to win their bid, they fudged the proposed weight of the vehicle.

Consider the ethics of the source for the action. And weigh the action against the stakes. When those stakes are the very highest, it is perhaps possible that the greater good of all humanity is served. How honourably? It is complicated.

Bantam's Bid Proposal—July 21, 1940

The Bantam team took the statement "bidders are cautioned to read carefully all instructions contained herein as well as those in Standard Government Instructions to Bidders (Standard Form No. 22)" to heart and completed their bid forms to the Quartermaster's exacting demands.

The Butler firm's response contained the completed "standard government form of bid" cover page for invitation for bids No. 398-41-9 which had a proposal opening date of 10:00 AM EST on July 22,

1940. The form dated July 20, 1940 stated it was completed in Butler, Pennsylvania which confirms Probst's account that the documents were completed in Butler, but as he related, the questionnaire was retyped in Baltimore in the middle of the night to correct the weight requirement.[272] The Bantam team stated:

> In compliance with your invitation for bids to furnish materials and supplies listed on the reverse hereof or on the accompanying schedules, numbered: Sheet No. 1b, and Q.M.C. Tentative Specification ES- No. 475 dated July 2, 1940, the undersigned American Bantam Car Company a corporation organized and existing under the laws of the State of Pennsylvania a partnership consisting of … an individual trading as … of the city of Butler, Pennsylvania hereby proposes to furnish, within the time specified, the materials and supplies at the prices stated opposite the respective items listed on the schedules and agrees upon receipt of written notice of the acceptance of this bid within AT ONCE days (60 days if no shorter period specified) after the date of opening of bids, to execute, if required, the Standard Government Form of Contract (Standard Form No. 32) in accordance with the bid as accepted, and to give bond, if required, with good and sufficient surety or sureties, for the faithful performance of the contract, within 10 days after the prescribed forms are presented for signature.[273]

The upstart small car manufacturer offered a 1% discount and Francis Fenn signed the form as President of the American Bantam Car Company, Butler, Pennsylvania.

In accordance with the bid instructions a schedule was included which contained a main bid and two alternative bids as follows:

Table 2: Bantam Main Bid and Two Alternative Bids

Item No.	Articles or Services	Quantity	Unit	Unit Price	Amount Dollars	Amount Cents
1.	Trucks, Motor, Gasoline, Light Reconnaissance and Command Car (Four Wheels—Four Wheel Drive), in accordance with Quartermaster Corps. Tentative Specification ES-No. 475, dated July 2, 1940, attached	62	each	2260.50	140,151	00
		70	each	2260.50	158,235	00
a.	Alternative bid is requested for Trucks under Item No. 1 equipped with Full-Floating Type Rear Axle (Par. D-14.a.)	62	each	2415.50	149,761	00
		70	each	2415.50	169,085	00
b.	Alternative bid is requested for furnishing eight (8) Trucks under Item No. 1. Or 1.a., equipped with Four-wheel steering mechanism (pars. D-14.b. and D-22.a.).					
	Item #1	8	each	2673.00	21,343	00
	Item NO. 1.a	8	each	2823.00	22,584	00

All vehicles were offered f.o.b. (free on board/freight on board) Manufacturers Plant for shipment on Government Bill of Lading or Driven away by Government personnel. The bidder included the following stipulations, the first recognition of the greatest risk to the project, the development of a front axle that would meet the military's four-wheel drive requirement, as well as agreeing to the second greatest risk, the incredibly short development time[274]:

> At the present writing no four-wheel drive equipment in this size is in production. The actual design and layout for this equipment is practically complete however. We will deliver the Pilot model to Holabird forty-nine days from the date of order as this is the best time that can be made because of the necessity of waiting for the new four-wheel drive axles.[275]

The carefully developed proposal next contained the completed instructions to bidders page (which stated in capital letters at the bottom – DO NOT DETACH THIS SHEET) that obligated the bidder to the stipulations contained on the page and had Fenn signing a clause that read:

> It is hereby warranted that all unmanufactured articles, materials or supplies furnished under this agreement have been mined or produced in the United States, and that all manufactured articles, materials, or supplies have been manufactured in the United States from articles, materials, or supplies mined, produced or manufactured in the United States, except as noted below or otherwise indicated herein.[276]

The bankrupt Butler firm's award-winning response to the questionnaire based upon the exacting specifications in section D provided the foundation for the contract. This document also guided the way the team built the pilot model and provided the basis of how the Army tested the vehicle upon delivery.

Table 3: Bantam's Response to Army Requirements

F-1. Truck. Make Bantam, model 40, overall length 126 inches, overall width 54 inches overall height 71.5 inches shipping weight 1,273 pounds (exactly as Probst remembered!), 4 wheel steer shipping weight 1,323 pounds, dunnage in shipping weight 85 pounds.
F-1a. Trucks loaded on freight car, item 1, 8, 50' Auto Box Car, item 2, 8 50' Auto Box Car, item 3, 6 – 9, per truck by our own transport trucks
F-1b. Weight of truck fully equipped, 1,300 pounds, 4-wheel steer 1,350 pounds, gross weight allowances specified.
F-1c. Wheelbase 79 inches, with truck fully equipped and loaded: ground clearance under following units, front axle 8.5 inches, rear axle 8.5 inches, transmission 11.25, transfer case skid shoe 9.5 inches, gas tank 21 inches, battery 21 inches, propeller shaft brake 9.5 inches, angle of approach 45 degrees,

departure 36 degrees, truck will comply with overall height specification, driver vision requiremen will be met.

F-2. Frame will support maximum gross loads and be suitably braced.

F-3. Power unit – Will the engine, clutch and transmission be embodied in a unit power plant yes; will the engine be so mounted that it will not be damaged form distortion, yes; will the transfer case be mounted as a unit with the transmission, yes; will it be so mounted that it will not be damaged by frame distortion, yes.

F-4. Engine make Bantam 40; model 40; number of cylinders 4; displacement 113.1 cubic inches; maximum peak horsepower 40H.P.at 5500 r.p.m.; maximum operating speed guaranteed by the engine manufacturer 3300 r.p.m.; maximum torque, less only fan and generator operating 79 lbs./ft.; will this torque be developed while using fuel having a knock rating of not more than 68 octane, yes; will engine operating be satisfactory using fuel of this octane number, yes; the torque quoted above was developed employing what compression ratio, 5.4 plns to 1.0; is this the compression ratio that will be furnished, yes; cylinder head material, cast iron; will the crankshaft be counterbalanced, yes; number of main bearings, three.

F-4a. Will a governor be provided on the engine, no.

F-5. Cooling system – will the requirements of paragraph D-5 herein regarding cooling, be fully complied with, yes; will a thermostat be provided, yes.

F-6. Lubricating system – Method of lubricating: crankshaft main bearings, pressure; connecting rod lower bearings, pressure; camshaft bearings, pressure; piston pin bearings, splash; cylinder walls, splash, timing gears or chain, spray; capacity of engine oil reservoir, 5 quarts; is this capacity sufficient to meet the cruising range requirements of paragraph C-3 herein, yes; lubrication system will function satisfactorily on side slopes up to, 22%; and on longitudinal slope to, 59%.

F-6a. Oil filter – Make, as specified; model, as specified; type, as specified; will the filter comply with the requirements of paragraph D-6 herein, yes; will the requirements concerning oil lines be fully complied with, yes.

F-6b. Type of chassis lubricating system, alemite; type of fittings alemite h.p.; will the system be of a design that will permit the ready attachment of the grease gun, yes.

F-7. Ignition system – Make, auto-lite; potential 6 volts. Is automatic or hand control for spark advance provided, automatic.

F-8. Fuel system – fuel tank, capacity ten gallons; will this capacity be sufficient to meet the cruising range requirements of paragraph C-3 herein, yes; will the tank be so mounted that it will not be damaged by frame distortion, yes; tank mounting location, rear of body; fuel pump make, A.C.; model, 1523306; type A.F, will it include sediment bowl or chamber, yes; strainer, yes; hand primer, yes; will the pump be so located that its operation will not be objectionably affected by exhaust heat, yes;

F-8. Fuel system – auxiliary filter, make Zenith; model M22X-2-B2; recommended mounting location, at tank; air cleaner, make, A.C.; model, as specified; is it oil bath type, yes; oil capacity, as

specified; will it meet the efficiency requirements of paragraph D-8 herein, yes; will fuel line requirements be fully complied with, yes; will the lines be arranged to prevent vapor-lock, yes; the fuel system will function satisfactorily on slide slopes up to, 20%; longitudinal slope to, 50%.
F-9. Muffler – will the requirements of paragraph D-9 herein be fully complied with, yes.
F-10. Clutch – Make, long; model, 8½ CB-C; type, single plate; guaranteed to transmit torque of 90 lbs./ft.; will automatic means be provided for lubricating the throwout bearing mechanism, no; if not, will a lubricating fitting be provided at a readily accessible location which does not require the removal of toe or floor board, yes.
F-11. Transmission – Make, Warner Gear; model, T 84 E; guaranteed to transmit a torque of 80 bls./ft.; reductions, 1st 2.93 to 1.000; 2nd, 1.70 to 1.000; 3rd 1.000 to 1.000; reverse, 3.90 to 1.000 to 1.0.
F-12. Transfer case – Make, Spicer; model, 40; reductions, high range 1. To 1.; low range 2. To 1.0; guaranteed to transmit a torque of 325 IN lbs./ft.; will the transfer case include front axle drive declutching mechanism, yes; will the declutching mechanism be properly lubricated from the transfer main case, yes; will controls be readily operatable from the driver's seat, yes; will the controls detract from driving comfort; no; will transfer case noise be effectively minimized, yes.
F-13. Propeller shaft – Make, Spicer; model, 40; front Spicer 23 ¾ inch; rear, Spicer 23 ¾ inch; between transmission and transfer case, none; guaranteed to transmit a torque of, front, 325; rear 325; transmission-transfer case, none lbs./ft.; maximum angle at which universal joints are guaranteed to continue operation, 20 degrees; maximum angle that will exist in universal joints with truck in the fully equipped, loaded and level position (for momentary operation, 10 degrees; are the joints all of the same make and type, yes; are they of metal construction; yes; will the propeller shaft lengths conform to the manufacturer's recommendation, yes.
F-14. Axles – type, hypoid reduction; gear ratio, 5.25 to 1.0; Ratio of impact resistance between horizontal and vertical planes of axles housing, 1. To 1. To 1.0; will axle bowl covers be so constructed that they will not be damaged in cross country operations, yes; will they be bolted to the axle housings, yes; will differential assemblies be interchangeable between front and rear axles, yes; will housing breathers be provided, no; will gear lubricant be confined to the differential bowls, yes; will high pressure lubrication fittings be provided in the hubs, yes; will high pressure lubrication fittings be provided in the hubs, yes; if so, will the hubs include the required relief fittings, yes.
F-14. Front axle – Make, Spicer; model, 40; input torque capacity 325 lbs./ft.; will it be of the full floating type which a wheel will not be released if an axle shaft fails, optional; axle shaft diameter over the splines, 1.125 inches; number of splines, 10; steering drive ends, joint make, Bendix-Weiss; type C.V.; size, 3 ¼ inch; outside spherical diameter, 6 inches; will steering pivots be equipped with roller bearings, yes; offset between king-pin center and tire center, at ground 1 ¾ inches; front wheel maximum cramping angle, at the wheel on the inside of the turning circle, 30 degrees; will axle stops be of the required design and welded, yes; steering tie rod, outside diameter, 1 1/8 inches; wall thickness 3/16 inch; will the ends be threaded as required …; tread 47 ½ inches.

F-14. Rear axle – 2 wheel steer trucks – make, Spicer; model 40; type, optional i.e. full floating o semi-floating; if a semi floating rear axle is offered at the bid price, has the increased cost (per truck been quoted in the bid, for the provision of a full floating axle of a type with which the wheel wil not be released if an axle shaft fails, yes; input torque capacity, 325 lbs./ft. axles shaft diameter ove the splines, 1.125 inches; number of splines, 10; tread, 47 ½ inches.
F-14. Rear axle – 4 wheel steer trucks – make, Spicer; model 41; will the steering drive ends be identical to those provided on the front axle, yes; input torque capacity 325 lbs./ft.; tread, 47 ½ inches.
F-15. Springs – will the requirement concerning spring to spring stop clearances be fully complied with, yes; will the required spring leaf clips be provided, yes; is it guaranteed that the spring suspension will be suitable for the required service conditions, yes.
F-16. Shock absorbers – Make, Gabriel; model, 40; total number provided, 4.
F-17. Does not apply.
F-18. Wheels, tires and tubes – wheels, make, motor wheel; type, steel ventilated; will they be so constructed that they will not be damaged in cross country operations, yes; will they be interchangeable on all axle hubs, yes.
F-18. Rims – Make, Motor Wheel; size 16 – 5.50; type, Dr. Center; will they permit proper mounting of tires containing bullet seal tubes, yes.
F-18. Tires – Make offered for selection, Firestone; type, Ground gripper; size 16 X 5.50; number of plies, 4; type of tread design, ground gripper; loaded radius, 12 ¾ inches.
F-18. Inner tubes – Make, Firestone; type, regular.
F18. Tire, tube, flap wheel assemblies will be balanced to within 35 inch-ounces. Will the tires be balanced dotted, yes.
F-19. Brakes – Service brakes – application type, hydraulic; brakes and drums provided on 4 wheels; hydraulic line maximum pressure 1000 lbs. per square inch; brake size, front 9 X 1-1/2; rear 9 X 1-1/2
F-19. Parking brake – make, Spicer; type, external band; actual location, rear of transfer case; will the parking brake be operatable at all times on the rear wheels, yes.
F-20. Electrical equipment – potential, 6 volts; battery – capacity 80 ampere hours at a 20-hour rate; make U.S.L; model, AB-13; generator, make, Auto-Lite; type, voltage controlled; guaranteed maximum output capacity (when hot), 25 amperes; generator regulation apparatus box, make Auto-Lite; model, as specified; type, as specified; will the requirements concerning wiring be fully complied with, yes.
F- 21. Chassis equipment – will the requirement concerning engine hood, bumpers, instrument panel, tool, tire chain and accessory equipment be fully complied with, yes; are the requirements concerning lighting equipment thoroughly understood, yes; will they be fully complied with, yes; will reflectors be furnished as required, yes.

F-22. Controlling mechanism – Steering gear – make, Ross; model T 12; rated for easy steering in connection with a driving front axle and a load of, 724 lbs on the front tires at the ground; is the control mechanism guaranteed to be of a capacity adequate for the intended service, yes; steering wheel diameter, 17 inches.
F-22. Controlling mechanism – 4 wheel steer trucks – will the steering mechanism provide delayed steering on the rear wheels, yes; maximum cramping angle on front wheels, 30 degrees; on rear wheels, 23 degrees; will the design of the steering mechanism preclude weaving of the rear end of the truck and any tendency to over-steer, yes; will the mechanism be substantially constructed and so installed that it will not be damaged in cross country operations, yes.
F-23. Operating mechanism – will the requirements of paragraph D-23 herein, be fully complied with, yes.
F-24. Name, caution and shifting plates – will the plates be provided, inscribed as required, yes; will drawings of the plates be submitted for approval, yes; will they be mounted at approved locations, yes.
F-25. Body – will the body conform to the requirements of drawing 08370-Z, yes; is a body drawing being furnished for approval, yes.
F-26. Special operating equipment, rear pintle, make, as recommended; will it be installed as required, yes; will towing hooks be furnished, no; if not will the front bumper be so designed and mounted that it can be used for towing purposes, yes; will the truck construction permit the satisfactory installation and use of tire chains, yes.
F-27. Painting – will the painting requirements be fully complied with, yes.
F-28. Markings – will the trucks be marked as required, yes.
F-29. Maximum road speed, truck fully equipped and loaded, 50 m.p.h.
F-30. What grade abilities will be demonstrated with the truck fully equipped and loaded – with transmission in direct gear and transfer case in high range – 2 wheel steer truck 15%; 4 wheel steer truck, 14%; with transmission in low gear and with 2 speed transfer case in low range, 2-wheel steer truck, 75%; 4-wheel steer truck, 70%
F-31. Will a pilot model truck or trucks, be produced for inspection and tests at the Holabird Quartermaster Depot, yes; describe the type of trucks that will be produced for pilot model tests, light reconnaissance and command car 4 X 4
F-32. Has the service facility list been included with the bid, no; if not has it been filed with the Purchasing and Contracting Officer, will be.
F-33. Have drawings been included with the bid, chassis assembly, yes; frame, yes; body, yes; have engine certified power curves been included with the bid, yes; do the curve sheets indicate what compression ratio and octane numbered fuel were employed, yes.
F-34. Bidders shall signify compliance with the requirements of this specification by supplying herewith the following data required as proof of the fact that compliance is intended:

F-34a. As required by paragraph E-2. Specification ES- No. 459, has the manufacturer of the truck offered under this bid been continuously engaged in the production of motor truck chassis for a period of 2 years immediately prior to the opening date of this Invitation to Bid, yes; and does he possess the facilities necessary to produce trucks meeting the requirements of this specification, yes

F-34b. Have the guarantees as required by paragraph E-3 specification ES-No. 459, been carefully considered and are they fully agreed upon, yes.

F-34c. If any exceptions are contemplated in the specifications requirements, have they been completely listed below, as required under paragraph E-3 specification ES-No. 459, yes; is it clearly understood that in the event exceptions are not listed below, the right is reserved to demand a full and complete compliance with the specification requirements, yes.

F-34d. Exceptions to specification requirements are listed below:

Tie rod will be placed in front of the front axle and above the center line. It is impossible to place the tie rod in the rear of the axle and secure the minimum ground clearance as specified.

We can supply spare tire mounting and bumperettes as specified. We would prefer, however, to extend the side rails of the frame to the rear and to mount a rear bumper duplicating the front. We would then propose to mount the tire between the rear bumper and the body. This change will raise the tire 1 ¼ inches, but will have the advantage of better rear protection and also the ability to mount the pintle hook so as to be accessible without the removal of the bumper or the spare tire.

We can provide the instrument panel with two glove compartments as specified, but it is our opinion that it would be better to use the instrument panel we are now using in Bantam cars, as we feel this would make it possible for the men in the two bucket seats to enter and leave the car much more easily.

In all preliminary conversations upon which the 4-wheel drive equipment were based, there was no mention made of the parking brake on the rear of the transfer case; in as much as parking brakes are already included on the 4-wheel hydraulic brakes and we naturally assumed the parking brake properly shielded against brush, etc. would be entirely satisfactory. We believe this specification should be changed as the specified parking brake will, in our opinion, not be effective or meet your requirements.[277]

The RFP had described in great detail what the Army required of the vehicle in both performance and parts as laid out in specification ES-No. 475. This document referenced a number of other specifications, as well as laying out extensive service requirements. The overall general requirement, referenced in section C, Service Requirements, as C-1 was as follows:

> The trucks described in this specification are intended for use as tactical vehicles by the United States Army. They will be required to transport the rated payload, which will consist of personnel and ammunition, at relatively high rates of speed over all types of roads, trails, open and rolling cross country, with the driving wheel tires, at times, equipped with tire chains,

> under all conditions of weather and terrain. The truck shall be of such a design and construction as to permit of its servicing, adjustment and repair, with the minimum practicable difficulty, time and tool equipment, under difficult field service conditions. The following service and detailed requirements must be fully complied with to insure that the trucks will satisfactorily perform the required functions.[278]

Bantam also completed the one page "Standard Government Form of Bid" as well as the front page of the "Instructions to Bidders" document. Bantam was the only bidder to complete all the documents and submit a conceptual drawing of their proposed vehicle.[279]

The Butler upstart clearly intended to attempt to meet the Army's desired specification with the exception of the weight requirement.

Camp Holabird, Maryland—July 22, 1940

The American Bantam Car Company was not the only manufacturer to arrive at Camp Holabird the morning of July 22, 1940. Willys-Overland (the phantom "other interested party" referenced in the Quartermaster's July 10, 1940 memo seeking the Adjutant General's permission to proceed with the bid process) had hastily prepared a bid package, though handwritten and was a time and cost bid only: no plans, weights or specifications.[280] Willys had sent a letter to the Quartermaster Corps on July 20, 1940 stating:

> We have been rather rushed in preparing this bid due to the fact that we did not receive complete information until Wednesday of this week. Therefore if there are any additional facts that we can supply or any questions which you may have concerning our bid I would greatly appreciate if you will call me collect at Willys-Overland Motors, Inc. Toledo, Ohio.[281]

While the David company in Butler had also not received the complete information until "Wednesday of this week," (July 17, 1940) Fenn and Probst were able to load a full sling shot completed bid package, while the Goliath from Toledo couldn't muster the same competency, a testament to Fenn's, Payne's, Crist's and Probst's talent.[282]

At the depot four companies were present when Major Lawes called for bids, Ford, Crosley, Willys-Overland and American Bantam, an unusually low number for a procurement. At the bid opening time of 10:00 AM, Ford and Crosley declined to submit arguing the impossibility of building the prototype in forty-nine days, Willys offered their incomplete package and Fenn, Payne and Probst tendered their proposal.[283]

As Probst later described:

> On that sweltering July 22, 1940 we waited only thirty minutes for the decision. I thought I was sweating it out but discovered later that the temperature hit 101 degrees that day and two people died of the heat.
>
> Major Lawes, the purchasing and contracting officer for Holabird, called us into his office at 10:30 with the Willys people. He started by saying, "Willys has the low bid," and paused. The bottom dropped out of me. Frank turned white. Payne cracked his knuckles. "However," Major Lawes continued, "our requirements are forty-nine days delivery for the pilot car. Bantam has bid forty-nine days; Willys has bid seventy-five days. The contract will be awarded to the company that commits to our delivery requirement – Bantam."
>
> Dismissing the Willys group, Lawes said to us, "We know you have no engineering department left. Probst will have to find one quickly. It will take ten to eighteen days to process the contract through the various departments. But from then on, you must, under penalty, deliver in forty-nine calendar days; seven weeks, no more."[284]

Lawes then laid out the salient details for the execution phase of the project:

- Bantam had to create engineering resources immediately;
- Two weeks to complete the award and then Evans' and Fenn's team would have seven weeks, forty-nine days, to deliver the prototype; and
- If the vehicle survived the testing phase the firm would receive an order for the seventy vehicles for field testing.[285]

At this juncture the active role for Commander Charles H. Payne ended. He had accomplished his mission, begun in February 1940, to interest the United States Army in a lightweight vehicle and have the American Bantam Car Company build it. His tireless efforts in the successful completion of the project cannot emphasize enough the value of a "project champion" which can come from any level of an endeavor. The former naval aviator's contribution was recognized by Colonel Oseth:

> Well, Mr. Payne, as a representative of the Bantam Company, furnished the opportunity that we (the Infantry) had been looking for to have an infantry battlefield vehicle manufactured and designed. He did extremely valuable work as a high-pressure salesman, and he was a good one in lining up, in removing objections within the War Department itself.
> There are a great many things that stand in the way of a project of this kind when it is initiated. There is a natural conservatism sometimes, here and there, on the part of individuals. Mr.

> Payne worked continuously. He was practically ubiquitous in getting in touch with these people that objected, either having them overruled by the next higher person, or removing their objection. His contribution was that of a salesman and promoter, who furnished us with the opportunity which we hadn't previously, of getting what we wanted in a battlefield vehicle.[286]

Bantam was the winner of the RFP process, and while the Quartermaster Corps drafted a contract based upon the RFP and Bantam's response, the team in Butler began preparations to build the prototype.

Questions for Educators

Why is it important to understand the procurement process of the buyer?

What are ways to find out the procurement process of a particular purchaser?

Discuss the ethical choice made by American Bantam to "fudge" the weight requirements on the bid forms.

Discuss the challenges of having a short timeframe to produce a bid package and how to overcome identified items.

Discuss what Bantam did right, and what could Bantam have done better, vis-à-vis putting together their bid package.

Chapter 8: Project Execution—Contract and Building the Pilot Model

While successfully completing the initiating, planning and RFP processes are crucial to project success, the rubber hits the road (pun intended!) during project execution and monitoring / controlling. The proper completion of initiation and planning will pay off during project execution; however, the team still has to deliver what was promised. For the American Bantam Car Company "official" planning was not conducted in the current use of the term in project management methodology. Once the Ordnance Technical Subcommittee left the little city just north of Pittsburgh, the record shows that Frank Fenn and Harold Crist of Butler's small car manufacturer had teamed with Fred Hall and Robert Lewis of the mission-critical Spicer manufacturing company, and they were not idle.

Entrepreneurial Lesson 32
Analyzing an RFP

A lover sends to the loved one a request for a proposal of marriage, putting the onus upon the latter. It requests an engagement. It might lead to nuptials if the requirements are met from both sides.

The beloved looks for the traps, the deal-breakers. What is the lover really asking for? Can satisfactory delivery be made? Will the couple live and work together successfully until the end of the project they doth part?

The Entrepreneur receives an RFP that might lead to a match made in heaven, but the government is playing the field with all the Entrepreneur's rivals. A back-handed bit of flattery—We may do business with you. Then again, we may not. Show us what you got.

What are the enterprise's strong suits that attracted the RFP initially? The Entrepreneur looks for traps and deal-breakers. Often an RFP ends up more work, and more costly than the actual work, being bid upon.

Washington, D.C. —July 23, 1940- August 5, 1940

While the Bantam team returned to Butler after the bid award to prepare to attempt the seemingly impossible, the Army's bureaucracy churned out the appropriate paper work. A technical analysis of the winning bid was quickly completed. The table below contains the key findings of the review.

Table 4: Technical Analysis of Bids Submitted
In Response To
Invitation For Bids No. 398-41-9

Bidder No. 2 – American Bantam Car Company, Butler, Penna

Findings / Exceptions / Deviations	Recommendation
Shipping weights	The shipping weights quoted appear reasonably correct.
Exception: Tie rod will be placed in front of the front axle and above the centerline. It is impossible to place the tie rod in the rear of the axle and secure the minimum ground clearance specified.	The tie rod location offered is contrary to the specification requirements but is the most desirable place available. Mounting behind the axles housing will result in less than the minimum ground clearance, which is believed will be more hazardous than the mounting offered. It is recommended that the specification requirement be waived and the construction offered considered acceptable.
Exception – We would prefer to extend the side rails of the frame to the rear and mount a rear bumper duplicating the front, this in lieu of furnishing spare tire mounting and bumperettes as specified.	Demand compliance with specification requirements.
We can supply the instrument panel with two glove compartments as specified, but it is our opinion that it would be better to use the instrument panel we are now using on Bantam cars.	Require two glove compartments be supplied as called for in the Invitation for Bids.
Exception – A cut-in type parking brake is offered in lieu of the transmission brake specified.	It is recommended that the specification requirement be waived and the parking brake offered be accepted provided it meets the performance requirements of paragraph D-19. b.
Deviation – The chassis drawings which accompanied the bid discloses a number of features which do not conform to the requirements of drawing 08370-ZA (is this the drawing we have?) a. Thermo-syphon type engine cooling system instead of pump circulated system. b. Same volume radiator core apparently will be used with the larger engine that is used with the engine of less than one-half the size of the one offered.	Hand written notes acknowledging deviations

c. The cooling fan diameter is shown to be greater than the height of the radiator. The blades extend below the core.	
d. The head lights are not placed in a protected or desired location.	
e. The engine hood does not slope as required to give road vision. However, this is probably due to the use of the larger engine.	

General Recommendations
1. The product described in the bid submitted by the American Bantam Car Company most nearly meets the specification requirements, is lowest in price and since this is an experimental development, award is recommended to be made to this firm.
2. There are a number of controversial questions which can and will be adjusted at the time of award.
3. It is suggested that the personnel of the interested using arm be consulted regarding the importance of the Exceptions and Deviations and their reactions thereto incorporated in the directive award.
4. This office recommends acceptance of the alternate bid which includes full floating axles.
5. If the alternate bid which covers four wheel steering is acceptable, it is recommended that the delivery time be extended the amount requested by the bidder.
6. The bid submitted by Willys-Overland, Inc. while basically low, actually is higher, due to the addition of liquidated damages because of excessive delivery time over the limit of seventy-five (75) days.
Suggested changes in specification – this specification should be reviewed as soon as the results of field tests are available.[287]

Bid Endorsement

Official endorsement of the technical analysis came on July 25, 1940:

1. Award under invitation for bids No. 398-41-9 will be made to the American Bantam Car Co., Butler, Pa., as follows:

Item No. 1.a. (Alternate) —For sixty-two (62) Trucks, Light Reconnaissance and Command Car 4 X 4, at a unit cost of $2419.50, less 1%-10 days, plus $8.06 per truck for furnishing one (1) spare wheel, tire and tube; Total Net Cost: $148,763.11.

Item No. 1.b. (Alternate of Item No. 1.a.) – For eight (8) Trucks, Light Reconnaissance and Command Car, 4 X 4, at a unit cost of $2823.00 less 1%-10 days, plus $8.06 per truck for furnishing one (1) spare wheel, tire and tube; Total Net Cost: $22,422.64.

Entrepreneurial Lesson 33
Contract Negotiations

A contract is anything to which all the parties agree, rarely getting all they wanted. Contracts usually involve compromises on all sides. First ponder best case/worst case scenarios. If the parties can live with the worst case, then a contract is possible. In fact, contracts are written from a worst case mindset.

Parties begin talking informally, developing talking points. These resolve into what the parties will do together. The horse trading begins. No party talks numbers unless another flinches first. Almost every negotiation comes down to one of the parties acting as if to walk away. It is an old tactic to discover how seriously the others really want it. Power here lies with the one who can take a deal off the table and live without it. The tactic might backfire, but not as often as it succeeds in getting a contract executed.

Total net value of award—70 Trucks ….. $171,185.75.

2. Recommendation of your depot contained in the Technical Analysis of Bids are concurred in, except that the offer made by the American Bantam Car Company under exception noted in Par. F-34. D. 2 (spare tire location), should be accepted, and complete compliance with the requirement of Par. D-5. should be required.

3. Necessary funds, Tr-Authorities and route orders will be furnished under separate cover at an early date.[288]

Contract

The Army sent official notification of the award to Bantam by telegram on the same day (July 25, 1940) that the Butler manufacturer's bid was accepted.[289] The contract was dated August 1, 1940 and finalized on August 5, 1940. This document provided the final information the squad in Butler would have to build the pilot and included some changes and additional information as reported in the technical analysis.

The agreement first specified the number of vehicles ordered as well as their cost as follows:

ITEM NO. 1.a:-62 Each TRUCKS, MOTOR, GASOLINE, LIGHT RECONNAISSANCE and COMMAND CAR (FOUR WHEELS-FOUR WHEEL DRIVE), in accordance with Q.M.C. Tentative Specification ES-No. 475, dated July 2, 1940. To be equipped with FULL-FLOATING TYPE REAR AXLE:

Unit Cost	$2,415.50
Gross Cost of Item 1.a	$149,761.00

Less discount of 1% for payment in 10 days	1,497.61
Net Cost	$148,263.39
Plus $8.06 net per truck for one (1) spare wheel tire & tube	499.72
TOTAL NET COST OF Item 1.a	$148,763.11

ITEM NO. 1.b:-8 Each TRUCKS, MOTOR, GASOLINE, LIGHT RECONNAISSANCE and COMMAND CAR (FOUR WHEELS—FOUR WHEEL DRIVE), in accordance with Q.M.C. Tentative Specification ES-No. 475, dated July 2, 1940. To be equipped with FULL-FLOATING TYPE REAR AXLE and FOUR WHEEL STEERING MECHANISM:

Unit Cost	$2,823.00
Gross Cost of Item 1.b.	22,584.00
Less discount of 1% for payment in 10 days	225.84
Net Cost	22,358.16
Plus $8.06 net per truck for one (1) spare wheel tire & tube	64.48
TOTAL NET COST OF Item 1.b.	$22,422.64
TOTAL GROSS COST	$173.070.56
TOTAL NET COST	$171,185.75[290]

The amount of the arrangement was just under the $175,000 that the Army had budgeted to procure the vehicles. The Quartermaster Corps between July 22, 1940 and August 1, 1940 had completed a more thorough analysis of Bantam's bid and included twenty-four additional stipulations, requirements, and requests for information in the contract.

Table 5: Contract—Additional Requirements

1. You took exception to mounting the tie rod behind the front axle. You will be permitted to mount the tie rod ahead of the front axle housing, provided that it is adequately protected from damage.
2. You will be permitted to extend the frame side rails to the rear to support a full width rear bumper, provided that the front and rear bumpers will properly overlap. If necessary, bumper guards may be used to provide compliance with overlap requirements.
3. The two (2) glove compartments are desired and it is requested that you make an effort to supply compartments that will not interfere with entrance and egress from the vehicle, Additional data are desired covering the compartments.

4. Regarding the parking brake it is desired that you submit for approval a layout portraying clearly the type of cut-in brake you would provide, bearing in mind that the control mechanism must be effectively protected from damage.
5. You have quoted an engine compression ratio of 5.4 plus. It is desired that you quote the actual compression ratio figure you intend to employ.
6. In your bid questionnaire you state that the cooling system requirements of paragraph D-5. will be complied with. However, your chassis print R-100001 indicates that the thermo-syphon system of circulating the cooling medium will be employed. This is contrary to the specification requirements. A circulating type pump must be furnished on the vehicles.
7. The chassis print shows the cooling fan extending above the radiator core necessitating a housing in the radiator upper tank. Also, the fan blades extend below the radiator lower tank which indicates that the installation is one in which a large engine and fan assembly are utilized with a radiator core designed for a smaller engine. While the design as illustrated, is acceptable, you are cautioned that the cooling medium temperature differential requirement at the top of the radiator must be complied with.
8. You have not named the brand of oil filter you intend to furnish. In this connection it is suggested that you investigate the metal edge type filter now under development by the Zenith Carburetor Corporation. It is understood that a filter of light weight might be obtained suitable for use on this light weight vehicle. Comment and data are desired.
9. The specification drawing requires a gasoline tank having a capacity of at least ten (10) usable gallons. Your chassis print shows a tank of ten (10) gallons capacity but it may be possible that all ten (10) gallons are not usable. You are cautioned that the usable gallonage must be at least that required.
10. You have quoted the transfer case torque capacity as 325 inch-pounds. It is assumed that this is an error. It is desired that adequacy of this unit be substantiated.
11. It is requested that data covering the propeller shaft universal joints be furnished together with the shaft angles that will actually exist with the vehicle in the level and loaded position.
12. You have quoted the steering drive and universal joints as of 3-1/4" size, and outside spherical diameter of 6". Obviously steering drive universal joints of the spherical diameter stated could not possibly be assembled in the axles offered in the vehicle. It is requested that the correct size joint together with a print of same be furnished this office.
13. The steering tie rod must be threaded to permit a fine toe-in adjustment, i.e. fine and coarse threads at the right and left hand ends of the rod respectively. You have failed to answer this question but it is assumed that you contemplate such a construction.
14. You offer Firestone "Ground Gripper" tires. The specification stipulates that the tread design must not require directional operation. Will the tire you contemplate using be one that does not require directional operation to insure satisfactory life? It is desired that data covering the tread design be furnished this office for approval.

15. The chassis assembly print shows only one auxiliary shift handle. Since the two speed transfer case requires separate shift handles for range gear and declutching mechanism two shift handles must be furnished and provided with simple means to prevent low range gearing being utilized when the front axle drive is disengaged. This can be in the form of a lip extension placed on the range gear shift handle so that the transfer case cannot be shifted into low range unless the front axle drive is engaged.
16. It is desired that a more suitable location be selected for the mounting of the auxiliary gasoline filter. The filter must be accessible for servicing.
17. With the 3300 r.p.m. engine maximum operating speed, tires having a 12-3/4" loaded radius, and 5.25 axle ratio, the vehicle road speed will be less than 50 m.p.h. It is desired that the road speed at the 3300 r.p.m. engine speed shall definitely exceed 50 m.p.h. Accordingly, it is requested that you advise whether an axle ratio of approximately 4.7 to 1.0 can be furnished in lieu of the 5.25 ratio.
18. The construction and arrangement of the tool boxes are not in accordance with bid drawing #08370-ZS. You are advised that the construction must be that shown on the above mentioned drawing.
19. It is desired that the body be made slightly wider to more properly cover the rear tire equipment. This as you have increased the axle tread beyond that contemplated. It is further desired that the wheel housing side panels be moved closer to the tires resulting in a wider cargo space between the wheel housings and wider rear seat.
20. In the case of the four wheel steer vehicles it will be necessary, of course, to provide proper clearance for tire chains when the rear wheels are cramped either to right or left.
21. It is noted from your layout that when the front wheels are cramped there does not appear to be sufficient tire chain clearance with respect to the frame. You are cautioned that sufficient clearance must be provided.
22. You are requested to furnish as promptly as practicable detailed prints of the engine, transmission and transfer case, front and rear axles, and a print clearly showing the four wheel steer layout actually installed in your chassis.
23. A sample of the dull and lusterless paint you propose to employ together with the name and address of the manufacturer, must be furnished this office.
24. The headlight mounting location you selected is not considered the most appropriate one, It is requested that you submit sketches showing any optional mountings you could provide. The tail lights must be mounted flush in the body rear panel.[291]

The final section of the deal would detail the final overall requirements including the stipulation that would make history: delivery of the pilot model in just forty-nine (49) days:

As set forth in your bid you agree to complete deliveries as follows: Pilot Model within forty-nine (49) days, that is on or before September 20, 1940; Sixty-one (61) vehicles under Item 1.a. to be delivered twenty-six (26) days after delivery and approval of Pilot Model; an additional two (2) weeks will be granted for delivery of the eight (8) vehicles under Item 1.b. To enable this office to have an inspector at your plant when these vehicles are ready for shipment it is requested that you notify this office at least five (5) days in advance of the date same will be ready for Government inspection. War Department Registration Numbers will be furnished as soon as they become available to this office.[292]

September 20, 1940 was forty-nine days from the contract date of August 1, 1940. However, it took a little more time to iron out the details and the Quartermaster set the clock ticking on August 5, 1940. The deadline to supply the pilot model to Camp Holabird was September 23, 1940, no later than 5:00 PM.

Butler, PA—June 22, 1940-August 5, 1940

As mentioned in chapter 7, Fenn believed in June 1940 that Bantam would receive the work to attempt to build the new vehicle through negotiated contract. Having no idea when Army would award the contract for the vehicle, or their expected delivery date for the trucks, the Bantam President did not delay in beginning preparations:

Figure 50: Pilot Chassis Rail—September 3, 1940. Photo Courtesy of Robert Brandon, Butler, PA

I told them (Bantam personnel) to immediately get to work and compile all possible data with the view to assisting drawing specifications on the proposed vehicle. We had several draftsman and detailers, and I didn't feel that the thing was far enough along to warrant us in employing any engineers on the job.

During the first and second days that the members of the technical committee were there they laid down certain performance characteristics that the car should have, so we went to work to see how many Bantam components could be used to meet those performance characteristics. We were constantly in touch with Mr. Hall and we immediately began to call in manufacturers of small engines, such as Hercules and Continental. Hercules were very much on the ball and were in our plant quite frequently. In fact, they were in there two and three days at a time.

Now, they had one particular engine that if you were to look at it you would say, "Well, it is that engine." The bore was different in respect to several sizes which would give the engine a greater cubic displacement and consequently more power. As we were shooting for weight, however, we were not quite satisfied with the weight of the Hercules engine, and we asked Continental to come in. Continental came in, and we found we could get more horsepower with less weight by making certain changes, such as changing the Bell housing.

Entrepreneurial Lesson 34
Problem Solving

In business there are no problems, only situations to handle. It is purely a matter of handling interruptions as smoothly as possible. Problem solving has the wallpaper effect. Put up new wallpaper on one wall in one room and suddenly the whole house needs remodeling. Medication, too, solves one physical condition but causes another, and so on.

One's day is constantly interrupted by a chain reaction of associated problems stemming from putting out fires. Progression from emergency to crisis to flow to routine to resolution requires a nimble balancing act—holding water in a sieve.

To end emergency and crisis and to lead the enterprise into flow, the Entrepreneur solves problems by first stopping the bleeding. Once flow is restored it allows for time to assess the damage in order to achieve resolution. Solving a problem might initiate a new problem, but then one learns to handle interruptions that spice up every day.

Another thing that was very important was the fact that Hercules were reluctant to make any changes in their standard engine and Continental were willing to make the changes. For example, it was brought out during the conference between ourselves and the technical committee that this car would have to operate at impossible angles, that is, it might be tilted up 15 to 20 degrees on one side, and such as that, and it might have to climb grades as steep as 60-degree grades. That would necessarily mean that in order for the engine to have a proper supply of oil that we would have to have a deeper oil pan; and Hercules weren't particularly anxious to go along with the changes in their standard engine that would be necessary to meet those requirements.

So we began to swing to Continental, because of their willingness to make those changes, and the lighter weight, although at the time the tender of bid was made (July 22, 1940) we had not reached a conclusion as to whether we would use Hercules or Continental. From the standpoint of clearance the Hercules engine offered some advantages. We had not reached a decision as to whether those advantages outweighed the advantages offered by Continental.

We had numerous telephone conversations with Mr. Hall and after the Spicer Manufacturing Company, who, after all, are specialists in the building of differentials and propeller shafts, items like transfer cases, after they had completely explored the thing they advised against the use of the Bantam axle.

Then followed a lot of shuffling around to see what axle could be used. They were in production of the Studebaker Champion axles, and it was decided that we would use that axle. Then came the problem of the frame, and weight of the frame, and the type of construction, and we decided the frame should be a box-type frame, which was not in use in the automotive industry, either the truck industry or the car industry, at that time. That meant additional weight. As a result of our work the box type frame was adapted and the whole construction of the car had to be canvassed.[293]

Figure 51: Chassis Coming Together—September 5, 1940. Photo Courtesy of Robert Brandon, Butler, PA

By the time of the award of the contract on August 5, 1940 Bantam had decided on the box-type frame; aero plane-type shock absorbers; the modified Studebaker axle with their transmission with certain changes in it and a transfer case to be built by Spicer; that the body could not be made to conform to the originally expressed desire for a 36-inch silhouette, and the silhouette would have to be at least 40 inches; the radiator and carburetor to use; the use of stock lighting ignition, and that the engine would have at least 85 cubic inches capacity.[294] Fenn also remembered that:

Pending the outcome of the bid he (Crist) started procedures for securing material from which to fabricate many car and chassis parts in advance of engineering. He also selected two other men to assist him in the actual construction of the first vehicle or prototype. Others were selected to provide backup assistance and supply to the three doing the physical creating.[295]

Figure 52: Body Tube and Rail Assembly—September 4, 1940. Photo Courtesy of Robert Brandon, Butler, PA

After the award of the bid to Bantam on July 22, 1940, Probst went to work building the engineering capacity that was not needed just one month earlier.

Bantam had no engineers at that time and it was necessary for me (Probst) to go to Detroit and find some engineers to do this job. It took me about a week to line up three or four men with any experience. I think I got them back to

Butler about the first of August, the engineers, and I believe the award came in the 4th or 5th of August, the official date.[296]

Figure 53: Ralph Turner Examining the Engine. Photo Courtesy of Robert Brandon, Butler, PA

The Bantam team had wisely used the six weeks from the time the Army committee left on June 21 to the award of the contract; however, as the dog days of the summer of 1940 wore on, the forty-nine day deadline still seemed impossible.

The Butler automotive manufacturer had two experienced hands in Probst and Crist to guide the engineering and hands-on building of the pilot model; however, the Bantam factory manager would need other experienced staff to pull off the almost unfeasible feat of building the vehicle from the ground up. Fenn's right hand man wanted to keep the core team small and he knew exactly who he needed to round out his group.

Butler, PA—August 6, 1940-September 17, 1940

Chester Hempfling was born and grew up in Butler and after graduating from high school went to work at the Armco Steel mill until 1929. He joined the predecessor to the American Bantam Car Company, American Austin, in 1930, and was gainfully employed by both establishments for the next eighteen years. He was another "can-do, jack-of-all-trades" automotive man as shown by his imaginative solution to directly delivering a vehicle to a customer during his time with American Austin:

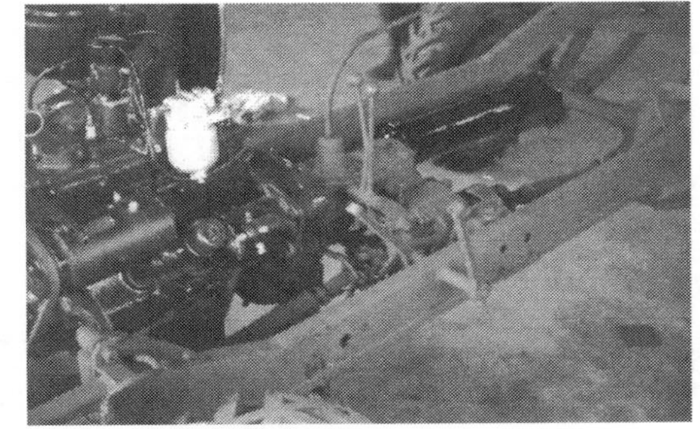
Figure 54: Chassis Drive Train Under Construction. Photo Courtesy of Robert Brandon, Butler, PA

We lined up the service car and the one to be delivered and attached a tow bar. Next we would tie-in the ignition of the new car to a toggle switch in the service car. I adjusted the throttle screw of the towed car so that the engine would be running about 30 – 35 mph, shut off the engine and set the car in high gear. To start off, I would tow the rear car, then cut in the ignition of it with the toggle switch. It would jerk a little, then settle down and off we would go. At a hill which might slow the Austin down, with that car pushing and no one in it, I'd go up the hill at 35 – 40 mph! At traffic lights I would shut off the rear car and control the front one. Once, in Pittsburgh,

I was too busy in traffic controlling the front car to shut the back car off and it jack-knifed and pushed me sideways up on the pavement. There was a lot of power in the hook-up![297]

Hempfling would form one half of a dynamic duo that would contribute greatly to the successful completion of the pilot model. The other experienced man Crist would have was Butler native Ralph Turner. During his high school years he worked in a watch repair shop and after graduating in 1928 he was hired as a salesman for the Hudson automobile company. He lost that job at the depths of the Great Depression and fell back on his time piece experience finding work at the Elgin Watch Company factory in Elgin, Illinois. He returned to Butler eight years later to take over the watch repair shop after the death of the man who had employed him during his youth. It was at this establishment that Crist made the acquaintance of this mechanically gifted individual. The Bantam factory manager talked him into joining the American Bantam Car Company and made him general foreman of the production line. In this capacity destiny would tap his shoulder as a key individual in building the Light Reconnaissance and Command Car prototype.[298]

The improbable had met the impossible and the core project team of Karl Probst, Harold Crist, Chester Hempfling and Ralph Turner had their work cut out for them. While all had vast amounts of hands-on automotive experience none had ever attempted something of this magnitude, building a revolutionary new vehicle with strict requirements, in the seemingly unimaginable time of forty-nine days. The doubters were many, including the legion of experts in Detroit, who were betting 5 – 1 against Bantam.[299]

Probst had laid out the general game plan for completing the vehicle in forty-nine days:

> We can find the engine; I'm thinking of a commercial engine (A Hercules was specified first, then a Continental) I've used before. I know the clutch and transmission we'll buy, the Spicer transfer case and, of course, the axles from Studebaker. To make that ridiculous forty-nine days, we've got to lay our hands on every possible part that's already available in production today.[300]

Figure 55: Transmission and Transfer Case. Photo Courtesy of Robert Brandon, Butler, PA

Probst knew he had a top-notch leader when he was introduced to Harold Crist: "On Thursday the 17th (of July) I met with Frank Fenn and his factory manager, Harold Crist. Crist was a human dynamo. He and his four key men (Hempfling and Turner the most important) could produce tools and parts—some with no drawings. We needed that ability for sure."[301] The prototype's building would be a design, build, design, build iterative process with rework the norm.

> **Entrepreneurial Lesson 35**
> **Doubters**
>
> Doubt everything. Doubt what's written in the previous sentence. Doubters are not pioneers. Unlike visionary Entrepreneurs, they care about what others will think about them, so they layer on a bunch of dubious criticisms about achieving things that have never been done before.
>
> Amidst a ferocious hailstorm of doubt, with all the odds stacked against them, seven people worked twenty-four/seven for seven solid weeks to build the Bantam Jeep prototype. The builders were themselves doubters. Not that they ever doubted they could do it, but the unending stream of problems to solve and having to wait on outside entities to deliver key parts, made it seem like they would never make the deadline.
>
> You, the reader, probably know by now that they delivered the prototype Jeep with a half-hour to spare. To the seven and their visionary leader, the outcome was never in doubt.

> As with any completely new prototype, everything had to be made by hand. Even stock items, such as brakes and steering gear, required alterations. The shaping and fitting of sheet metal was accomplished by trial and error. Hundreds of parts, including jigs and fixtures, were fabricated from rough sketches. There had been no time for the preparation of detailed drawings.[302]

The team's responsibilities were broken down as follows:

> Crist was the boss. Turner was responsible for the chassis and the engine. I (Hempfling) was responsible for fabricating the sheet metal parts. I would like to say at this time that Ralph and I were "mechanics" not engineers. Engineers are college graduates who do drawings, and the drawings are sent to the workshop for production. Most engineers have no idea of how to work the machines used in production. We mechanics hand made the parts. They were then laid out on a block and pictures were taken. They were then sent to the drafting department and blueprints were then made. The blueprints were made after the part was made.[303]

Figure 56: Chester Hempfling with the tin snips the German metal smith used to cut the rounded hood on the pilot model. Photo Courtesy of Robert Brandon, Butler, PA

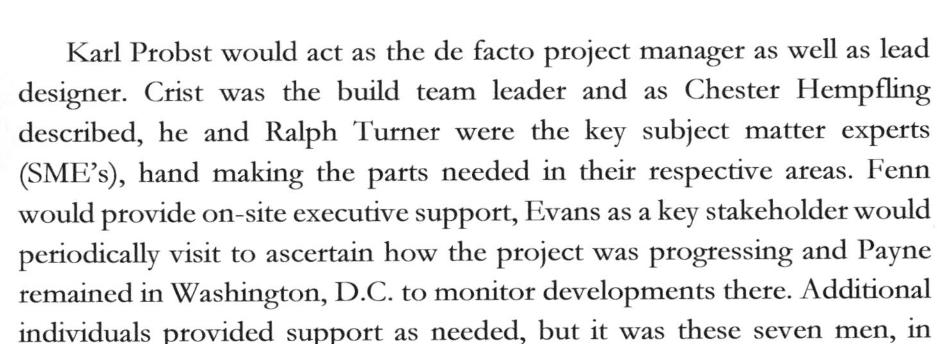

Karl Probst would act as the de facto project manager as well as lead designer. Crist was the build team leader and as Chester Hempfling described, he and Ralph Turner were the key subject matter experts (SME's), hand making the parts needed in their respective areas. Fenn would provide on-site executive support, Evans as a key stakeholder would periodically visit to ascertain how the project was progressing and Payne remained in Washington, D.C. to monitor developments there. Additional individuals provided support as needed, but it was these seven men, in particular, Probst, Crist, Hempfling and Turner who were tasked with building the pilot model on time and to specifications.[304]

One writer characterized this group of intrepid, talented individuals thrust into the center of history as follows:

> Gathered at American Bantam's Butler factory, north of Pittsburgh, was a group of ingenious seat-of-the-pants engineers, craftsmen, and inspired mechanics so typical of the early days of the automotive industry. One of them was Harold Crist, who had been an engineer in the heyday of the Stutz Motor Co. of Indianapolis, builders of the legendary, cutting-edge Stutz racing cars.
>
> Crist focused on the contract bid with two Butler-area natives, Ralph Turner and Chester Hempfling, both imaginative, resourceful, and highly skilled hands-on craftsmen / mechanics.[305]

Figure 57: Rounded Grill Added—September 6, 1940. Photo Courtesy of Robert Brandon, Butler, PA

Ralph Turner described the overall process of how the first Jeep came to life:

> I had the job of cutting the metal, and then putting it together. I can remember Crist sitting by the hour on a nail keg changing the design a little here and there as we finalized the first prototype.
>
> I first went to Armco Steel which was located next door to the Bantam plant to get steel cut in the shape that we wanted to make the frame. I took it back to Bantam, and made a "box frame." A box frame is light and strong because it has the ability to twist and give without breaking. We then cut the sheet metal to shape, and formed the body of the Bantam. Crist wanted a curved and rounded hood. No one knew how to make a rounded hood, so Crist hired a German metal smith to do the job. The man took an acetylene torch and a series of hammers, and pounded a perfectly rounded hood. The engine was provided by the Continental Engine Company of Butler (45HP). The differential came from the Spicer Company of Toledo, Ohio. I had to take each axle and cut it down to size. We had Ross steering, Stromberg carburetors, Harrison radiators, etc. All companies buy common components from specialty companies.

The next step was to make a transmission with a transfer case. I went down to a local junk yard and acquired two Chevy transmissions. I then cut the sides out of them and welded them together. I had to totally rework the insides to get the desired result. I had to re-drill some of the holes, line up the shafts, and, re-gear the transfer case, and make it work.

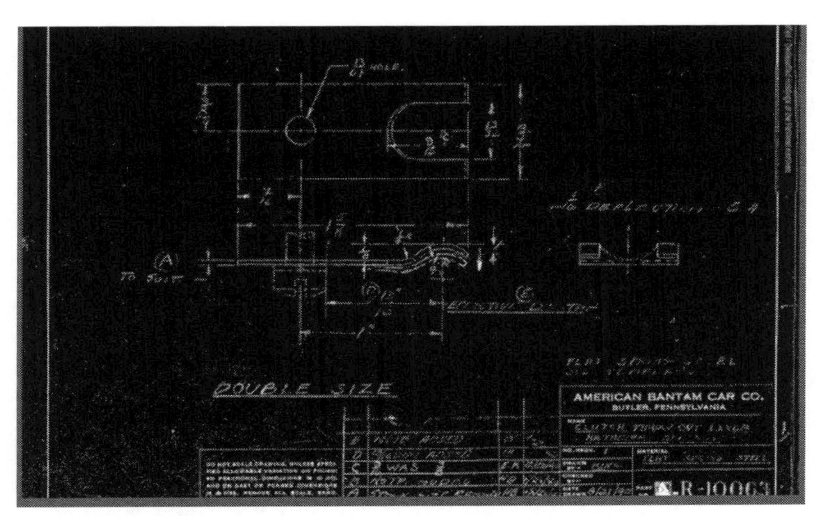

Figure 58: The Clutch Throw Out Lever Original Blueprint for the Bantam pilot model. Source—United States National Archives, College Park, Maryland

I remember once that Crist and Probst got into an argument about the front engine mount. Probst wanted a straight mount coming up from the frame- Crist knew from practical experience that the mount had to be angled to accommodate the torque of the engine. Crist won the argument and the Bantam was built with a front motor mount that set at an angle.[306]

The men worked tirelessly day after day seven days a week. He (Crist) was known as a "go-getter" and now he proved the phrase aptly applied. As he and his small group worked unremittingly day and night selecting components, assembling, adapting and adjusting parts, solving problems and ever racing time to complete the job within specified bid time limitations... the impossible was accomplished. Each morning the chief draftsman of the Bantam Company (Probst) had checked the progress of Harold and his crew, made sketches of the items successfully installed the day and night previously, and added them to the list of builders materials. The end result was a vehicle which incorporated, in all major areas, those ideas which later proved to be so fundamentally correct as to be used in that order even today some forty-odd years later.[307]

Crist, Probst, Hempfling, and I (Turner) worked almost 24 hours a day during these 49 days. Sometimes, the project would be on schedule, and I would go home to get some sleep. No sooner would I get to sleep than Crist would call and say "Come on back Ralph; We have a new problem." I never thought that men could get so tired and still work.[308]

Crist worked us day and night. He wouldn't let us leave. Ralph and I (Hempfling) slept many nights in the upstairs girl's restroom ... A German metal smith used an acetylene torch and a

> set of hammers to form the rounded hood. I still have the tin snips that the German "special ordered" to cut the sheet metal.[309]

> You can only put just so many men on a job like this, so working around the clock became more of rule for us all than an exception.[310]

> Late into the night, seven days a week, Crist and his key technicians – Chester Hempfling and Ralph Turner – worked with tireless determination. Evans visited the experimental shop whenever possible, often rolling up his sleeves and lending an extra pair of hands.[311]

Figure 59: Chassis Assembly as of September 10, 1940. Photo Courtesy of Robert Brandon, Butler, PA

> Under Crist's watchful eye, Turner and Hempfling fabricated some of the parts on the Butler factory floor and purchased others from the richly laden shelf of automotive products available in the American industry – axles from Spicer, a radiator from Harrison, a Continental four-cylinder engine, a Stromberg carburetor. Turner got steel from the neighboring Armco steel plant and personally welded and fabricated the sturdy box frame for the vehicle. At a Butler junkyard he bought two Chevrolet transmissions that he cut, welded together, modified, geared, and mated to a transfer case to provide four-wheel drive. In a way, Crist's team worked backwards, fashioning the vehicle almost ex nihilo, without a set of blueprints. Bantam draftsmen converted what they built into drawings.[312]

The team was operating by the seat of their pants, but their hard work and years of hands-on automotive experience was paying off. However, even with all their extraordinary effort and expertise, the work progressed slowly and the major risk (the front axle) remained unresolved as the dog days of August ended and the cool nights of September ticked by.

The two key risks that the team needed to overcome revolved around the front axle and the issue of the vehicle's weight. Early on Bantam decided to ignore the weight requirement and build the vehicle to specifications.

> "Karl," he (Fenn) screamed, "Are you ready for the kicker? Do you know what it's supposed to weigh? Thirteen hundred pounds! That's what our twenty horsepower job was supposed to weigh. And it's got to be delivered in forty-nine days under penalty!"

With the patience of an older person, as Probst was sixty in 1940, he waited before addressing the issues:

> When he calmed down a bit, I replied, "We can produce drawings faster than our competitors (allaying the forty-nine day fear). Of course we can't make the weight, but neither can anyone else."[313]

This left resolving the front axle situation, identified as the critical component from the very beginning of the project, based upon the fact Fenn had called Fred Hall of Spicer to Butler on June 20, 1940 (chapter 6). Probst related how he and Fenn determined the Army's specification had made Bantam's axle unusable for the prototype, which led to the choice of adapting the Studebaker axle:

> Wednesday, July 17th: Fenn called shouting so loudly that he almost didn't need long distance. "We have the formal bids. Somebody made just one little change. They raised the horsepower from the Bantam's twenty to forty! Karl, you know what that means. Our transmission won't take it; our axles won't take it; frame, suspension. We'll have to jack up the horn button so you can design a new car under it."[314]

However, Probst and Fenn did not fold their cards at the first sign of trouble. They brainstormed a possible solution on the spot, a characteristic the Bantam team would exhibit time and again:

> "Well", Frank said, "start now for Spicer (a specialty axle supplier which ironically had built axles for American Austin).[315] We'll have to get heavier axles; also the two-speed transfer case. Can you get here by nine Thursday morning?" I said I could by driving at night. I had made up my mind.
>
> In my '38 Buick Special coupe, I headed toward Telegraph Road to Toledo. At Spicer, I met with Bob Lewis, who had to give up any plans to convert the Bantam axle. Spicer made another axle, however, which was used by the Studebaker Champion, a 2,100 pound car with 65 hp; we decided to use that. We did some work on the transfer case and by three o'clock, I was driving east to Cleveland and then towards Butler, putting pieces together in my mind as I drove.[316]

Figure 60: Body Added Sometime After September 10, 1940. Photo Courtesy of Robert Brandon, Butler, PA

Probst and Fenn had laid the groundwork for mitigating this key risk, but could Spicer deliver?

Fred Hall and Robert Lewis were unwittingly propelled into the maelstrom of the light reconnaissance and command car project due to one single factor: Spicer Manufacturing was the only firm in the United States that could produce the axle, which transmits power from the rear of the transmission to the wheel. The Army required it, and the military, as well as American Bantam knew that only Spicer could manufacture the axle that would make the critical four-wheel drive function.[317] That capacity, combined with a powerful engine, would make the new vehicle truly special.

Fred Hall had worked at Spicer as the manager of the axle division since 1929 and Robert Lewis worked alongside him as chief engineer of the railway and axle division. These two men were the preeminent axle experts in the world at that time and fate had once again placed the right individuals at the right place at the right time to make history. Lewis provided a detailed account of the background of the axle that was eventually developed for the Light Reconnaissance and Command Car.[318]

> The history of the axle design and development goes back to our original basic patent on axles in 1933 and '35; all axles we manufacture are based on these original patents. In December 1939 we started the particular design for a four-wheel drive half-ton truck for the United States Army for Camp Holabird. Those designs were continued on until about the middle of 1940, and drawings submitted to Major William B. Johnson, and also, conferences were held with Major Johnson and Captain Newell. This design, although larger, was almost identical to present (1944) Jeep axles.
>
> June the 19th, 1940, I was in conference with Major Johnson and Captain Newell at Holabird when Mr. Hall was called to Butler in connection with a small Jeep. Hall was there to help in crystallizing the ideas as to what could be done, and the axles and transfer cases is one of the main units, and Hall was there to represent what could be done along that line. On Mr. Hall's return from Butler he brought back a tentative car specification of a small four by four car, using a small engine of 35 foot pounds torque, which he obtained according to his notes given to me, from Bob Brown at the conference in Butler, Pennsylvania.
>
> June the 28th, 1940, we started our first sketches of the four-wheel drive car, four-wheel drive axles for that car on our small model 10 axle, which was the original model axle used on the original Bantam car. These designs were carried along until we got word that they were stepping up the engine size to 65 foot pounds, which came out in the new Federal specifications. We received that on July 15, 1940, which has already been covered by Mr. Hall. On July 16, 1940, we started the same design carried along to the larger size axle, which was our Model 23 axle, and these drawings were submitted to American Bantam.

> On July 19, 1940 and July 23rd, we made sketches showing the proposed gear and shaft locations. On July 24th, 1940, we received the first Bantam print of the chassis layout showing the axle carrier on the right hand side. On July 29, 1940, we sent Bantam preliminary prints of our layout, axle layouts. On August the 7th, the Spicer final drawing of the experimental axle on the first job that was built.
>
> August the 9th, 1940, additional car specifications were received. On August 12, 1940, we released the first drawings for the material to be made for the very first axle. On August 20, 1940, we received a Bantam print of the body layout showing the axle carrier on the left hand side, and also a print of the drawing on the front axle assembly. On September 18, 1940, we finished assembling the first axles and shipped it to the American Bantam Company.[319]

By modifying the Studebaker axle that Fenn, Probst and Spicer had determined could do the job, and through a Herculean effort that Lewis downplayed, the two axle engineers supplied the key component five days before the pilot model was due at Holabird. It was the delivery of this key part that allowed for the completion of the prototype.

Butler, PA—September 18, 1940–September 22, 1940

As the days grew colder, the leaves began to turn autumn colors and with time running out the combination of preparation, hard work, and talent finally began to come together. Destiny was in the sights of the unknown men laboring in the background of history.

> Sunday, September 15th (8 days before the deadline) was the day the sun shone on Bantam. Bob Lewis at Spicer came through with our axles and we could see the last of our potential bottlenecks. I wired our ten major suppliers, "On Sunday, September 22nd, you will have up to one hour with our car and a driver to discover any required changes and adjustments …" late the following Saturday (September 21, 1940), it all came together. We filled the tank with gas for the first time and rolled the car out. It had been forty-seven days since we'd started with what seemed like nothing more than a horn button. "Get a Kodak," somebody shouted and we crowded into and around the car, all sixteen of us, nearly all the people who had worked so hard to get the job done. In the snapshot, I'm leaning on the spare tire.[320]

After the photograph was taken the team had the first of many issues to resolve and that was what to call the new vehicle. After some discussion they agreed upon, Bantam Reconnaissance Car, and the BRC was born.[321]

Figure 61: Bantam #1—The Very First Jeep—Minutes After Assembly Completed on September 21, 1940. Crist is driving, Fenn is in passenger seat, Probst leans against the spare tire at far left. Photo Courtesy of Robert Brandon, Butler, PA

The pilot model was created, but the project was far from over. The team had just one day to assess the vehicle and work out any issues they could before delivering the pilot model to Camp Holabird, 400 miles away, no later than 5:00 PM on September 23rd. For a revolutionary new vehicle that was to face, as Probst described, "the most grueling proving test imaginable," two days of check out amounts in practical terms to no time at all. However, once again, the team had to work with what fate had provided.

Probst described what happened during the first day of testing, late on Saturday, September 21, 1940. Without knowing it Harold Crist would have the honor of being the first person to drive a Jeep.

> Without any preliminaries, we started it up. Crist and I drove out of town looking for the steepest hill we could find. "Lucky we're in Pennsylvania rather than flat Detroit," I told Crist. We sighted a hill, must have been forty-five percent. No road, of course, because cars don't go up forty-five percent inclines. I cut in the four-wheel drive and we crested the hill with power to spare. "Whatever it is," I told Crist, "it's a performer."[322]

The following day, Sunday, September 22, 1940 would prove hectic for the Bantam team as they crammed in as much testing as possible.

Figure 62: A Quick Test Spin Around the Factory. Photo Courtesy of Robert Brandon, Butler, PA

> Sunday was a ninety-degree day in Butler, Pennsylvania. Everybody drove the car. It did not overheat, but I told Crist, "To hold down the weight, I put in the smallest radiator I figured would work. We'll take the slightly larger one with us to Holabird to be sure it doesn't overheat on the long hills." We also selected heavier springs as spares and decided we could improve the angle of the steering arm. The suppliers came up with their adjustments, but on the whole, the way we built it was the way we took it to Holabird. Sunday was a great night to sleep.

> Further testing by ten suppliers on the 22nd was concluded without incident. By the end of the day the odometer indicated 150 miles, scarcely enough to warm up the oil, much less reveal any shortcomings in the design, but no time remained to find out if it would stand up under prolonged abuse. That night some minor changes were made to improve the steering and brake system, and a final coat of olive drab paint was applied.[323]

With the application of the paint the vehicle was ready for delivery to Holabird.

Camp Holabird, Maryland, September 23, 1940

Monday, September 23, 1940 dawned, the 49th day, and it was time for the team to deliver their "miracle of the 49 days at Bantam" to Camp Holabird.[324]

The honor of driving the Bantam Reconnaissance Car to Camp Holabird would go to Ralph Turner. Fenn, Crist and Probst followed the former watch repairman in the Bantam factory manager's car.[325] Probst described events as follows:

> Before eight o'clock on Monday morning, we were on the road to Maryland. We drove slowly at first, telling ourselves it was important to break the vehicle in. But as we wound through the hills of Pennsylvania, the five o'clock deadline we had worked toward these seven weeks seemed to come closer. To make Holabird come closer too, we were soon pushing the car to the limit, and it really was fun. At 4:30 we drove through the gates of Holabird. It was the forty-ninth day.[326]

The Bantam crew was met by a group of soldiers, officers and civilians who were waiting to see if they would deliver. About 100 individuals, including the Ford, G.M.C. and Chrysler test crews, converged on the strange little car. They were accustomed to seeing experimental vehicles of every shape and description, but here was something uniquely different, even for Holabird. With a tread of only 47 ½ inches and a wheelbase of 79 inches, it looked more like a fugitive from a rich kid's playroom than a combat car.[327]

Probst recalled the on the spot initial test of the vehicle:

> We made a demonstration at Holabird on the field there and climbed the sixty-percent grade, and Major Lawes, who, I believe, was head of Holabird at that time, asked permission to drive it. He took it out for about twenty minutes and went out around and down in the holes and every place, and then he came back and asked for the man who had produced the vehicle and Mr. Fenn introduced me, and also Mr. Harold Crist, as the factory manager.
>
> Major Lawes said he had tested Army vehicles for almost twenty years and he said he could tell in twenty minutes whether a vehicle was good or not. He said he thought this vehicle was going to be absolutely outstanding.[328]

The intrepid "band of brothers" of the American Bantam car company had done it! In a period of eleven weeks, beginning in July 1940, this group of never-say-die individuals had designed, bid and then built, a revolutionary new vehicle that would, in the prophetic words of Major Lawes, "be absolutely outstanding." However, before Bantam's creation could step into destiny, the BRC would have to pass the rigorous tests the Army had planned for it.

Epilogue—Parts Analysis

The request for proposal had required that, "all unmanufactured articles, materials or supplies furnished under this agreement have been mined or produced in the United States."[329] The table below presents a sampling of the parts included in the first seventy BRC's built.

Table 6: Parts: ¼ Ton, 4 X 4 Truck ("Jeep")

American Bantam Car Company Butler, Pennsylvania
Contract W-398-QM-8269

Part No.	Part Name	Vendor	P.O. No.	P.O. Date	First Date	Receipts Quantity
R-10259	Fuel Pump	A.C. Spark Plug Divn.	13617			
10044	Clutch Throwout Bearing	Aetna Ball Br. Mfg. Co.	13516	8/23/40	9-9-40	70
10290	Rear View Mirror	American Automatic Device Co.	13528	8-27-40	8-23-40	1
10027	Accelerator Pedal	American Automatic Device Co.	13528	8-27-40	8-23-40	1
	Wiring	American Wire Division, Electric Auto-Lite Co.				Wiring for Pilot model made at Bantam and fitted on car by representative of American Wire Division, Electric Auto-Lite Co.
10048	Gas Tank	O.L. Anderson Co.	13521	8-23-40	9-4-40	2
	Wheel & Rim Assemblies	Budd Wheel Company	13521	8-23-40	9-19-40	2 sets
	Hand Brake Assembly	Butler County Motor Co.	13535	8-28-40	8-28-40	1
	Tail Lamps-Service, Stop & Blackout	Corcoran-Brown Lamp Divn.	13583	9-19-40	9-17-40	1 Pr.
	Head Lamps	R.E. Dietz Co.	13555	9-5-40	9-1-40	1 Pr.
	Ignition Lock	H.A. Douglas Mfg. Co.	13548	9-3-40	9-15-40	2
	Side Rails	Dreyer Metal Products Co.	13510	8-23-40	8-29-40	4
	Tires & Tubes	Firestone Tire & Rubber Co.	13532	8-28-40	9-10-40	1 Set

10015	Brake & Clutch Pedals	Fort Pitt Steel Casting Co.	13534	8-28-40	9-5-40	4
	Front Axle	Spicer Manufacturing Company	13509	8-22-40	9-18-40	1
	Speedometer	Stewart-Warner Corporation	13541	8-23-40	9-16-40	2
	Fuel Filter	Zenith Carburetor Divn.	13525	8-26-40	8-30-40	2
10107	Pedal Shaft Bushings	Cleveland Graphite Bronze Co.	13578	9-18-40	9-23-40	13
	Hood & Fenders	Cutler Metal Products	13580	9-19-40		Sheet Metal Parts for Pilot model made at Bantam and fitted on car by their representative.[330]

Note: In addition to this list of components, many small items were picked up at local automobile supply houses, numerous small parts were fabricated in our plant and some standard Bantam parts were used. Some sample parts were also used and standard nuts, bolts, washes, etc. were obtained from our inventor, or purchased locally.

The detailed list of components clearly indicated that Bantam followed the guidelines as specified in the Invitation to Bids to use only American made parts. Therefore, the pilot model, in many respects, was "America's Car."

Questions for Educators

Discuss the lessons learned from American Bantam preparing before actually having received the contract.

What strikes you the most from the story of how the axle risk was overcome?

Why is it important to have highly skilled subject matter experts on the project team?

What are the pros and cons of all subject matter experts being the highest skilled?

Why is it important to incorporate a reasonable testing period before handing over a project deliverable to a client?

Chapter 9: Project Execution—Testing

Producing a deliverable represents a major milestone in the course of a project. However, creating something and having actually met the requirements, represent two separate issues. To achieve success, the stakeholders must determine that the product or service meets their needs. Professionals in the information technology world call this process "user acceptance testing," and in 1940 the United States Army had its own version of this concept in place, and ready for the BRC. Victory would come only after successfully completing this rugged and brutal phase, and the military formally accepting Bantam's creation.

September 24, 1940-October 29, 1940—Testing

The intrepid Ralph Turner was assigned the task of servicing the pilot model throughout the testing period and he stayed on post twenty four hours a day seven days a week from the time of the delivery of the vehicle to when he drove it back to Butler after the evaluation was completed.[331] The testing was assigned to E Company, 23rd Quartermaster's under the direction of Captain Eugene Mosley, chief of the test section. Assigned to this unit was Sergeant Lawrence H. Ross, a test driver and team leader for six of the thirty-five men assigned to this unit.[332] Turner would work closely with both these individuals, and the former watch repairman, who had helped hand build the BRC, would prove indispensable in helping the new vehicle successfully traverse the myriad of difficult tests the Army had planned for Bantam's creation.

Sergeant Ross described the general testing practices and the overall evaluation process for the BRC.

> Pilot models that came from different factories were to be tested. We had six drivers and myself, seven men. We drove according to the schedule that was put out in the different places in camp on the test course on the highway cross country, through mud holes, in general tried to tear up the truck.[333]
>
> I think it (the BRC) came in September, the latter part of September, and we drove it every day for about five or six days, I believe, and then we had a breakdown. It was laid up for a couple of days for parts and then we started back driving it again. I drove it approximately eight hours a day. We worked Sundays, Saturdays, and other days, every other day for eight weeks.[334]

The Army wasted no time putting the latest vehicle in their arsenal through its paces after its delivery on Monday, September 23, 1940.

Figure 63: Troops Testing the Bantam Pilot. Source—United States National Archives, College Park, Maryland

On the following day (September 24, 1940) the Bantam was demonstrated to the procurement heads of the Army and Marine Corps, who had come up from Washington. The weather had turned foul; it was cold and rained constantly. Capt. Eugene Mosley, chief of testing section, shuttled the brass around the test track until early afternoon:

The Holabird proving grounds featured a mud pit called "the hell hole," an artificial bog about 300 feet in diameter and several feet deep in the middle. Only large six-wheel-drive trucks and tanks had succeeded in traversing the treacherous quagmire. The Washington people wanted to see how long the Bantam would last in the muck.

> Mosley backed far enough away for a running start and was on the point of assaulting the pit when several high-ranking observers motioned him to wait. The captain was riding alone and the officers insisted the test be made with a full crew aboard. In the absence of volunteers, the officers themselves climbed in and Mosley stomped on the throttle. Half-way across, the Bantam was hopelessly swamped, its carburetor choked with mud and water. The marooned passengers could do nothing but sit in the drizzling rain and contemplate the wisdom of their decision. Possibly the idea of installing a canvas top occurred at that this time.
>
> Lawes summoned a six-wheeled rig and the gumbo-plastered Bantam and its occupants, wetter and wiser, were hauled to solid ground. While the mud was being cleaned from the carburetor, Probst remarked that he thought the car could push through the muck if Mosley skirted the center and went in no deeper than two feet. After all, it had to

Entrepreneurial Lesson 36
Impress Top Executives

The easiest way to impress top executives is to make more money for them than they are already making. If the Entrepreneur is exceeding the expectations of a board of directors, shareholders, stakeholders, venture capitalists, or all at once, it makes a difference as to whether or not any of them will buy into the next venture with either sweat or real equity. Good is not good enough.

Someone will do business with an Entrepreneur if the latter has made the former or others a boatload of money in the past. It does not matter whether the Entrepreneur had made nothing or a killing. It has to with using other people's money with which to make other people money. More power to the Entrepreneur, then, that finds a way to profit mightily from the enterprise, too.

The top executive to impress is oneself. Keep something in the head, in the heart, and in the pocket book.

have air, and beyond that depth the Bantam was practically submerged. This time Mosley coaxed the car all the way across. The observers nodded their unanimous approval.[335]

There was one final issue to resolve and that was the issue of the BRC's weight, the same concern that had bedeviled the Bantam team since the vehicle's design. Probst recalled this critical turning-point moment in Jeep history:

> It was now time for top-level appraisal. We drove out to a restricted area. After all the good things were said about its gutsiness and go, one of the generals rubbed his chins and asked, "What does it weigh?"
>
> "It weighs 1800 pounds now," Payne replied very quickly, "But Probst believes he can cut 350 pounds in production." As chief engineer for Bantam, I was on the spot.
>
> "Perhaps Commander Payne has misunderstood me," I said, looking straight at the general. "Less fuel, oil and water, about 100 pounds, this vehicle weighs 1840 pounds. We'll probably have to add thirty to fifty pounds to strengthen weaknesses that will show up in our tests. In time, with new designs of parts not now in production, it may be possible to get you a vehicle of 1300 to 1400 pounds." (Maybe that's why I'm not known as a company man.)
>
> Standing there I knew the question of approving the Bantam Reconnaissance Car was in the balance.
>
> The Cavalry general helped to decide it. "If two men can take it out of a ditch, we need it." He was about six-foot-three and weighed 250 pounds. In his shiny boots, he walked to the Bantam; grunting, heavy leather belts creaking, by himself, he lifted the rear. He nodded approval.
>
> Bob Brown – chief civilian automotive engineer for the Army – also helped decide it. "Today we've seen the remarkable performance of this unit. To ask Probst to cut the weight like that may make it far too weak to take the punishment it is going to receive. Don't cut the weight." Under the circumstances, approval of the car at its weight had to be one of those "great decisions."[336]

Entrepreneurial Lesson 37
Admitting a Mistake

It takes a big person to admit a mistake. No bigger a person than Obama has consistently faced the world and admitted when he and his administration have blown something. He said as much during his first presidential campaign when he predicted he will not be a perfect practitioner. This is rare for the leader of any nation, let alone a chief executive of the United States.

Everyone makes mistakes. Casting blame everywhere but where it belongs, little people never admit that they do anything wrong. The ones who have the courage to take responsibility for all of their actions are the really big people.

With one lift from a general, and one affirmation from Robert Brown, who had attended that already long ago June meeting where the idea for the BRC was birthed, and the issue of the vehicle's weight was settled. Payne was proved right to bid the project at under 1300 pounds or Bantam would not have won the award due to bureaucratic rules; however, when it came time to "put up or shut up" Probst's honest approach was effective. The customer could now see what the BRC could do and on-the-spot reevaluate this critical requirement. While not the most scientific approach, the lift test won the day.

Figure 64: Bantam Pulling a 37mm Howitzer the exact weapons carrier role the Infantry had so long searched for in a lightweight vehicle. Source - United States National Archives, College Park, Maryland

An official report of further tests on September 25, 1940 also was favorable to Bantam's creation:

Memorandum For The Chief of Staff:
Subject: Demonstration of Light Weapons Carrier

1. On Wednesday, September 25, 1940, Lt. Col. Earl S. Hoag, of this Division, together with officers from interested arms and services, witnessed a demonstration of the light reconnaissance and weapons carrier vehicle built by the Bantam Company, at Camp Holabird. This is the first item on a production order of 70 vehicles ordered by the Army.

2. The vehicle is powered by a 113 cu. in. displacement engine, is 4-wheel drive, has six forward speeds, a maximum speed of approximately 65 miles per hour, an overall height of 40", and will carry 4 people. A towing device is installed, and it is contemplated the vehicle can be used as prime mover for the 37 mm. gun.

3. In the demonstration yesterday, it appeared to have ample power for mobility provided conditions were such as to provide traction for the wheels, and it appears to be able to do everything previously contemplated for the motor tricycle, if not more.

4. Representatives of the Bantam Company (Mr. Fenn, President) stated that present production capacity, with slight additional tooling, is 20 cars per day. He also stated that given 45 days

additional tooling production could be established at the rate of 50 cars per day and that the unit cost in quantity orders should be around $600.00 each.

5. The plans are being made to demonstrate the car in Washington, probably on Sunday, September 29. Definie informattion as to the exact place and time will be furnished later.[337]

With the first two days of testing behind the intrepid Bantam submission a difficult path lay ahead for the audacious little car. The question on everyone's mind was if, and how long, before, Lawes, Mosley, and their crews could destroy this upstart truck.

On September 27th, the Bantam was handed over to the testing section. In the weeks ahead it would receive an unmerciful pounding at the hands of Capt. Mosley and his drivers. It was their job to break prototypes as soon as they could. In the end they seldom failed. The Bantam would be driven full tilt over log roads and plowed fields, through sapling forests and across sand traps calculated to tear the heart out of a vehicle. Mosley would try every trick in the manual and devise a few of his own for good measure. Sooner or later, something had to crack.

> On one occasion Mosley thought he could fracture the frame or tear the body loose if he drove the Bantam off the end of a four-foot freight loading platform. He tried it time and again at speeds of ten, twenty and thirty miles per hour. Nothing failed. Mosley would have gone off at forty, but his back ached from the bone-rattling jouncing. Lawes told him to give it up and try something else.
>
> Another time the Bantam was being demonstrated before Army engineers at Fort Belvoir, Virginia. A 75mm field piece had been attached and Mosley began towing the heavy weapon across the parade grounds. He had gone about 100 yards when he realized that observers, who were watching from a distance, were shouting frantically. The gun crew had neglected to lock up the recoil sprig and it had plowed a deep furrow across the field. Clearly, the Bantam had tractor-like pulling power.
>
> Once, on the way to Butler for a factory inspection, the Bantam was forced off the road and slammed into a drainage ditch, nearly turning over. With the help of two motorists, Mosley and a corporal were able to extricate the battered vehicle. A hasty inspection revealed that a front wheel had been knocked out of alignment, otherwise the car was reasonably intact. Despite violent wobbling of the wheel, the Bantam finished the trip under its own power.
> Finally, on October 16th, Mosley succeeded in putting the Bantam temporarily out of service. After twenty days of continuous abuse, the body was beginning to sag in the middle. Both

frame side-members had cracked under the severe strain. By this time, however, the vehicle had proved itself to the Army's satisfaction. [338]

Crist supported Turner's 24 hours a day seven days a week assignment by visiting the base three to four days every week.[339] During one of his visits, on October 4, 1940, he was present at a publicity demonstration for the BRC, which showed just what Bantam's creation could do.

Well, the fact is the photographers, I was present at this demonstration and that particular day we had such a rough test on another car Captain Mosley drove up to me and told me, he says, 'Crist, you don't have to take this treatment of your car if you do not want to, if you say so we will stop it,' and I says, 'You give her the works, we want to find out what she will do, and if she fails in these tests we will correct the condition.'

Figure 65: The Bantam Proving Sergeant Ross Correct—it could do anything. Source: United States National Archives, College Park, Maryland

And he very courteously thanked me and he said, 'That is the spirit,' and then he gave the fellows a very severe demonstration, his driving ability was very good, and then when he was making one of these runs through the mud and jumping out of one of the holes there, which represented a shell crater, the news photographer said, 'Do it over,' and he said, 'give it a little more speed,' and this Sergeant Ross, he came forward, in the company of his commander, and put up a very stiff argument with the news man, and during this argument with the news reporter, the photographer, said he did not believe the car was any good and it was a little more than this man Ross could stand so he immediately exploded and said that the Jeep could do anything.[340]

Turner was his usual "jack of all trades" fixing the oil pan after the Army had ripped a hole in it and realizing that this part was too low to the ground he put a skid plate under it. During the rugged tests the one piece windshield was broken. A new two-piece part (a divided windshield) was shipped down from Butler and installed by the Butler firm's general foreman of the production line. The chassis was also broken late in the testing (as related above, around October 16, 1940) and as Ross recalled, "I do not know every darn thing that broke. There were a lot of breakdowns but I know a lot of things that broke." Turner fixed them all. It was his destiny to act as the first Jeep mechanic servicing the pilot model through successfully completing some of the most rugged treatment any vehicle has ever endured.[341]

Bantam would have to wait until the reports on the testing were written and reviewed before learning if their pilot model had actually passed the Army's trials. The placement of the order for the next 70 vehicles as stipulated in their contract with the military would confirm acceptance.

TEST REPORTS

The final reports on the test were contained in three separate documents, Inspection Report on Pilot model 1/4-Ton, 4 X 4 (Bantam) Chassis Light Reconnaissance and Command Car (October 23, 1940), Test Report on Bantam, ¼ Ton, 4 X 4, Pilot model Contract No. W-398-QM-8269 (Invitation for Bids 398-41-9) American Bantam Car Company (October 23, 1940), and Final Inspection Report on Pilot model 1/4-Ton, 4 X 4 (Bantam) Chassis Light Reconnaissance and Command Car (October 28, 1940).

Table 7: Inspection Report on Pilot model 1/4-Ton, 4 X 4 (Bantam) Chassis
Light Reconnaissance and Command Car
October 23, 1940
Comments Broken Down By Paragraph Section Specification ES-475

Par. B-1. The truck as received had one-sixteenth (1/16) inch toe out on the front tires, loaded. Care must be taken to see that wheel alignment is correct on the production trucks.
Par. D-1 Weights – Vehicle – front – 975 lbs, rear 1,055 lbs., total 2,030 lbs. Gross – front 1,060 lbs., rear 1,570 lbs. total 2,630 lbs. Note – The specification limited the vehicle weight to thirteen hundred (1,300) pounds, based on the provision of an engine developing approximately sixty-five (65) lbs./ft. torque. Every effort was made to minimize weight, but in the hand built sample vehicle a two thousand thirty (2,030) pound weight resulted when material was used of a size adequate for cross-country service. To offset this, eighty-three (83) lbs./ft. engine torque was provided. The weight that will result in production is not yet known, but efforts will be made to keep the weight under two thousand (2,000) lbs.
Par. D-2. Both side members in the frame failed at the point of support of the rear of the engine, transmission and transfer case. The strength of the side member at this point is not adequate for the load imposed. The design of the side member must be suitably altered and adequacy guaranteed. The right side member was damaged by the right front spring striking the engine front support bolt. This interference must be eliminated. The frame lower flanges were damaged by severe bottoming of the rear spring bumper blocks. Alterations to be made in spring and bumper block designs must prevent the frame members being damage. The engine rear mountings, transmission and transfer case support member failed at the points of attachment to the frame side member. The member design must be altered and so reinforced as to

adequately support the load imposed. As this member also serves as a skid-shoe under the transfer case, its lower edges should be generously rounded to permit the member skidding more readily over obstructions in the terrain.
The left front spring bracket failed. The bracket design is not considered satisfactory. The manufacturer must suitably alter spring bracket designs.
The engine right front support bracket failed twice during the tests. A suitable type bracket must be furnished on the production vehicles.

Par. D-4. The intake manifold carburetor attaching flange cracked and had to be repaired. It is understood this was caused by the mounting of the air filter, which was not equipped with the brace, and is to be included in production. The thickness of the flange stock shall be increased and the brace provided in the production trucks.
To prevent damage to the engine oil pan, a skid plate, of the general type of the one added during the must be furnished on the production vehicles.
The crankcase oil filler pipe opening must be accessibly located.

Par. D-5. Truck cooling system originally furnished did not meet the specification cooling requirements. Several cooling tests were run using various combinations of pulleys, fans and radiator cores. It was finally decided that the most satisfactory combination of meeting the requirements was a six (6) blade fan, assembly and high efficiency core. The production trucks must include the six (6) blade fan and the improved radiator core. To increase the cooling efficiency, louvers more provided in the right hood side and in the fender skirt. An adequate number of louvers must be included in the production trucks.
The radiator upper unit was fractured and had to be repaired. It is believed that the fracture was caused by the location of the radiator tie rod bracket. A suitable tie rod bracket of improved design must be provided.

Par. D-7. The ignition system is not effectively weather sealed. On several occasions the system failed because of water accumulating on the spark plugs and coil. Means to effectively weather seal these units must be provided.

Par. D-8. The auxiliary fuel filter must be installed in the fuel line between the fuel tank and the fuel pump.
The carburetor throughout the test became inoperative due to the entrance of water and dirt. This was due to an unnecessarily large hole where the accelerator plunger link enters the carburetor body. This difficulty had not been satisfactorily remedied at the time of the completion of test.
Flexible fuel line from the fuel filter to the carburetor was damaged due to connecting adjacent units. It was necessary to replace the line. On the production trucks, fuel lines shall be placed in a protected position.

Par. D-9. The exhaust muffler originally furnished with the truck was damaged beyond repair. A muffler of smaller diameter which provided more ground clearance was installed, and was found satisfactory.

Par. D-13. The front propeller shaft front universal joint cross failed during the tests. The broken cross must be inspected by the joint manufacturer, the cause of failure determined and remedied. The front propeller shaft tube strikes the engine bell housing. This interference must be properly corrected.
Par. D-14. Axles: Caskets must be supplied under axle drive shaft flanges. The front axle steering drive universal joints were removed at the completion of the tests and found to bind unduly when cramped. The axle manufacturer must see that the joints operate satisfactorily when installed in the front axles. In the production vehicles the front axle stops must be set to limit the cramping angle (at the wheel on the inside of the turning circle) to 26 degrees, plus 1 degree, minus 0 degrees, and the stop screws and check nuts must then be so welded that the setting cannot be readily altered. The horizontal rib on the right hand side of the front differential housing, struck and damaged the fan drive pulley. The shape of the ribs was altered to eliminate the interference. The interference must be properly eliminated.
Par. D-15. Spring eye bolts and nuts should include cotter pins. Double nuts must be provided on front and rear U bolts. Springs of the type furnished as original equipment were not satisfactory for cross-country operation. Several springs were broken and, due to front spring weakness, fan blade tips, fan shroud and fan drive pulley, were damaged by contacting the axle housing, and spring bumper blocks failed due to continual bottoming. The manufacturer must provide springs that will eliminate objectionable bottoming, install bumper blocks that will prevent interferences that cause damage, and guarantee the adequacy of the spring suspension and bumpers furnished in the production vehicles.
Par. D-16. The manufacturer must see that the shock absorbers are properly installed and adjusted.
Par. D-18. Wheel mounting studs must include serrated shoulders, to prevent the studs turning in the brake drums and hub flanges. Tire wear on the pilot model vehicle was considered excessive. In view of this it is recommended that the manufacturer consider furnishing approximately fifty (50) percent of the vehicles with the Firestone mud and snow tread as furnished on the pilot model, the remainder to be supplied with Goodyear All-Service mud and snow tread, without delay in delivery and additional cost to the Government.
Par. D-19. The emergency brake handle lever pall will not release properly. The contractor must properly improve this construction. Emergency brake system as furnished on pilot model was not satisfactory in operation. A proper emergency brake must be provided.
Par. D-20. Trouble was experienced with the lighting cable harness assembly. To expedite the test certain of the electrical units were rewired. It is understood that harness is not the one that will be used on the production vehicles. A suitable wiring harness must be provided. The ammeter is not registering properly. It shows "discharge" when a test ammeter indicates a "charge." Indicating instruments must operate accurately.

The generator pulley exploded during operations. This was apparently due to a bad pulley as the second one installed went through the remainder of the test without failure. Suitable generator pulleys must be furnished on production vehicles. The voltage regulator should be properly grounded directly to the generator, providing a separate wire for this purpose.
Par. D-21.a. The front bumper length does not comply with Q.M. Drawing 08370-Z. The bumper shall be suitably altered. Hood side panels must be reinforced by the addition of a transverse tie-rod. b. The speedometer cable must be properly installed and clipped. The cable as installed is too sharply bent where it connects to the transmission. This condition has damaged the cable case. c. A front and rear axle wheel bearing nut wrench was not included with the tool equipment. This item must be provided in production tool sets. Inspectors will be instructed to check the wrench for suitability. The pliers and adjustable auto type wrench were not branded with an identification number. The marking must be applied. This requirement also applies to the above wheel bearing nut wrench. d. The horn should be mounted in a more suitable protected position. e. The entire black-out wiring system is not working properly. This is probably caused by failure of certain wiring in the harness. The dimmer switch must be so positioned that the proximity of the emergency brake lever will not prevent its being readily operated. Loom should be provided on tail light wires. Tail lamp plugs must include the required metal parts.
Par. D-24. Name, caution and shifting plates were not installed on the pilot model truck. The plates must be mounted at the appropriate locations where they will be readily seen by the operator.
Par. D-25. The body, cowl, windshield, hood, front fenders, headlights, gas tank and brush guard, will be commented on in a supplemental report, which will be forwarded from this office on October 23, 1940.
Par. D-28. The vehicle marking shall be applied using blue drab color paint complying with specification ES-No. 510. A sample color chip was furnished Mr. Frank Fenn. Production of the chassis only is authorized subject to proper correction being made of defects enumerated herein.[342]

The BRC was subjected to the severest tests the Army could devise, and while numerous failures, corrections and comments resulted from the trials, the BRC had held up remarkably well considering it was an experimental vehicle built in an incredibly short time. The critical issue of weight, a challenge from the initial specification, demonstrated that Probst was right all along, a vehicle with the specifications the Army desired was not feasible at a weight of 1,300 pounds. The military realized this during the course of the test and as outlined in Par. D-1, most likely reluctantly, accepted a more realistic weight requirement of 2,000 pounds. Otherwise the majority of the findings were issues Bantam could address before building the next sixty-nine BRC's.

There was nothing in the first inspection report to disqualify the car from passing. However, two more reviews remained, the official "test report," and the final inspection report on Par. D-25 referenced above. If the prototype passed these two final hurdles the Bantam team would officially have met the requirements specified and have completed the project successfully.

Table 8: Test Report on Bantam, ¼ Ton, 4 X 4, Pilot Model

Contract No. W-398-QM-8269 (Invitation for Bids 398-41-9) American Bantam Car Company (October 23, 1940)

1. The operations test on the Bantam Pilot model was commenced on September 27, 1940 and terminated on October 16, 1940. The types of operations were as follows:

Highway operation:	247 miles
Test truck operation:	1,894 miles
Cross country operation:	901 miles
Bad road operation:	244 miles
Miscellaneous tests:	124 miles
Total:	3,410 miles

2. The following difficulties were developed during the operation test.
   a. Tire wear was very excessive. This could have been due to operation on the test track which is very severe on tires but is believed that the wear as demonstrated was excessive.
   b. Interference of the crank shaft fan pulley with a reinforcing web of the front axle caused breakage of the pulley. This was corrected by the manufacturer's representative by grinding away a portion of the web and installing stiffer springs. The corrective action was sufficient as no more difficulty was experienced.
   c. The generator pulley exploded during operations. This was apparently due to a bad generator pulley as the second one installed went through the remainder of the test without failure.
   d. The windshield was inadequately braced and failed early in the test. The windshield wiper needs stops to prevent its being pulled off the windshield during operation.
   e. The carburetor throughout the test became inoperative due to the entrance of water and dirt. This was due to an unnecessarily large hole where the accelerator plunger link enters the carburetor body. This difficulty had not been satisfactorily remedied at the time of completion of test.
   f. Considerable difficulty was experienced in grounding out the ignition system at any time the vehicle entered water above a foot and a half in depth. This is due to the fan turning the water and splashing it about the spark plugs and distributor coil. Proper shielding of the

ignition system with rubber shields should correct this difficulty. This had not been corrected at the completion of the test. g. The emergency brake as furnished on the pilot model was not satisfactorily in operation and it is understood that a new type of emergency brake will be furnished on production vehicles. h. The headlight bracket tore loose from the fender during the test. This must be braced more adequately. i. The crank case was fractured on two occasions by rocks and other obstructions on the course. A skid plate was brazed to the crank case and no more difficulty encountered. A proper skid plate protecting the crank case is a necessity on this vehicle. j. Chain clearance on the rear wheels is inadequate. Space between the rear wheels and body must be increased. k. No satisfactory springs were submitted for test. The last springs furnished were the best but require more strength. The mortality on rubber bumper blocks was very high. The weak springs used may have contributed to this bumper block failure. l. The exhaust muffler was torn off during the test. m. The fenders and grills loosened during the test. n. Difficulty was experienced keeping the headlight lens in its frame due to loosening of the clamping screw. o. There was interference between the front drive shaft and the clutch bell housing. This interference was not serious but should be corrected. p. The rear motor support cracked twice. This needs to be strengthened. q. One shock absorber had to be replaced at the end of the 3,394 miles of operation. r. Several shorts developed in the electrical system. This may have been due to the fact that this was a hand built vehicle but care should be exercised in production vehicles to prevent chaffing of the electrical system. s. The rear spring hanger of the left front spring failed during the test. This unit should be strengthened. t. The test was terminated due to the failure of both frame side members at the rear motor support. This was undoubtedly due to the combined weight of the operating personnel, the transfer case and the weight of the rear end of the motor, all of which are supported at this point. The frame must be reinforced to prevent this type of failure.
3. Remarks a. Some type of handle at the rear and side of the body to assist in lifting the vehicle when it becomes mired in mud or extreme terrain conditions will materially assist in removing the vehicle when it becomes bogged down. b. The vehicle demonstrated ample power and all requirements of the Service.[343]

The most sophisticated vehicles testers in the United States had driven the BRC the equivalent of across the country, in the toughest conditions they could conceive, and the pilot model had stood up remarkably well. There was just one more obstacle to overcome, the inspection on the chassis mentioned in Par. D-25 of the initial inspection report.

Table 9: Final Inspection Report on Pilot model 1/4-Ton, 4 X 4 (Bantam) Chassis

Light Reconnaissance and Command Car

October 28, 1940

1. The following comments covering body, cowl, windshield, hood, front fenders, headlights, gas tank and brush guard are furnished in addition to the Inspection Report on Pilot model 1/4 –Ton, 4 X 4 (Bantam) Chassis, Light Reconnaissance and Command Car, submitted under date of October 23, 1940:
Par. D-25. a. The brush guard must be of stronger construction and shall include the headlight guards required by Drawing 08570-Z. The original front fender equipment was not suitable and will be replaced by fenders of a designed stipulated below. The hood catch would not remain latched when the car was resting on uneven terrain. A suitable catch shall be provided at the front and safety catches must be mounted on each side of the hood. Louvres must be inserted in the hood sides on production trucks. The design of the windshield is not satisfactory. The manufacturer shall furnish a windshield assembly of adequate strength and suitable design on the production trucks. The windshield wiper was placed too near to the left side of the windshield. Stops must be provided to prevent the blade being rotated off the windshield. The headlight brackets cracked the fender skirt to which they were attached and the headlight lens clamp screws loosened from vibration, permitting the lens to become loose. The left front headlight interfered with opening and closing of the hood. Headlights properly placed and brackets of a suitable design must be provided. Running boards required by Q.M. Drawing 08370-Z., extending from the front fenders to the side panels with their outer edges extending in a straight line with the outer edges of the fenders and extending rearward for a distance of at least fifteen (15) inches shall be provided.

The body was not mounted squarely on the chassis. Bodies must be properly mounted.

Sufficient body clearance must be provided at the tires for the use of tire chains. It is suggested that at least one and one half (1-1/2) inch additional clearance be provided between the tire and sides of the wheelhousings. The body as provided did not have sufficient tire clearance when operating without tire chains.

The bucket seats were not sufficiently rugged and must be of stronger construction. Both original seats supplied were in bad condition at the end of the test.

The seat cushions have a semi-circular front, the forward portion of which is useless. It is requested that the front of the seat cushion be cut back approximately two (2) inches.

The forward edge of the wheelhousing must be well rounded or shaped to prevent tearing of clothing or hurting occupants when entering truck.

The body rear corner braces prevented the proper lowering of the lazy back as required. The lazy back must lower as shown in Q.M. Drawing 08370-Z.

The bucket seat backs are three (3) inches higher than shown in Q.M. Drawing 08370-Z. It is desired the seat backs extend eighteen (18) inches above the seat cushions.

The canvass cover and fasteners did not fit properly. The cover was poorly sewed with edges not properly hemmed. A serviceable cover must be provided. It is desirable to have two (2) straps over the right wheelhousing, arranged to hold the cover when not in use.

The tool box drawer under the driver's seat should be increased in size to accommodate the hand tools (excepting the jack, wheel wrench and crank), including the hammer and monkey-wrench.

The stud threads on the tire carrier and nuts were not protected from rust and the threads of one stud were stripped.

The gasoline tank filler spout is inaccessible. The spout must be accessibly placed on production vehicles.

New springs must be of a design that will not raise any portion of the truck beyond the specified limits.

The body floor shall be reinforced adequately for the mounting of a machine gun midway between the rear panel and cowl, approximately on the chassis longitudinal centerline.

The pintle hook was mounted incorrectly. The rearmost portion of the pintle must be one-half (1/2) inch forward of the rear surface of the rear bumper and be accessible for testing.

Channel section at rear of body to which tire carrier bracket is attached shall be twelve (12) gauge instead of twenty-two (22) gauge.

2. In addition to the corrections listed above, you are authorized to proceed with the following design changes. The cost of these was quoted in our letter of October 17, 1940 and agreed upon in conference with your Mr. K. K. Probst, Mr. C. M. Payne and personnel of this office. A formal Change Order will be forwarded to you at the earliest practicable date and will cover a total of sixty-eight (68) trucks, complete with bodies, the remaining two (2) chassis to be shipped to the body manufacturer, as outlined in our letter of October 26, 1940.

Two braces extending from the dash to the instrument panel shall be provided.

The glove box in the instrument panel shall have the bottom cut back two (2) inches to provide more leg room.

Larger pedestal on driver's seat shall have a two (2) inch side drawer beneath.

A two (2) inch Latex pad on each front seat and a one (1) inch Latex pad on the adjustable back rest over the rear seat to be properly applied and covered with O.D. Duck

Clips shall be provided for retaining the wheel nut wrench and crank.

Two (2) handles shall be provided on each side of body. The handles shall be applied so that they will enable lifting of the rear of truck by crew.

The rail forming the top bow shall be 1-1/16 inch O.D. pipe instead of ¾ inch O.D. pipe and its brackets changed accordingly.

Provide a 1-inch Latex covered pad at each side of each bucket seat back; also an 18 X 18 inch (approximate) pad at each side of body interior directly adjacent to each front seat. Panel pads shall have a plywood backing and O.D. Duck covering corresponding to that used on the seats.

Driver's seat to be stationary.

Assistant driver's seat must have a stationary back. The seat must be hinged to fold forward.

Fenders, hood and brush guard as shown in Cutler Metal Products Company Drawing E-5.[344]

All the reports were in; however, these documents did not provide a recommendation one way or the other on if the BRC was accepted. However, the analyses were written in language that made changes, suggestions, additions, etc. to include in the next batch of vehicles. It would remain for the committee responsible for the procurement, the Transport Subcommittee of the Quartermaster Corps Technical Committee to make the final determination.

That committee, on October 18, 1940, did not even review or discuss the field inspection reports or the test report on the Bantam pilot model as they were in the process of being prepared. In one of the greatest understatements in history, the Army approved Bantam's vehicle:

> The pilot model has been examined by the interested arms except for Armored Forces and is being tested at the Holabird Quartermaster Depot. The Commanding Officer of the Depot has informally reported that the test is practically completed *and the vehicle found satisfactory (emphasis added)*, subject to modifications found necessary as a result of the test.[345]

Bantam's vehicle so perfectly met the Army's requirements, and had met every testing challenge, that the BRC received the Army's stamp of approval even before the final test reports were issued. The incredible project that created a revolutionary new vehicle in forty-nine days was officially a success!

Entrepreneurial Lesson 38
Celebrate Success!

After the British defeated Rommel in Egypt, Winston Churchill said, "Now this is not the end. It is not even the beginning of the end. But it is, perhaps, the end of the beginning."

Along the bramble-bushed path of a venture, however, moments of unexpected goodness come to life—high points where the norm is drudgery and "slodging" through very, seemingly uneventful, hard work. They pop up at random times, and those rare moments in which they do, should be savored.

When the final battle is won, then it is time to celebrate. Until then, enjoy the happy little moments. They are far and few between and give one the feeling that something can eventually be accomplished, perhaps even in the category of greatness.

How do Entrepreneurs enjoy their accomplishments? By moving on to the next.

Bantam's vehicle so perfectly met the Army's requirements, and had met every testing challenge, that the BRC received the Army's stamp of approval even before the final test reports were issued. The incredible project that created a revolutionary new vehicle in forty-nine days was officially a success!

Questions for Educators

What are the most important lessons to learn from the Army's testing of the Bantam Reconnaissance Car?

Discuss the pros and cons of having an on-site expert, like Ralph Turner, during customer testing.

Chapter 10: Kim and Duncan Rolls—The Pilot Model Redux

Entrepreneurial Lesson 39
Life Prepares You for Your Work!

Everything one learns in school and in living is used at some point. Were you a biology major and did not see the point of English literature? What about the English literature major who never thought that algebra would ever be of any use, until having to calculate ratios for a bank loan?

Children learn what they live, and grow up to become what they learned. Take the true story of Johnny A. His mother was a junkie/dealer who paid for dope through prostitution. As a boy, Johnny's mother hoisted him through windows in order to steal drugs and cash. Johnny was an all-A student who wanted to grow up to be in a legitimate profession. Ten years after the fact, under no suspicion, unable to live with the guilt, he confessed to being the driver for two others to commit a murder. Johnny is now serving fifteen years to life in prison. The others have never been caught.

The original BRC was lost to history after the United States Army completed its testing and placed the order for the additional seventy vehicles. The pilot model was severely worn by the Army's testing and also suffered damage to the axle and front sheet metal in an accident in October 1940. BRC #1 made it back to Butler on its own power, but after returning to its birthplace no one knows what happened to it.[346]

The Jeep pilot model was a one-of-a-kind creation as American Bantam incorporated changes requested by the Army in the next group of BRC's manufactured known as the BRC-60 line. For over seventy years only one copy ever existed of Bantam #1 until a Jeep restorer and his wife, Kim and Duncan Rolls, decided to undertake their own "project impossible" and recreate the BRC pilot model.

Every project contains a certain level of challenge; however, at times a project manager may encounter an endeavor singularly unique to their career. This was the case for Kim and Duncan Rolls when they decided to attempt to build a recreation of the original Bantam pilot model, an accomplishment not achieved since the original BRC was created. Their four year undertaking, their endeavor, analyzed from a project management perspective using the five process groups from the PMBOK® (Initiation, Planning, Execution, Monitoring and Controlling, Closing) holds valuable lessons applicable to other 21st century undertakings.

Project Background

Australian by way of Great Britain Duncan Rolls began working on Jeeps at age eighteen when he purchased a CJ3B which he believed was a World War II vehicle, but in actuality it was not: "I had my first Jeep at eighteen. It was a CJ3B, but I thought it was a World War II Jeep, because when I was younger all the Jeeps you've ever saw [sic] were basically on war movies and you just thought a Jeep was a Jeep and it was from World War II. This thing was green and had Willys on it, and I thought I found myself a war Jeep. It wasn't."[347]

As he worked on his purchase he realized that the Jeep world ran deeper than his youthful enthusiasm understood, "Once I did more study and built it, I kept looking at it and saying to myself, 'Man, it doesn't seem to have enough grille bars and the headlights seem too big. I don't see Willys on the hood.' So I figured it wasn't a war Jeep and I thought, 'Oh man, I cheated myself,' so then I started to look for one."[348]

Before Duncan could continue on his journey with the iconic car, he had to make a living as a stonemason, a trade which would support his passion for automobiles and Jeeps for a lifetime.[349] He has also worked in a number of other fields including driving armored cars and chasing celebrities as a paparazzo, but his trade provided the grounding to pursue his passion for vehicles of all kinds. "One thing about having a trade, it doesn't matter what you go and do, you can always come back to your trade. You never forget your trade, it's just like riding a bike. You might not ride a bike for twenty years, but you sure as hell know how to do it as soon as you get back on it. And so, (his trade) it's always been there for me."[350]

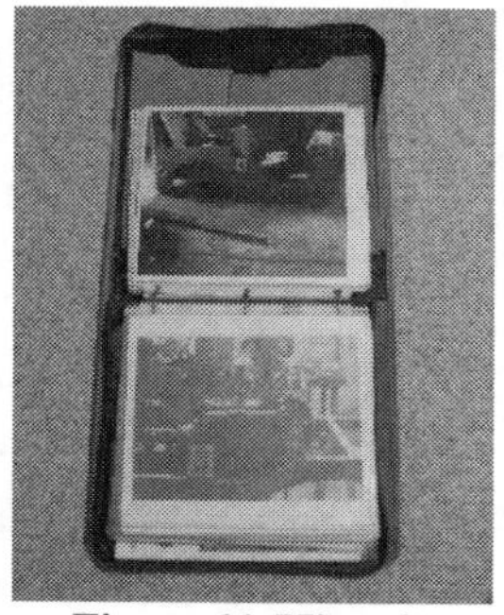

Figure 66: Historic Photos of the Pilot Model In Kim and Duncan's Bible. Photo Courtesy of Kim and Duncan Rolls

The Australian tradesman's eclectic occupational background proved valuable over the years as skills learned in these jobs transferred to his work on cars and Jeeps. "Being a sub-contractor, you're always conscious of time because time is money. The second thing is you have to quote, you have to find out prices, you have to find out availability of what the client wants. You have to get all the pieces together, do the job then get paid. It's a contract; every job is different, you're always in a different place."[351]

These talents proved invaluable in his developing ability in working on cars and Jeeps, "that's why when it came to building the Jeep it was basically the same sort of thing; you had to find out what it is, where to get the parts from and assemble it. I did it like I would anything, I always set a goal. The main thing as a sub-contractor is you get paid by what you do not just by standing around looking pretty."[352]

With the CJ3B the car bug had bitten Duncan completely and he pursued working on vehicles as a hobby and, "eventually I gained the skills by starting with that first little Jeep, learning how to oxy weld and how to make adaptors, how to do a bit of body work and how things worked on vehicles. Plus, my friends and the guys I worked with were into cars. There were always old cars and they broke down, so I'd always volunteer. You go around and you get fed and you just hang out with your mates, work on the cars. I learned a lot."[353] He concluded that, "in the end I learned more by doing it hand on than you would just reading it. Eventually, they used to come to me and say, 'Duncan, how do you do this?' It swung a big 360 right back."[354]

When not helping his buddies with their vehicles and building his own hot rod he continued working on Jeeps. "After my hot rod I had another Jeep. I had a 43 Willys, I had a 42 Willys. I had quite a few World War II Willys. My brother had a GPW and I worked on that for him. We modified that one. I did a lot of modifications. I'm not afraid to modify vehicles either. Restoration is restoration. Anybody can pull something apart and put it back together, but modification takes a lot more ingenuity because everything you move or change is a snowball effect which affects every other piece down the line. You move the engine this far, then you realize that you've got no room for a throttle or the drive shaft is going to be too short, or this, that and the other. That teaches you to problem solve."[355]

Duncan realized that the Jeep, while a special vehicle, was also relatively simple in its construction as the metal work was minimal, the painting basic with very little glass work.[356] In addition, "you don't have a top, you don't have any chrome and you've got canvas for seats. I wanted to drive them. I wanted a four-wheel drive, I wanted to get out in the bush and drive them around." While the Jeep had a reputation for indestructability the Australian stonemason found out differently: "They (the Jeep) had this persona that they're invincible. Well I realized straight away they're not invincible at all. You break everything on them. Of course they don't talk about that because they've got the Army Corps of Engineers that bring them back and repair them and back into the field they go."[357]

Despite learning the venerable war machines' idiosyncrasies he grew to admire the World War II Jeeps, "for what they are and how they were built, they're absolutely unbelievable where they will go for such a little vehicle with such a small amount of horsepower, 40 horsepower. Of course the little four-wheelers we have today have twice as much horsepower, but they basically have got the same size as the original Jeep."[358]

> During his journey Duncan landed in California during the 1990s, and as previously mentioned, worked as a paparazzo. There he met an unlikely kindred spirit, a French woman named Kim. As they got to know each other they discovered they shared a similar passion for the Jeep with her fondness for the historic vehicle having developed during her youth driving one in the French countryside.[359] They eventually married and their devotion to each other and the Jeep steadily grew.

Kim remembers, "You know something? When I saw him actually, the first time he took me to a junkyard I was in L.A. I was looking at this guy, it reminded me of an artist who is looking at the color that he's going to use, the shape of the things that he can use. Definitely he was an artist." She also expressed the viewpoint that their relationship worked because, "my love of Jeeps was also so genuine since before I met Duncan. It was not something I was trying to fake because he became my husband, 'Oh I'd better like what he likes.' It was something that was also in my heart, deep down.[360]

Duncan recalled, "Here I am with this sophisticated French lady and taking her to wrecking yards and looking for bits and pieces, scrounging around, we're going down to Pomona Swap Meet, which she had never seen. To most women that would be, 'What's all this rusty junk?' You've got to look through it. It's not rusty junk, it's something that you can use" and Kim added, "I was wearing my Army boots and my Army pants, and would go with him and just follow him around."[361] The Jeep duo would go to military shows and find that the World War II Jeeps were all the same.[362] While Duncan possessed the hands-on skill, Kim would provide invaluable talent on a project neither of them yet envisioned, as Duncan related, "You have to have a partner—in the true sense a partner—has the same goals and ideas."[363]

Entrepreneurial Lesson 40
Partners

Partners…? Who needs 'em?

Partnerships never work—so "they" say. Marriage partners—forever until divorce doth they part. Do Rogers & Hammerstein, Hewlett & Packard, and The Rolling Stones prove the rule or are they exceptions?

Entrepreneurs do not trust having partners, because of the drag on visionary progress it usually engenders. Like the saying, "Get out of here stay by the door," indicates, they love their freedom but cannot stand to always be alone. Partners are brought in to finish the job. Entrepreneurs are starters, rarely finishers. They like letting others complete something that to them is already old the moment they conceive it. For success, partners are a necessary evil or blessing.

Almost an oxymoron, a contradiction in terms, it is rare when two partners are both visionaries. The image of the Entrepreneur is that of a loner-pioneer, a solo act, slowed only by practical partners putting the vision to worldly, hopefully, very profitable use.

While still living in L.A. they discovered a part of Jeep history they had no idea existed. While driving around town Kim and Duncan spotted Roy Van Wicklin's Jeep business in Calabasas and decided to visit. Roy was a long-time Jeep expert and during their visit he showed them a BRC-40, something neither had ever laid eyes on and he told them, "it's a rare Jeep and you can't get anything (parts) for them" and he added, "It will take you a long time to restore that. However, for Duncan it was love at first sight, "But I just really liked it. I just thought it was great," but the Australian was a bit incredulous that parts could be that hard to find." Later events would prove Mr. Van Wicklin's words prophetic. However, logistics and funding would stop Kim and Duncan from purchasing the vehicle which they lament to this day, "I should have bought it, but at that time it just was not viable and I didn't have a place to put it." However, the genesis of an idea formed that day, "I think that was the seed right there that … to get in and do it."[364]

That seed was a fascination with the Bantam pilot which Roy introduced them to that day. "I remember he took me in the office and he had a little Bantam roadster. He said, 'That's where the first Jeep came from.' Now I'm looking at this little roadster going, 'Yeah, right. I can't see any Jeep in that.' Until you really start to study, then you see it."[365]

Duncan continued to build hot rods, off-road vehicles, rock crawlers, just about anything with an engine and tires. In 2004, after moving to Texas, having learned more about the Bantam Jeep and having done all he wanted to do with the Willys and Ford World War II Jeep lines, Duncan came back to the idea germinated all those years before in Roy Van Wicklin's shop. He wanted to recreate the Bantam pilot. As Duncan himself recalled the events just described, "In 1996 I had just finished restoring a 1943 GPW for a client in France. I was reading an article on the BRC 'Pilot' and wondered why no one had ever tried to recreate it." The idea remained in the back of his mind for eight years when in 2004, "I decided that it would be a real challenge to try and build it." He proposed the idea to Kim who enthusiastically endorsed the project. Little did they both know that their love of Jeeps and unique abilities and partnership would lead them on a long journey in which they would create their own history.[366]

Figure 67: Duncan Rolls in his shop looking again for measurements. Photo Courtesy of Kim and Duncan Rolls

Initiation Process

The initiation of the project was straightforward as Kim and Duncan decided early on to keep the project a secret; therefore, the project team was small, consisting of the Texas couple and one close friend identified as the "Harley Davidson Guy." As Duncan related, "The reason I kept it secret is first of all, I knew it was going to cost a lot of money. Second of all, the second guy is the first loser and it would be pointless. There was a lot of talk on the Internet on, 'I am going to build this,' and I've heard it all before. 'I'm going to build the pilot.' There are a bunch of guys, 'I'm going to build a pilot.'"[367]

However, for the Aussie stonemason saying something and accomplishment do not necessarily go hand-in-hand, "I thought, 'Yeah well, first of all you don't even have these pictures so how are you going to do that?' I had a lot of stuff sitting there and I had a lot of time and money invested, so it was in my own interest to just be hush-hush about it. Actually nobody knew about it except my one friend."[368]

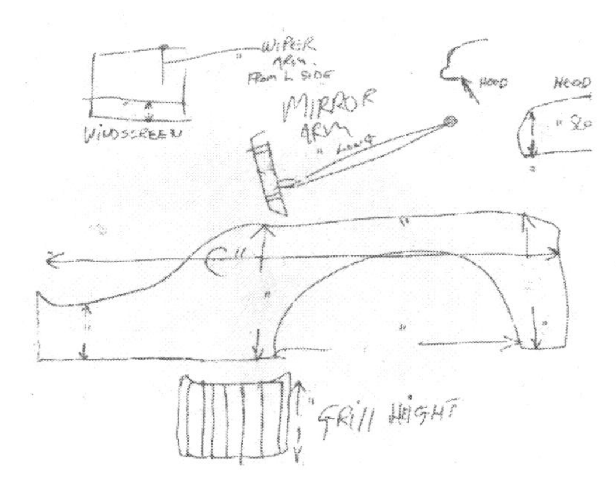

Figure 68: Drawing and Measurements taken from "Gramps" at the Smithsonian Institution. Photo Courtesy of Kim and Duncan Rolls

Duncan was the de facto project manager as well as the (and only) subject matter expert (SME). As the hands-on Jeep expert he would decide which steps would occur during the recreation of the Pilot. While not written down, his approach toward the subject constituted the project work breakdown structure or project plan. In his role as SME the Outback former armored car driver would do all the work necessary to recreate the pilot. While rare, he truly was the indispensable man on the project.

Kim would act as administrative support handling research, procurement, photographic documentation (she was also a portrait photographer in Los Angeles) and team morale. She was all-in for the endeavor from the start, "To me, I was fascinated by the project so it was never something that was imposing on my schedule. I was part of it. I felt 100 percent part of the project. We were both living, eating, and drinking the project I think. It was our baby."[369]

Her work in the research area was critical. "My role was actually more into … I'm pretty good at this, in the research … the research and development of the project. Looking at wholly … I would prepare for Duncan so he wouldn't waste his time on the computer, 'Look at this. Look at this. Read this or read that.'"[370] This support allowed Duncan as the automotive subject matter expert to concentrate on what he did best.

The French Jeep enthusiast related in terms of purchasing support. "I kept receipts, but I tried not to … Duncan hates receipting, he hates anything like that. I was really there to come back to reality and, 'Come on, do we really need all this stuff.' I still have that. It's in a big, big pile of receipts for the baby there (the pilot). A lot of the diapers."[371]

Kim's photography talents were essential to provide project progress and documentation as written records were not kept due to the small project team size. "My role, which was very important, since I was a photographer in the past, was to really take as many pictures as possible. I was always there to record everything he was doing. That's why actually we have so many pictures of the recreation of the pilot, because I was always there to do it. To me it was my problem, my most important role."[372]

Duncan concurred, "Kim would be working and I'd just knock on the window, I'd knock on the window and she knew, 'Come out with the camera and take pictures,' because I'm always dirty and I don't want to come into the house. I'd just knock on the window and she knew straight away, 'Come right now and take pictures. If I'd do something else you're not going to get to see it.'" Kim concluded concerning her photographic documentation role, "He doesn't have patience, I can assure you. You either come while I'm doing it right now or you'd miss out; continue doing what he's doing. You better come and do it immediately." This dynamic provides evidence of the close working relationship this intimate project team possessed.[373]

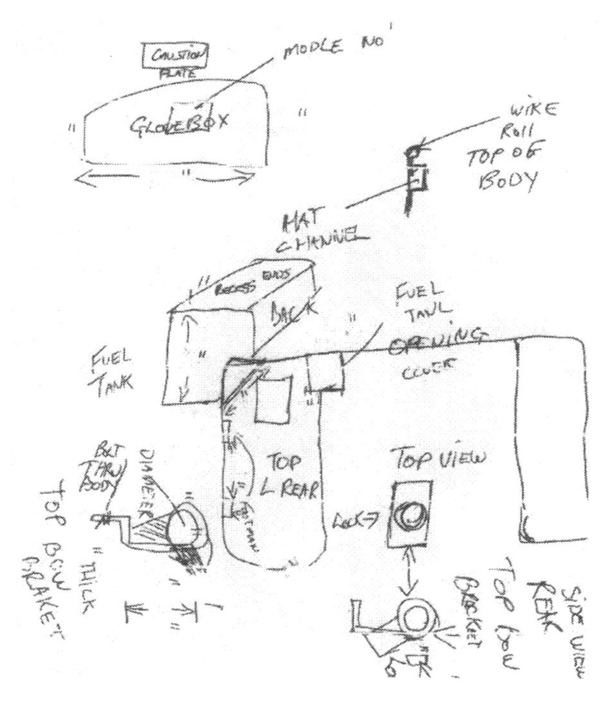

Figure 69: More Measurements Taken from "Gramps" at the Smithsonian Institution. Photo Courtesy of Kim and Duncan Rolls.

Kim's final role was to ensure that the key project team member was fit to work on the project, "Everything was geared towards achieving this project. My role was to make sure that Duncan was just fed and had enough sleep and was just happy, because he was really working hard. With his job as a stonemason, he came home, the first thing he does is go to the shed, Saturday, Sunday, in there. I had to make sure that we had a good balance to be able to continue and be happy, because you cannot be cranky. He cannot come home cranky and tired and nothing to eat. You had to have a very smooth atmosphere in here. So it was always sane, most of the time."[374]

The Harley Davidson guy, a Vietnam veteran who restores World War II versions of these iconic vehicles acted the role of quality control.[375] As Duncan explained, "The only other guy was, like I said, my friend with the Harley because he's a fabricator as well and he restores. I wouldn't tell him anything, I'd just give him the pictures and I'd say, 'What you think?' He'd say, 'You got it,' or 'You haven't got it." Between the three, it was good. He is a Vietnam Vet, he loves old cars and he was in the navy. He was really excited. He was sworn to secrecy and he never told anybody."[376]

The project objective was straightforward; recreate, not replicate, the pilot as it was delivered to the United States Army Quartermaster Corps on September 23, 1940 before the Army placed license plate 302 on the vehicle. The difference between recreating and replicating was important, and were the only options as to restore a vehicle you have to possess the actual car and the original pilot was lost in 1940. Kim and Duncan chose the more difficult path of recreating the pilot which would require as many original Bantam parts (which we shall shortly see proved difficult to find) as they could possibly include. Duncan recalled, "I wasn't going to do it unless it was exact because I thought that would just bastardize the project, start putting things on it that weren't quite right or a 'that will do' attitude.' I'm not a 'that will do'. If I'm going to do it, I'm going to do it properly. It didn't matter how many times I would make something, if I wasn't happy with it then it was in the scrap and I'd do it again."[377]

Figure 70: Kim and Duncan's "Bible" Containing the Key Information to Recreate the Pilot Model. Photo Courtesy of Kim and Duncan Rolls

The definition of a recreation can prove problematic, but in the end it all comes down to parts, "yes, because the more original stuff (parts) you use makes it closer to being a real vehicle. A lot of judging, even at Pebble Beach, if you use a certain amount of the car and the rest of it's a replica – they still classify it as a restoration. I figured there's so much original stuff on it, it's just basically nearly the real thing." Kim added, "I think at Pebble Beach it's sixty percent. If you have sixty percent of the original parts then it's considered a restoration, not a recreation or a replica. That is what Duncan's trying to achieve, to have as much … as many parts as possible."[378]

The Pilot would consist of a complete re-creation with as many original parts as possible of the American Bantam Car Company's first Bantam Reconnaissance Car, Bantam #1 as it was delivered to the American military on September 23, 1940. Figure X represents a project charter for the Rolls' effort.

With project team in place, and the objective (recreate the Pilot) and deliverable (a recreated Pilot) defined Kim and Duncan were ready for what they believed was a relatively easy execution phase and accomplish what no one else had since the original American Bantam team delivered their vehicle to the Army on September 23, 1940; however, as with many projects, Murphy's Law (what can go wrong will go wrong) was waiting for them.

Planning Process

Detailed planning was not undertaken. However, their efforts did conform to project management methodology with specific phases and tasks within the phases. The planning phase would consist of

Entrepreneurial Lesson 41
Attention to Detail

Is it God or the Devil in the details? Or both? Is a great writer really great if their are lotz of errs and typose? One listens to a piano sonata by Beethoven and wonders: how can someone write something like that and in the same breath asks how on earth could someone play that. From memory, no less. Every note, every change in tempo, every movement is on paper.

A Stephen Wright joke: "Last night somebody broke into my apartment and replaced everything with exact duplicates..." The details of laws argued by attorneys and interpretations of them made by actors determine the fates of lives on and off screen.

Divine or demonic, the details in the parts make the whole of a work of art or an Entrepreneur's invention that much greater.

general research, an analysis of a BRC-60 housed at the Smithsonian institution to develop requirements, parts acquisition and obtaining a pattern maker, and machine parts.

At this juncture, just after the close of the initiation phase, given the uniqueness of the project and the apparent challenges, a prudent project manager would conduct a risk analysis to provide input to a possible go – no go decision. Given the trials Kim and Duncan would later encounter it was probably best this was not done (they may have decided not to do it!), but an analysis of the risks brings into perspective the enormity of the project.

From discussion with Kim and Duncan it became apparent the top risk to the project was parts acquisition, an extremely arduous task as the last American Bantam Cars were manufactured in the late 1930s (with only a few thousand ever built) and only a scant 2,675 Bantam Jeeps were built during 1940 and 1941, the majority of which were sent to the USSR and Great Britain as part of the Lend-Lease program, and lost during the war.[379]

The next major risk was funding. As Duncan recalled, "Money was an issue. If it got to the point where you had no money there was still things to do, but you didn't have to … I didn't have to break myself to do it because it wasn't all done in six weeks. If you tried to do it in six weeks, well I can't find 100 grand in six weeks, but if I have four years it's not that much. You break it down per month, but you still have to have income coming into your door."[380]

Another challenge the Texas couple faced was the possibility of failure: "the risk was I might not be able to get it done. If I couldn't get a basket case (a trashed BRC-40, discussed more in project execution), I couldn't have built it, simple as that. Because there was no way to get the most important parts I needed like the bell housing, the flywheel and the timing cover. You just couldn't get that stuff. It's not available."[381]

Lastly Kim and Duncan understood the risk that someone else might build a pilot and they would be the first loser. As Kim related, "I have to admit, not one second did he doubt that someone could, but I did. I was, 'Let's go, we have to hurry up. We have to hurry up. It has to be finished. It has to be finished.' … I was so afraid, I was probably more afraid than him."[382]

Entrepreneurial Lesson 42
Commitment to Excellence

The motto of NFL team, the Oakland Raiders, declares "Commitment to Excellence." Anyone not committed to excellence in any enterprise will fail to pay attention to detail, be a poor partner, and remain ill-prepared to use the lessons that should have been learned during a lifetime of just punching a clock.

Excellence is obtained by trial and error. Watch the world champion figure skater. The performance appears effortless, as if any human being can just naturally do it. Excellence requires absolute indefatigable focus on detail and is mandatory for success.

How many millennia did it take to figure out the number of days there are in a year, and why every four years there is an extra one? The Entrepreneur does not count what it takes, only doing what counts.

Success only looks easy.

As the project progressed Duncan believed this risk was minimal. Kim remembers, "He was always confident, 'I'll be the first one to come out with this thing. Nobody else is going to do it' He said, first of all, as he said, the cowl. Where can you find one? He says, when this guy had another one to sell, Duncan went and quickly bought it. He said, it's hanging in the garage, it's there, at least it's there … because he knew it is the most important part. If you don't have it, you cannot even start the car." Duncan added, "after two years I said, 'No I don't think I've got a risk,' because here I am super passionate and I had nothing. Thirty-nine, 40 roadster cowls aren't exactly on every street corner. If a guy's got one who's restoring it, then, 'You're not going to get it.' That was a big problem straightaway, to get the cowl."[383]

The key phase in the planning effort was defining the requirements for the vehicle. The requirements documentation for the project would take on a unique form consisting of photographs and measurements from both a BRC-60 (the second model built by Bantam incorporating changes the Army requested after testing the pilot) and a BRC-40, Bantam's final production model. Some of the photographs and all the measurements diagrams were placed in book form and affectionately named the "Bible" by Kim and Duncan.

Requirements gathering would prove problematic as Karl Probst's original bid drawings were lost and photographs constitute the only archival evidence of Bantam #1. (Army Motors, page 21) Displaying initiative and determination similar to the project team of 1940, and that would characterize their efforts, Duncan undertook to develop his own set of requirements using his understanding of the Bantam Jeep line and his own expertise honed from decades of Jeep restoration projects.

Duncan took it upon himself to learn as much as possible about American Bantam history as well as the original prototype and credits William Spear's website (one of the foremost experts in the world on American Bantam Jeeps, www.williamspear.com) with providing invaluable information which formed the foundation of the Bible.[384] As Kim recalled, "We started to look on the computer on

Bantam and you couldn't find too much stuff. All of a sudden when we found out about Bill and this whole thing he had at his website, it was absolutely incredible and I looked at it and said, "Look at this! We are going to be able to do this. We have to contact this guy." After contacting Mr. Spear, and at his suggestion, subscribing to the Austin Bantam Society club publication "Rooster Tails" they came upon the first big break on the project: an advertisement in that periodical for Bantam parts.[385]

Kim and Duncan followed up on the information in the Rooster Tails' advertisement which led to the completion of the requirements and the first major step in the project execution the acquisition of the first batch of parts. Kim explained, "This is how it happened. When we saw the ad in the Rooster Tails, Duncan called the guy and said I want to buy some of your stuff. Then Duncan explained what he wanted to do. At the time actually, Bob Brandon (a Bantam Jeep enthusiast who lives in Butler, PA) was pretty impressed with the idea. He said, 'You know that the … this BRC-60 is in a museum not too far from my house' 'Oh really? We have to go and see it.' He says, 'Well you know what, I can probably arrange a visit there for you. When we went to pick up the parts, the cowl, diffs, gear box, transfer case and everything else, the whole thing was set up for us to spend a day at the Smithsonian and take all the pictures at the museum."[386]

Figure 71: Duncan Rolls Measures 'Gramps' at the Smithsonian. Photo Courtesy of Kim and Duncan Rolls

That "BRC-60" Bob Brandon referred to represents the oldest remaining Jeep in the world, the seventh ever built, Bantam #7 or known in the Jeep world as "gramps." This vehicle was built in November 1940 shortly after the prototype was approved by the Army. Duncan knew he had a goldmine because if he could measure and photograph "gramps" he alone would possess the closest actual dimensions and photographic record of a car in the direct lineage of the pilot. After visiting Bob, purchasing the parts and closely examining "gramps" (using a dress makers tape so as not to harm the aged machine) Duncan had his requirements. "I called it the bible because it had everything in it that I needed. That was my blueprint, all those pictures. Two hundred photographs I had taken of 'gramps,' the sixteen pages of drawings and about a dozen or so unseen black and white photographs of the Pilot build."[387]

The last item, "a dozen or so unseen black and white photographs of the build" constituted rare pictures of the original pilot's construction in 1940. Duncan recalled, "When I finished at the Smithsonian I had a pickup full of Bantam stuff and I said, 'This is going to be easy. Look, I found all this stuff in one trip.' (laughs) Not only did I get the Bantam cowl, not only did I get to go to the Smithsonian and measure everything, this guy (Bob Brandon) pulls out the original photographs taken in the factory and took me down to Kinko's®. We blew them all up, eight by ten and that's what went into my bible."[388]

Duncan also gained an invaluable insight during the requirements gathering as he com- pared the photos he had of the original prototype to the ones taken of the Smithsonian BRC-60; and that was while there were numerous differences in the body between the pilot and "gramps,“ the chassis was the same.[389]

Figure 72: First Bantam Parts Acquired in Butler. Photo Courtesy of Kim and Duncan Rolls

This was a critical observation as Duncan explained, "You have to have the chassis right. You have to have the wheelbase right. Once you've got that, then you know as you build the body, 'Hey, that is where it's got to go.' You've got this certain amount of distance around the wheel arch, the wheel has to sit here and the front fenders are here. You can start scaling everything."[390]

Working in parallel within requirements gathered from the Rooster Tails article, as related, Duncan acquired from Bob Brandon: the front and rear differentials; gearbox; transfer case; steering wheel; and one solid rim from a collector who had a BRC-40. Most astonishingly he located a 1939 Bantam Roadster cowl (the most critical part as related above) which was the part which the original project team used as the base for the entire prototype.[391]

The final efforts in the planning phase and the initial acquisition of parts was the selection of a pattern maker who would manufacture parts during this phase and project execution. After some effort Duncan found an individual to build the patterns and commissioned him to recreate the bell housings, steering boxes, engine timing covers, thermostat housings, clutch forks and hand brake parts.[392]

Execution Process

The majority of the project was contained in the execution phase. To meet their exacting standards, throughout every phase of the project's execution, most parts were made a minimum of three times to a maximum of thirteen which added time and uncertainty to the project as Duncan would never know until he started working with a part how many times it would be made. [393] As he remembers, "Thirteen was the most … Kim couldn't believe it when I'd throw them out in the scrap.

She'd say, 'Can't you use it?' I'd say, 'No, it's scrap,' because you can't do anything else with it and I don't want to look at it because it's a mistake."[394]

This was a difficult part of the project execution for the couple, as Kim expressed, "It's a shame. He should have kept all these pieces. He'd say, 'Thirteen times for this.'" Duncan added, "It's depressing to look at stuff you have worked on and it's not right."[395]

Figure 73: Duncan Making Parts. All Parts Were Hand Made. Photo Courtesy of Kim and Duncan Rolls

However, as with all projects, challenges set in, making a mockery of Duncan's original euphoria of finding a cache of Bantam parts that, "this is going to be easy." Two years slipped by and the project was stalled. Duncan remembers during that time, "I was just trying to collect parts. I'd been looking … I got NOS[396] stop, tail lights and black-out lights. Then I managed to get the gauges, which was the speedometer and the four-gauge cluster. I got some light switches and a couple of bits and pieces. That was it. I was going nowhere."[397] After his initial success and over an eighteen month period Duncan only acquired two NOS tail lights, ignition and light switches and most importantly the very rare instruments (odometer and four case cluster which includes oil, temperature, AMP and fuel gauge).[398]

In the end the Rolls' realized they needed a 'basket case' (a junked BRC-40, the last model manufactured of which approximately 2,600 were made) to copy for parts. As Kim recalled, "this is when you realized also that everything was expensive. Everything that we could get was expensive. You know it was just absolutely incredible. After two years you said, "Oh my God, the only way for me to progress is to buy one." The task would prove difficult as Duncan knew, "there were roughly at the time there was supposed to be sixty-nine BRC-40s left in the world. That makes it pretty difficult because now you've got to find one that is not restored; two, you've got to find a guy that is willing to sell it."[399]

That is when fate, which shined on the project at various times, stepped in, as Kim related, "Because it was such a genuine project that he had, it was almost like there were things made easier for him along the way for some reasons that came up. Honestly, we had a little angel again there, a guardian angel was there because we found this, we found that, when we were looking for it."[400]

At this juncture the Rolls' guardian angel stepped in, as Duncan explained, "As I said in the story last night, Howard Thompson in Florida had had that hurricane go through. It demolished all his out buildings and he lost his aircraft and his Jeeps. He was willing to sell it (a non-restored BRC-40). I eventually got a basket case (Thompson's) for $11,000 at the time—$11,000 would have bought me a fully restored Willys Jeep, fully restored." With the basket case secured it was now possible to truly recreate the pilot.[401]

Figure 74: Duncan Pounding Out a Hand Made Part. Photo Courtesy of Kim and Duncan Rolls

Due to the sheer enormity of the number of pieces in this jigsaw puzzle of a project Duncan decided to use a design-build methodology (similar to the original prototype project team!), ignoring the big picture and focusing on the tasks at hand on a daily basis. [402]Duncan was able to do this as he knew in his mind from his extensive expertise on Jeeps, automotive knowledge and from all the research and photographs what the completed prototype would look like. Similar to a jigsaw puzzle he had the photograph of the final product, but had to fit all the pieces to complete the puzzle.

A key component for building the recreation for the Rolls' was not only to have as many original parts as possible, but to recreate it as the 1940 project team would have built the original pilot. Duncan explained, "There was a guy saying he was going to build the Pilot. However, he was going to build it from a modern point of view. Obviously, he wasn't a guy that built stuff with his hands. He was going to scan the chassis and recreate stuff by CNC machines and things like that. Everyone said, 'Well, why don't you do that?' I said, 'Well, that's not the way they built the Pilot.' When I built that Jeep, I only used oxy acetylene and a stick welder. I didn't use migs or tigs or all of this fancy new stuff because they didn't have it ... I wanted to do it exactly how they did it; hammers, dollies, the equipment they had. A drill, grinders, that's it. Exactly how they did it, that's how I wanted to do it."[403]

Figure 75: Duncan Carefully Crafting a Hand Made Part. Photo Courtesy of Kim and Duncan Rolls

The other critical issue for Duncan was ensuring the rebuilt pilot was to scale, which doing so from photographs alone could prove problematic: "maybe you could build it from the pictures if you could scale it. Of course, the problem I had even when I had all my pictures is the guys were much shorter in those days. I'm six foot two. Every time I'd look at the picture, I'd have to sit down or kneel down because my perspective from my eyes was different from the picture that was taken. It doesn't sound like much, but if you stand up and look at it from a different perspective, you're not going to see the same curves … I had a heck of a time trying to get them. Of course, none of the photographs are ninety degrees. To do a scale, you need ninety degrees with a known factor."[404]

However, as with so many issues that arose during the project, Duncan found an answer "The known factor is I knew how big the wheels were, and the tires. I could scale everything off the wheels and the tires. You could say, 'That is a sixteen inch rim with a 550/16 tire.' Then you could scale everything else on that Jeep from that if you have a ninety degree shot, but none of them were ninety degrees."[405] However having the measurements from "gramps" was critical as they supplemented for the lack of ninety degree photos.

In the end the measurements, photographs and Duncan's skill solved the scaling problem. "See, it's a funny thing when you look at pictures in your mind. You've only got a picture and there are parts of the picture missing. But you have pictures of the other pieces and so your mind actually fills in the blanks for you and says, 'Well, this has to flow in to there. That has to move into here. How does that work?' Like I said, constantly, every day, looking at those pictures until I could see it was in my head. Eventually it was like it was in my head. That was the key."[406]

After two years of searching for parts the building phase of execution began with a second parts manufacture effort which included shock absorber mounts, clutch and brake pedal shaft, master cylinder brackets, various cross members, front and rear bumpers, pintle hook mount, springs and chassis rails which would form part of the chassis assembly. That proved a major effort as the prototype and the BRC-60 had the same chassis while the BRC-40 had a different chassis.[407]

Chassis / Rebuild Front-Rear Differentials / Springs

Using the color photos from the Smithsonian BRC-60 and the black and white pictures of the original prototype, as stated, Duncan had concluded the chassis were identical. "I eventually worked out that it was the same chassis. There was nothing really different between the two (pilot to BRC-60).[408]

The examination of the chassis also bore fruit for later phases of the project. "Once I got back from the Smithsonian I was still looking for parts. Every day, Kim can tell you, I would be studying my photographs. I'd lay out the two hundred photos of 'gramps,' I'd lay out all of the black-and-whites of the original pilot. Then I would study the differences. Now I had some good chassis shots in those pictures of the guys standing there (original project team) with the chassis. I'd look at it, where the position of the shock absorbers and the brake lines and all of the brackets and the clutch; everything that they had set up in there. Then I'd come in and I'd get my pictures of 'gramps', roughly

Figure 76: Chassis Finished. Photo Courtesy of Kim and Duncan Rolls

the same era or area that I had that was closest as I could get; because don't forget 'gramps' had the body on so it was very difficult to get those shots with the fenders in the way and stuff like that, stick the camera down there and take pictures."[409]

He knew he had to build the chassis first as that formed the foundation of the vehicle, "you have to have a chassis to build the body because you have to have it to sit the body on, you have to have your wheels there. You have to have wheels on the correct rims with the correct tires. I made sure they were 550 16's. That way I could make sure that when I moved the fenders, especially the front ones, backwards and forwards so, that the radius and everything else was like the pictures."[410]

The intrepid Rolls' improvised their first of many solutions to seemingly impossible problems as Kim remembered, "There's something about the chassis. We were lucky to find a guy who had one (a BRC-40), when Duncan asked if he could borrow the chassis, the guy probably said, 'Why would you want to borrow this? It is totally rusted out.' Duncan said, "I'll bring it back to you in three months. Could you give it to me for three months?' He knew he had three months to figure out the chassis. We brought it back to him exactly on the date of three months after."[411]

"I figured I haven't enough of it (parts for the Pilot), but I can start building the chassis. Because I had all the pictures of the chassis, I had the pictures of 'gramps' chassis, I said, 'Let's start with all the brackets that go on the chassis.' That's what I did. I started with the very little pieces, the brackets of the chassis. The borrowed, really rusty BRC-40 chassis, had the same techniques of build and that way I could get the measurements of that channel and the bumpers and all that stuff. There were differences, in the lengths. The 60s and the pilot had a seven inch longer chassis at the back than a 40, that was the only real difference, the gear box transfer case cross member and the pintle hook … It was invaluable in the way they constructed it, the actual dimensions, the gauge of the metal. Because you couldn't go to "gramps" and start cutting through it going, 'What gauge is that?' It showed me where they put rivets, what size rivets they were. That's how I built the chassis."[412]

In the end the Rolls' recreated prototype looked slightly different from the photographed original pilot, but for good reason, "Of course my Jeep was a little bit higher because all of the pictures were taken after they had six guys in it, beat the crap out of it, jumped off the landing docks and flattened the springs. I figured because I had the length of the springs, original springs, so mine sat a bit higher. But I'm sure if you put six guys in it and took it out and beat it up, it would sit a little bit lower because the springs would eventually settle."[413]

He built the two outside frame rails and the cross members and welded the latter to the former. Using hot rivets and welding, the bumpers and pintle hook frame were affixed to the structure as well as the spring hanger brackets, transmission and transfer case cross member and the engine mounts which completed the chassis.[414]

With the foundation in place Duncan had the springs built and put in place (an arduous task), the rear differential which included the challenging task of recreating the brakes unique to Bantam and these difficulties were the same for the front differential which was built next. The gearbox and transfer case were then remanufactured with the transfer case proving relatively simple to build, but the gear box proved challenging as many pieces of that part were different on the pilot from the Willys, but once again Duncan was up to the task of overcoming all challenges.[415]

Engine

The heart of the prototype, the engine, was next which was comprised of NOS long block, NOS inlet exhaust manifold and carburetor. The bell housing, timing cover, steering box and thermostat housing were cast and the bell housing provides an example of how Duncan had many of the parts constructed for the project: "the casting, I sent the original bell housing to a pattern maker, which is an old fashioned trade. He would copy the pattern in wood, and then he would have a cast made. He would check the castings against the original then he'd send them back to me. I would take them to a machinist, a friend of mine, to his machine shop, and give him the original. He would machine all the holes, all the threads, everything else into it, cut out all the holes to exact dimensions." He added, "that stuff I didn't do because I don't have the equipment to do it. Why would I want to learn when I've got somebody who has done it for fifty, sixty years that knows exactly?[416]

The flywheel was Computer Numerical Controlled (CNC) made. The inlet exhaust manifold, starter motor, updraft Zenith carburetor, fuel pump, fuel filter, water pump, distributor, voltage regulator, generator, coil, and clutch, were NOS. A reproduction cloth covered wiring harness, the inlet tube from the carburetor to the oil bath and air cleaner were handmade and an original oil bath air cleaner was purchased. The recreation of the oil pan provides an example of Duncan's attention to historical accuracy, "I made the oil pan just exactly how these guys (the original project team) would have done it. The stock one wasn't exactly like that, so they would have gone to the parts bin and said, 'Right, we need to make an oil pan. It's going to be off-road, so we better put a skid pan on it and we need more oil capacity because this model is going to work harder. They didn't go to a CNC machine. The guys just took an old pan, cut it up and then welded the pieces together. That's exactly how I did it.'"[417]

There was one other perspective Duncan built into the recreated prototype, "I tried not to make my work look too pretty because these guys were in a hurry, forty-nine days. Do you think they were grinding and cleaning and making it look really nice? No. Well, it doesn't look really pretty like nice tig weld,' but that's exactly how it would have been done. I would tell Kim, you cannot be too refined because in forty-nine days they had to produce this for the military. Can you imagine?"[418]

However, as he built the chassis he used a mock-up to ensure the engine compartment was correct. "I dummied up the engine. I knew where it was, I had the right area there to make sure that all the measurements would fit. Because don't forget I had the BRC-40 (the basket case) so I could measure where the engine mounts were, where the gearbox mounts were. It was all the same length engine gearbox and transfer combination. I didn't actually have all the stuff at that time, but dummied it up, figured out where it would go and then I just did the sheet metal."[419]

Duncan also ensured the placement of the engine met his exacting standards. "When I had the BRC-40 chassis and had the cast engine mounts. The engine mounts on the pilot, I hand fabricated out of 3/16th metal. There was a big discussion when they were actually doing the engine about the angle of the engine mounts. One of them wanted them horizontal, but the other guy wanted them on forty-five degrees. They wanted them at forty-five degrees, but in the Bantam BRC-40 they are all horizontal."[420]

"I have the pictures of them. I know what size the doughnut engine mount is. I had to make the front engine cradle and change the angles. Again, going back to the 40, looking at the differences, see how it was made ... making it like it but not exactly because it was different. I had the measurements of the engine mounts, and the gearbox mount, I had the measurement on the chassis where the gearbox mount was, which was completely different on the Pilot and the 60's versus the 40s. You knew where the cowl was and I knew how much distance at the back of the head to the firewall was. When I fitted it all in, it's exactly the same. You could just get your finger in the back. At the appropriate time Duncan would drop the engine in as one unit, "I assembled all the engine. I assembled the gearbox, the clutch, pressure plate, put it all together and put it in as one unit."[421]

With the engine built, the gearbox and transfer case were fitted to it and the exhaust built from photographs while the drive shafts were made and fitted. The fuel tank, fuel lines and brake lines were next all of which were made of stainless steel for longevity and rust prevention purposes. The steering box was built cast, worm gear machined and topped off with an original steering wheel all based upon an original BRC-40. The entire structure sits atop four solid rims supported by 5.50 Firestone ground grip tires. This work marked the completion of the inner workings of the vehicle.[422]

Body Work

The outer parts of the vehicle were completed in the body work phase. The cowl was built first using the part obtained from the 1939 Bantam Roadster which was split down the middle between the gauges and six inches added. Kim remembers this as a very stressful moment, "Do you remember when you extended the cowl … you cut it. I came to take a picture and I was like, 'I don't want to see this.' It's like watching a surgery, an open heart surgery. When I saw the 6 inches there, welded, I said, 'Ahh … Oh, it looks so great!'"[423]

Duncan added, "There are so many guys that are afraid to cut rust out. It's metal, it's cancerous, it has got to go. You can't do anything with it. Apply body filler over it; it's a waste of time. You've lost the integrity; you have to replace it. I was lucky, there was only a little bit of rust in the bottom of the cowl. I repaired bottom sections, and I didn't have the exact measurements. I did it twice. There were a few mistakes along the way, but it's metal. Make a mistake with metal, cut it out and do it again. No one ever knows. You could do it one or a hundred times. That's what you got to do. Remember, anybody can restore a car; it takes a man to cut one up."[424]

The firewall was built and the overall height of the cowl was shortened to match the measurements taken from the BRC-60 at the Smithsonian and all rust damage was repaired. With the measurements from the firewall to the radiator in hand Duncan had the ability to approximate the distance to place the cowl on the chassis.[425]

Figure 77: Forming the Hood on the English Flywheel. Photo Courtesy of Kim and Duncan Rolls

He also built the radiator, copied the flywheel on a Computer Numerical Controller (CNC) and had the generator and starter motor recreated form photographs.[426] With these final parts obtained Kim and Duncan were ready to move into the project execution phase which constituted the majority of their effort to recreate the prototype.

Grille / Fenders

The grille came next and was built using a combination of the photos from the pilot, the BRC-40 radiator bolted to the chassis and measurements from the BRC-60 once again showing the multidimensional nature of the project incorporating pieces from all Bantam Jeep models and Bantam civilian models (the 1939 Roadster). The grille was not a simple proposition as Duncan explained, "The grille is difficult because it only looks small in the picture, but it actually comes right back to the cowl. That's how it's supported. Once I had the cowl positioned on the chassis and the grille, I knew the distance. The next major thing was the side panels, then the filling panels, the fenders and then the hood."[427]

Photos from the original prototype were the guide to building the left and right side panels which tied the cowl to the grille. The fender braces were put in place with much effort and then came the difficult task of filling in the pieces between the fender and side panels which was complicated by the compound curves unique to the pilot model; however, eventually the pieces came together and with the fenders bolted to the side panels the inner fenders were made.[428]

Entrepreneurial Lesson 43
Overcoming Challenges

Does there exist a more perfect example of overcoming challenges than that of the Bantam Jeep prototype creation team? Anything more entrepreneurial? Fraught with disaster, impossibly tight deadlines, and the notion that, literally, the history of the world hung in the balance?

See if these come close. Mount Everest. A mountainous pile of challenges to overcome. In the known history of climbing the queen of the sky, a double amputee—both legs removed at the knee—summited on carbonized titanium peg legs and feet. As hard to imagine as that is, what about the blind man who summited? How about twice?

The Entrepreneur does not see problems or difficulties, but rather the opportunity to meet challenges head on. If there is no way around, under, or over it, one has to plow through the obstacle. The words, "I don't know," are not in the Entrepreneur's vocabulary.

Windshield / Filling Panels / Side Panels / Fenders

The windshield frame was built next using a cardboard template of the Roadster cowl, measurements for the BRC-60 and the acquired Roadster windshield frame as Duncan exposited on, "I built the windshield frame using the original roadster piece because it still uses a roadster staunch. Of course I added about twelve inches of windshield. They cracked it in testing. That's why they changed the windshield on the 60 and put another piece on it. Then eventually they two-pieced the windshield so they wouldn't break as much glass."[429]

The filling panels would prove challenging as Duncan remembered, "the fill-in panel, absolutely the most frustrating and difficult, that panel between the fender and the cowl because the cowl is on an angle, the side panels are on an angle; the fenders are straight, but they are round. The right one, it took me thirteen tries on one, which was day after day making it. The other side, a mirror image, was a half a day."[430]

The front floor section, the rear floor, and support for the rear seat, which covers the ten gallon gas tank, were completed. The body work on the side panels would also prove difficult, but Duncan was up to the task.

"The only differences between the Pilot and the 60 are the front sheet metal and the double-cutout in the body. The height above the rear wheel in the body tub is bigger on the Pilot. That's why it looks really fat in the back. When you look at the 60s, it's a little smaller. Then when you get to the BRC-40, they've trimmed it down even more. Without having the pictures and looking at them, you would never know.[431]

"At the Smithsonian I took a big piece of cardboard and I traced around it, where the swage marks were and the actual size of the opening. I made cardboard templates of the curve on the back of the body, because the pilot and the 60s all had curved bodies like Willys, but all the BRC40s are at a 90 degree angle, straight back."[432]

Panels for the rear wheel tubs and the tops (which contain the little toolboxes), the backrest for the rear seat (that slides up and down) were built. The rear side panels came next which were made in two pieces (due to their length of about nine feet) and welded together.[433]

Entrepreneurial Lesson 44
Mistakes Are Made

Are people mistaken about mistakes? In trial and error developments, there might be misjudgements in timing, but maybe not mistakes.

XYZ makes a straddle wager on a stock option, hedging against losses on either side of the price. Whether it rises or falls, XYZ is covered. XYZ also has a real estate investment in building a community fifteen miles away. While hoping for the stock to turn in one sustained profitable direction, XYZ receives a call from the plumber saying a toilet has been installed incorrectly.

The markets close in an hour. XYZ figures it all can wait until tomorrow, so heads up to investigate the toilet. While away from the computer, a sudden change in the underlying company's public behaviour creates frantic speculation both for and against its common stock, which wildly swings both sides of the straddle. XYZ misses all of it and the next day settles for fifty-per cent losses from a large investment.

Hood / Miscellaneous Parts

The hood was the next in the long series of challenges and did not disappoint. Duncan had to have a large portion of the vehicle built before tackling this challenge as he expounded, "I had to look at the vehicle. It was no point trying to build the hood without all that other stuff there; I had to get it right in my head. I would use cardboard, I cut the cardboard to shape, masking taped it around the cowl and around the front of the grill. I built it all out of tape and cardboard. To get some perspective, I sprayed it all grey to look like the metal. When you stand back, it looked real. I've got some faked photos, that I had, which is cardboard on the side and I sprayed it all grey. That's how I got my perspective on it."[434]

The hood construction process continued: "Once I made it out of cardboard, I just cut it and laid it out flat on a piece of metal, cut the shape out with an extra couple of inches all the way around. I built an English wheel and rolled it until it would come to the shape. On the front section of the hood there I had to cut and relieve it because it's too much metal. If you have a 500-ton press you can bend anything you want. It's just bang, that's done in one second."[435] He concluded, "I won't say exactly how, but I rolled it, played with it and I made mistakes. It's fairly flat on the pilot. It's a fairly flat round hood. When you go to the 60s, they're more pronounced. Definitely a lot more round shaped in the nose. They lifted it up. You can see the difference in the shape. The pilot is very flat and the 60 is definitely … has more rise on the front."[436]

During the construction of the hood Duncan took note of an historical anomaly as he recollected, "the story that I heard is some guy working there (original pilot team) all he did was make those (hoods) out of one piece of metal with oxyacetylene. I honestly don't believe that myself, I think it was probably taken off something, then modified, but he could have. You see that to add strength, they rolled a bead all around the perimeter at the edge. I always wondered when I looked at it, why a bead didn't align up with the cowl. Because the cowl wasn't designed for the Pilot. It was a roadster cowl and it had different swage marks on it. That's why they always looked odd to me, but the swage marks built into the hood is for the strength."[437] With the hood built Duncan built the rear hood brace which reinforces the hood hinges. He then completed the four top bow brackets the foot braces for the rear floor, driver and passenger front seat, glove box, steering column drop bracket and diamond plate transmission cover.[438]

Corrugated Floor / Body Work

It was now time for the last piece of body work, the corrugated floor, which of course, once again, was different from the BRC-40 corrugated floor. Duncan had the measurements from the Smithsonian BRC-60 and the number needed for the floor. As Duncan recalled, "I had the measure- ments between the rise in the corrugation and then I counted the amount of corrugations on the whole floor, because when I checked the pictures the corrugation had to line up in a certain area. I counted every single corrugation of the floor. The distance and then I tried to find the metal."[439] After two years of searching he actually found the proper corrugated steel in his hometown![440]

He fitted the corrugated floor to the main floor structure and then bolted the tub on the chassis for the first time.[441] For Duncan the body work was one of the easier phases of the project, "The bodywork wasn't really that hard to do because it's a lot of flat panels. It was just getting everything in perspective. Like I said, you didn't actually have to have the part to physically measure. I just kept looking at it from different perspective until I thought that it matched the pictures exactly."[442]

With the recreated prototype nearing completion Duncan began work on the final fitting processes which included the fitting of the fender side panels, grille and hood. Nothing lined up on the first try (surprise!), but after a week of finessing the pieces fit well. With the black and white original pilot photos in hand Duncan took the vehicle to an upholsterer to have the proper covers made for the top and seats.[443]

Painting

In keeping with the project objective of building a recreation versus a replica was paint. Duncan explained in detail, "The other problem was paint. The paint on the Bantam is nothing like World War II, standard Willys. It's completely different color. There was a huge debate on what color it should be. There was a guy that has a paint company called TM Ordnance, and he had original samples. The color on the Bantam is different.' He sent me all the samples. I said, 'You've got to put them on metal so I can see. It's no good sending me on a piece of plastic, it's not going to look the same."[444]

Duncan continued, "We had little bits and pieces that had original paint. You take something off that hadn't been off. The problem, of course, with military paint is that it changes every day. If you could put it in the weather it changes, you run your hands over it the oils out of your finger change the color. It's no good saying, 'That's the color,' on a seventy-year-old vehicle because it's not. We went through lots of different samples and in the end I settled on number 8. He had that paint. I painted every one of my restorations in that color and everybody loves that color."[445]

Figure 78: Duncan Sitting in His and Kim's Creation for the First Time: Photo Courtesy of Kim and Duncan Rolls

Kim recounted another issue with the paint, "In the earlier Bantam, the paint base was lead, and we don't have lead anymore. It did make a difference in trying to find the exact composition for the color. Duncan elaborated, "The EPA (United States Environmental Protection Agency) has changed the paints. I remember back in the day when I'd drive my old Willys. I'd take them out in the bush and they'd be dirty ... you can't clean flat paint. What I'd do is take a rag, pour gasoline on it, wipe my Jeep and it looked brand new. If I went up to the Pilot and wiped it with a gasoline rag, it'd take the paint right off. Every one of these Jeeps I restore I make sure everything works perfect before you put it together because the paint just won't hold up to gasoline."[446]

Engine Placement / Vehicle Testing

After four years the vehicle was essentially completed and the time came to bring it out in public for the first time at the Austin Bantam Society annual meet in 2008. Duncan did not test the engine when the chassis only was built (before putting all the body work on the vehicle). This led to unexpected issues and what Duncan considered one of his most serious errors of the entire project, "A big mistake that I made. The problem was the club was busting to see it. I was still waiting on the wiring harness being made in Australia. I couldn't start it, but you could push it and it looked the part, everything was there. I go, 'Well, I promised I'd bring it.' I assembled the whole Jeep, and then of course when I did put the wiring harness in, I had problems with the engine, leaking oil and this and that and the other; I had to dismantle it again and again."[447]

The engine problems would persist, "the original clutch plate came to pieces after a few miles and jammed and I had to pull it all back out. Got everything done for that show at Carmel, (2009) put it on the trailer and blew second gear. I only did 130 miles in that Jeep. I had to pull the gearbox and transfer case out and rebuild it again. It's not like the Willys, it's much harder to take the transfer case off because it's connected internally to the gearbox. Whereas the Willys, it's just unscrew bolts on the outside and pull it off. With the Bantam, you've got to pull half of the transfer case apart to get the gearbox and transfer apart, a real pain. Anyway, I rebuilt it and it is fine now. Yeah, that was the biggest mistake I made, was not testing it (the engine) in the actual chassis."[448]

However, Duncan's skill and ability would shine through during testing once the engine issues were worked out. On the initial test Duncan recalled, "Once it fired up, I thought it was going to go and it did, and I drove it." He continued, "everything worked … everything worked because it was a brand new car, just had the usual teething problems that aren't foreseeable like oil leaks … I hate oil leaks. Everyone knows Jeeps just puke oil out at every orifice, always have, always will; because the seals were so bad … The other thing about the early stuff too is the casting is very porous, the oil migrates through the actual case to the outside. I always wondered why it always looked so wet. Well the oil is actually coming from the inside out through the pores."[449]

Figure 79: Kim Taking Her First "Test Drive" of the Pilot. Photo Courtesy of Kim and Duncan Rolls

Duncan worked out the kinks and eventually the recreated prototype ran as smoothly as the original prototype delivered on September 23, 1940. Ironically, Kim and Duncan pinned the completion of the project as September 23, 2008 with a project start date of September 23, 2004. The Rolls' remained true to history honoring the September 23rd date in their work.[450]

Monitor and Controlling Process

The monitor and controlling process would involve budgeting, documentation (photos), quality control, morale and intangibles such as tenacity and sacrifice.

Kim and Duncan began with a rough budget estimate of $25,000 out-of-pocket expenses (over twice what it would cost to purchase a fully restored Willys) to complete the recreated prototype and this proved decidedly unrealistic. "I had a budget and then we broke it three times. I thought twenty-five grand, which was like a super expensive Willys. That twenty-five grand came and went before I even had the chassis built ... then the thirty-five came and it still ... forty came, at forty grand it started to look like a Jeep, I'm thinking to myself, "Forty grand, you're crazy.[451]

The budget challenges, however, cemented Kim and Duncan's commitment to the project. Kim recalled, "we don't think of the money anymore. There was no point anymore to thinking, 'Oh my God, how much money we have to spend' because it was too crazy then. You just have to keep going with your project. As we said, 'there was no more vacation, no more birthday presents, no more Christmas presents, no more nothing' because everything was invested in every piece we could find. It was a lot of money. In the end it was so much invested, we couldn't stop anymore" and Duncan concluded, "this thing was a half-million dollar project to me."[452]

Sacrificing every possible "extravagance" still did not cover the funds needed to complete the project. Duncan explained, "I had to sell all my toys in order to continue the project. I sold a half-track, I sold the V8 Jeep, I sold the Jeepster. I sold four of my projects that were finished, just to keep getting the money ... these are things that take you years to accumulate and I said, 'I've got to sell it.' You just keep selling and you've got some more money and away you keep going." In the end finances did not delay the project, "it wasn't the money factor that slowed me down because I would just sell something just at the right time I needed a major piece. It would just work out that way because there was so much work to do. It's like, "Well, you can do a lot of work with a couple of hundred dollars' worth of metal."[453]

Entrepreneurial Lesson 45
Cash Flow

How much money is there on hand right now? Without cash you are out of business. Enormous organizations transact billions upon billions of dollars. Yet it is possible for one to incur losses even when there are billions in revenues.

It comes down to the future value of money and the timing of incoming real cash. Cash flow rules the world. Governments cover cash flow gaps by borrowing and printing money. Gone now are the days when you never spend more than you have. Deficit spending became the norm everywhere. How does one get paid if everyone else is waiting to be paid, too?

Many rich people are cash poor. Cash seems always to be tied up, usually for tax reasons, but also for preservation. Even in times of living behind the credit eight ball, the fundamental rule is always the same. You have to take in more than you spend. Cash is not only king, it is everything.

The Rolls were all-in. "All your disposable income, like your holidays and everything else that you would normally do, the movies or eating out, whatever, that just all went in the Jeep, every single penny plus more. When we discuss now, there'll be no birthdays, no Christmas, what I meant was not buying any presents, we're not spending any money, we're not buying clothes or stuff that we don't need; just what you need to run the house and pay your bills. Every other piece of income was designated for the Jeep. That's why Kim and I discussed that, because I said, 'It could be tough.'"[454]

Kim summed up their attitude toward the cost of the project, "Remember you were still working as a stonemason at the time, so you were still making money. It was not like a, "Oh gosh, we have to find $1,000." It was part of everyday life. This became our baby. It's like when you have a baby, you don't think about the cost of money, right? You continue to spend money for that baby. To me this was the thing, so we keep going and going for the project until it was finished." This fiscal dedication was coupled with Duncan's tenacious attitude, "To me, if you start something … (I never abandon projects.) To me, that would be just a waste of time. Why would you start something and spend all that money and then what are you going to do with it? No, there was no quitting. I don't quit. I was going to do it one way or another, that's it. It was going to be done." Sacrifice, commitment and tenacity proved a winning combination in the recreation of the Bantam pilot vehicle. Duncan sanguinely summed the experience, "I could have had a mid-life crisis, had a new Corvette and a pickup sitting out there for what I paid for that, you know to drive around forty horsepower!"[455]

While Kim and Duncan kept track of out-of-pocket expenses they did not factor in the most significant cost for the project which was labor. A total project budget estimate would include the following:

A critical skill that would prove indispensable during the monitor and controlling phase was Duncan's ability to solve problems. Duncan's problem solving skills were put to such an extreme test that he not only had to find or make all the parts for the recreation, when he had to build a part and couldn't find the tool to make it he would build the tool himself! His method was unusual as Kim recalled, "when Duncan had a big problem he could not solve and he's really thinking about it and worried, 'What am I going to do …' Ninety-nine percent of the time, the answer comes in his sleep. It's so strange. He would wake up in the morning, 'I found the solution. I know exactly what to do.' It's so funny. It comes always when he needs it." [456]

Table 10: Bantam Reconnaissance Car Pilot Recreation—Project Budget

Project Budget 2004-2008

Item	Hours	Cost	Total Cost
Duncan Rolls (SME)	3,500	$75.00 / hour	$262,500.00
Kim Rolls (Support)	1,000	$35.00 / hour	$35,000.00
Out of Pocket Expenses			$80,000.00
Miscellaneous Expenses			$25,000.00
Total Budget			$402,500.00

Duncan added, "That's the mind, you see. When you're so preoccupied with one thing, I found it hard to sleep in the end because it's like the problem solving and you go to bed, you fall asleep and I'd be working on this damn Jeep in my sleep. Sometimes I'd just wake up and go, 'Oh, this is simple. That's it." Kim concluded, "It is so funny. It is so strange to me because he's been working out this problem for two to three days. Then, in a minute, without warning, 'That's it, I found it. He said, 'I've been working on the Jeep again.'"[457]

As previously mentioned during the execution phase, Duncan handled quality control with the Harley-Davidson guy acting as Duncan's quality "conscience," Kim kept her finger on the pulse of team morale (Duncan) and Kim acted as the official documenter for the project and assisted with quality control. They explained the team dynamic to ensure an exceptional finished product as follows, "He (Duncan) would always ask me (Kim) when he finished something. He'd say, 'Come and see this Kim," because he knew that he could see, but I could see it differently. He said, 'Look at this from your angle." Plus he wanted to know what I was seeing compared to what he saw. He would always ask me to come over and review or discuss. I would be very honest and I still am very honest, 'Darling, I think I can't see that much difference,' very brutal. I'll tell you exactly."[458]

Duncan added, "the problem is when you've made something, you think it's right. You spend that time, you don't want it to be wrong. If someone comes, 'I don't think it's quite right.' I mean, if I was angry about that, I got to do it again. I'd come out the next time and look at it and go, 'Maybe you're right," and just rip it off and do it again. It's very hard to do that after you've made something, 'It's good. It looks all right. It's getting there,' and then it's like, 'Oh no, it's not right. It's got to go."[459]

Duncan added, "the problem is when you've made something, you think it's right. You spend that time, you don't want it to be wrong. If someone comes, 'I don't think it's quite right.' I mean, if I was angry about that, I got to do it again. I'd come out the next time and look at it and go, 'Maybe you're right," and just rip it off and do it again. It's very hard to do that after you've made something, 'It's good. It looks all right. It's getting there,' and then it's like, 'Oh no, it's not right. It's got to go."[460]

Entrepreneurial Lesson 46
Sacrifice

While the enterprise is starting up and growing, Entrepreneurs make sacrifices, in particular with their home lives. There are not enough hours in the days, nights, weekends or holidays. The spouse, the children, the home maintenance all may languish in service to the vision.

All this just might not be true sacrifice in the religious sense, but rather an obsessive time-management issue. Look at RS, a Hollywood movie producer from South Africa. Back in her native country to supervise a Clint Eastwood movie, RS expected to be able to squeeze in maybe one or two rushed Sunday night family dinners while in production. Mr. Eastwood has evolved his enterprise to the degree that RS was home for early dinner every night she was in South Africa.

Eyes glazed over from too many all-nighters, the Entrepreneur might actually accomplish more by resting regularly. Ultimately, does it really make sense to sacrifice one's own health or *life* in pursuit of the vision?

Over the course of the four year project each member of the team knew their role and worked diligently to excel at their role while not infringing on another team member's responsibilities thereby ensuring the monitor and controlling phase was executed well.

Closing Process

After four years of highs, lows, sacrifice, pain, suffering, joy, heartache and everything in between the Rolls officially completed the project on September 23, 2008, exactly four years after they started and as previously mentioned the sixty-eighth anniversary of the delivery of the original pilot to the United States Army.

In terms of the final product meeting specifications Duncan estimates that the recreated prototype contains 70% original parts, and 30% manufactured and hand built parts. The key to having the recreation as exact as possible was the research. Having the photos of the original pilot combined with measurements from the Smithsonian BRC-60 proved invaluable.[461]

Figure 80: Finished Recreated Pilot Model with Canvass Top. Photo Courtesy of Kim and Duncan Rolls

The recreated pilot was only shown three times at shows after its completion and its subsequent purchase by a private collector, and these were the 40th and 41st Annual Austin Bantam Society (ABS) Trophy meets in 2008 and 2009 respectively, and lastly at the 2010 Military Vehicles Preservation Association (MVPA) Convention. At all three the Rolls' work won the highest award possible at the show including a gold award at the ABS events and the coveted Judge's Choice Award at the MVPA gathering providing official recognition of Kim and Duncan's extraordinary achievement.[462]

While the Rolls' learned many lessons along the way vis-à-vis how to recreate, restore, or replicate Bantam Jeeps it was the larger lessons that will stay with them. The first was the essentiality of the different personalities that led to successfully completing the project. Duncan explained, "I could have done it all by myself, but it would have taken way longer and it wouldn't have been this enjoyable because you'd have invested too much. At certain points, when I was really concentrating on doing stuff, Kim would say, 'somebody's on the phone,' and I'd say, 'I don't want to talk.' Often people call, but I'm busy. I'm really concentrating on what I'm doing; I'd rather not just break off to have a silly conversation.'" Kim added, "Really in this project, there are things that Duncan could not probably be as abrupt as I could because he is personally warmer. He called me his French pit bull because I would go to people and say, 'No, it's not going to be like this.' He couldn't do it so I was the one who was making a fence right there."[463]

Figure 81: Kim and Duncan Displaying Their Creation for the First Time in Boulder City, Nevada in 2008 Ironically Only Miles Away from the Home of Paul Bruno who would not find out about their work until 2009. Photo Courtesy of Kim and Duncan Rolls.

The second was why did they do it in the first place? In the end they both came to believe it was Duncan's calling to build the BRC pilot recreation as Kim mused, "I strongly felt this is why all along the way, there was this little help to coming along because he (Duncan) was the one who was supposed to do it. It was his destiny." Duncan added, "It was a labor of love for me really. I was passionate about it and it was something that I really wanted to do. It was not about bragging rights or being, 'Hey, look at this guy, he built the first Jeep.' It was about setting history straight. Now that vehicle will be around and then when my client that owns it now dies and it goes somewhere else, maybe it goes to a museum and in a hundred years' time some kids look at it and say, 'That guy must have worked hard to recreate that.'"[464]

Entrepreneurial Lesson 47
Make Life About More Than You

Jesus commanded: "Love the Lord your God..." and "Love your neighbor as yourself..."

The living Dalai Lama says: "The root of happiness is altruism—the wish to be of service to others."

Is there a clearer way to express the content of this lesson?

The third lesson they learned was how much the pilot really means to Jeep history and Jeep enthusiasts who have had experiences with the vehicle going all the way back to the original Bantams. As Duncan related, "It was at the next place we took it (the recreated pilot) to. I was there with the ABS and I had the little Bantam sitting there in the park and all of the public was coming in and having a look. This old man came up to me, he was old."[465]

"He was 91 years old and he said to me, 'That's a Bantam.' I said, 'How do you know that it's a Bantam?' He said, 'I drove one of those.' I said, 'Oh no, you didn't drive one of these.' He said, 'Yeah, I did.' I said, 'How do you know?" He said, 'Because I used to have a Bantam roadster.' He said, 'When I got in that Jeep it had the same gauges.'"[466]

"I took him around and I showed him the gauges. He said, 'Yeah, that's exactly it.' He told me what Army base he was on and when he used to drive it. I said, 'Would you like to go for a ride?' He said, 'Yes.' I helped him in. Kim was in the back. We got a guy in the club to video it, because he's probably dead now. I said, 'What does that remind you of?' He said, 'The sound and the smell.' That's the exact words he said. 'I remember the sound of the engine and the smell,' because they smell like canvass and olive drab and oil and everything else. I just took him for a ride around the block, around the park. His face just lit up. It was unbelievable. He said it had been seventy years since he had sat in one."[467]

For Kim and Duncan that was why they endured all the project had to offer. As Duncan explained, "that's the kind of stuff when you build it, that's why you build it. That image of him being in the car and taking it out there to actually drive a Bantam in America on the bases and it was a BRC-60; it was unbelievable. I said, 'Are you sure it wasn't a Willys?' He said, 'No, It had a round hood on it.' I said, 'That's a BRC-60.' The GP had the big square 39 Ford gauge, the Willys had the five instruments in it. Unmistakable to him. We have that on video."[468]

The last lesson for Kim and Duncan transcended the project to their life together. Duncan reminisced on the strain this type of project can place on a relationship, "You could end up having a divorce. How many women disagree with what their husbands do and just nag at him all the time until either you go or the car goes? Most of the time the guy capitulates and his car goes and he's miserable. I had one of them … I had one like that and I said, 'I'll never do that again,' because what gives you the right to tell me what to do with my life. You have to have a partner, in the true sense of the word, a partner, has the same goals and the same ideas."[469]

For the Rolls' that partnership had to have one foundation as Kim eloquently expressed, "We found out how much we love each other."[470] Thanks to the Rolls' love the original Bantam Reconnaissance Car, Bantam #1, exists again and just like the original pilot the Rolls' work represents a truly unique and remarkable accomplishment!

Figure 82: Author Paul Bruno and Duncan with Duncan and Kim's recreation of The First Jeep. Photo Taken at the 2010 Military Vehicles Preservation Association (MVPA) Convention.

Below: Gramps 1940 and Rolls 2009. Left: Bantam Serial Number 7, the seventh Jeep ever made, finished on December 7, 1940, now at Smithsonian. Right: Duncan & Kim Rolls' results from the measurements taken of Gramps.

Questions for Educators

What were the key attributes of Kim and Duncan that helped them achieve success?

Discuss the value of individual initiative in projects.

What lessons are there from examining the partnership of Kim and Duncan?

How important is it, and to what level, should project team members "sacrifice" to achieve project success?

Why is it important to make life, "more than about you?"

Chapter 11: Epilogue

The project that resulted in the creation of the Jeep demonstrates that when a dire need intersects with unusual circumstances (the beginning of World War II) the extraordinary can occur. The endeavor represents the right people, in the right place at the right time overcoming every obstacle to create a project deliverable so outstanding it was credited as one of the top three reasons the Allies won World War II. That legacy in and of itself would, for most products, rank as more than enough; however, the fact that descendants of Bantam's work still roam the highways and byways of the world, almost seventy-five years after the BRC's creation, provides further testament to the once-in-a-lifetime achievement these individuals brought to life.

When pondering the procurement of the first Jeep key items stand out that revolve around the weight requirement. This situation provides a lesson on the criticality of having subject matter experts determine technical issues. The weight was arbitrarily decided by members of the Ordnance Technical Subcommittee using the reasoning that since this truck would replace the motorcycle with sidecar it should weigh the same as that vehicle, or approximately 1,200 pounds.

The Committee, however, should have canvassed automotive experts on what they were contemplating versus the characteristics envisioned and identification of the weight as too low would most likely have occurred in time for adjusting the specification. The inclusion of the appropriate expertise during requirement gathering remains a critical success factor for projects.

The final item to consider relates to the controversy on exactly how and when the name Jeep was applied to the vehicle first known as the truck 4 X 4 light, then by numerous other monikers during 1940 including light reconnaissance and command car and then finally the Bantam Reconnaissance Car upon delivery of the pilot model. The testimony of Sergeant Ross from the FTC trial held during the war may answer that question:

> Now, when Hausman and Kenauer brought the Willys quarter-ton job down, what did you start calling it first? We called it a Willys, we called it a bantam, bantam Willys, a Willys 4 by 4 up until the time, it was about a week after they came there (November 1940) they had trouble with the front springs and we took out the front springs of the Willys. The front springs were too light and too long and they took them out and put in new ones, sent to Toledo and got them. I remember they came in on a plane and I was supposed to go out with the truck, with the Willys, 4 o'clock that afternoon, 4 to midnight on a road test from York, Pennsylvania, to

> Gettysburg, and from Gettysburg back to Baltimore, two road trips in eight hours. Well, the truck was not ready and it was time for me to leave.
>
> Am I allowed to swear in this court room? Say what took place. I asked them when they were going to have the God damn jeep ready and that is when they started calling the darn thing a jeep. To the best of your recollection, is that the first time you ever used the word "jeep" to apply to the quarter-ton cars. Yes. To the best of your recollection, is that the first time you ever heard anyone use the term "jeep" to apply to the quarter-ton cars? I never heard anyone use it. You never heard anyone use it before that? No. After that occasion to what extent was the name "jeep" applied to the Willys quarter-ton trucks? Well, they just called it a jeep, that is all. Who did you hear call it a jeep? All the test drivers? Sure. The garage personnel? Yes ... Now, in Holabird, as I understand your direct examination, you were the man that named the jeep, as far as your knowledge goes? Yes to the best of my knowledge and belief. And you applied that term to the Willys-Overland? That is right, I said it on the spur of the moment. Where did you get the name? Out of the funny papers. Did you ever see that "Popeye" column? Did you ever see that comic? That is where you got it? Yes. Why did you apply it only to the Willys-Overland model? It never came to mind before that. I was in a hurry to go out.[471]

Sergeant Ross' testimony confirms that the Jeep, as many have suspected over the years, came from Eugene the Jeep, a character in the *Popeye* comic strip who was a mysterious animal with magical abilities that first appeared on March 16, 1936 in the *Thimble Theatre* strip now known as *Popeye*.[472] Therefore, the best evidence we have suggests one of the most iconic vehicles in military and automotive history was named by a long-forgotten sergeant, on a base that no longer exists, in a heated moment, with no thought!

One of the most impressive characteristics of the first Jeep project was the tremendous number of individuals who contributed to the effort. It seems appropriate to conclude this history of that endeavor by naming them:

Colonel Atwood
William Beasley
Robert Brown
Harold Crist
Mr. Dowd
George Engler
Roy Evans
Frank Fenn

Chester Hempfling
Major Herbert Lawes
Major Robert Howie
Colonel W. C. Lee
General George Lynch
Captain Eugene Mosley
Colonel Ingomar M. Oseth
Charles Payne
Karl Probst
Sergeant Lawrence Ross
Major Tompkins
Ralph Turner
Edwin S. Van Deusen

Heroes all.

Figure 83: History Marker Dedicated in Butler in 1993 near the Location of the American Bantam Car Company Factory, Butler, Pa. Photo Courtesy of Robert Brandon, Butler, PA

Appendix

Bantam Reconnaissance Car Project—Time Line

1918 – January 1940:	Project Genesis, research into a light vehicle
February 1940 – Mid-May 1940:	Discussions on light vehicle general characteristics
Mid-May 1940 – June 6, 1940:	Coalescing and documentation of vehicle general characteristics
June 6, 1940 – June 20, 1940:	Initial work to develop a detailed vehicle specification
June 21, 1940 – July 2, 1940:	Development and documentation of detailed vehicle drawing and specification
July 3, 1940 – July 11, 1940:	Preparation and finalization of invitation for bids
July 12, 1940- July 21, 1940:	Bid preparation by manufacturers
July 22, 1940:	Bid opening and award
July 23, 1940-August 5, 1940:	Finalization of bid award and contract awarded
August 5, 1940-Sept. 21, 1940	Prototype built, assembled and christened "Bantam Reconnaissance Car" (BRC)
September 22, 1940:	BRC tested before delivery
September 23, 1940:	BRC delivered to Camp Holabird
September 24-25, 1940:	Initial BRC tests
Sept. 26, 1940-Oct. 23, 1940:	BRC tested at Camp Holabird

Oct. 23, 1940-Oct. 29, 1940:	Inspection, Test and Final reports on Bantam pilot model Completed
October 30, 1940:	BRC accepted and order for next sixty-nine placed Bantam Reconnaissance Car Project

Project Charter

Project Purpose, Background and Justification

Purpose

The development of a light weapons carrier / reconnaissance and command car, titled a truck ¼ Ton 4 X 4 light, suitable for use by all Using Arms, in particular the Infantry, Cavalry and Field Artillery, represents the project purpose.

Background

The United States Army has desired a light, mobile vehicle since the Great War to replace the mule and cart to move troops and light payloads including a weapons carrier for the Infantry, to enhance reconnaissance for the Cavalry and overall force mobility.

Numerous attempts to create or procure such a vehicle occurred since 1918 without success due to the direction to use up surplus World War equipment before procuring new items, budget shortfalls due to the Depression and a lack of prioritizing this vehicle for research and development.

The Infantry has conducted the most extensive work in this area having settled upon the Marmon-Herrington ½ ton 4 X 4 truck as suitable for their needs. However, issues during procurement of this vehicle through the Quartermaster Corps resulted in the obtainment of a vehicle that was unsatisfactory to that Using Arm.

Justification

German victories in Poland and the West have conclusively shown that high mobility, combined with maximum firepower, constitute key requirements of the battlefield. Therefore, the development of a light vehicle, at the quarter ton weight, has taken on greater urgency.

Objectives

The objectives of the project include:

Develop general characteristics for the ¼ ton truck 4 X 4 light,
Develop detailed specifications for the ¼ ton truck 4 X 4 light,
Bid and award contract to obtain a ¼ truck 4 X 4 light from qualified commercial manufacturer,
Develop a prototype ¼ ton truck 4 X 4 light for testing at Camp Holabird and,
Adjust prototype and approve a model for a ¼ ton truck 4 X 4 light for use by all Using Arms
Project Deliverables

The deliverables for the project include:

General characteristics for the ¼ ton truck 4 X 4 light developed,
Detailed specifications for the ¼ ton truck 4 X 4 light developed,
Bid and contract to obtain a ¼ truck 4 X 4 light from qualified commercial manufacturer developed, issued and awarded,
Prototype ¼ ton truck 4 X 4 light for testing at Camp Holabird developed and delivered and,
Prototype model for a ¼ ton truck 4 X 4 light for use by all Using Arms adjusted based on testing and final vehicle model approved

Project Sponsor

The United States Army Chief of Staff holds the title of project sponsor. This individual will provide the following services to the project:

Address high-level project issues as needed.

Project Contractor Sponsor – Assuming American Bantam Car Company Awarded Contract

Frank Fenn, President, American Bantam Car Company will act as the contractor sponsor.

His duties include:

Provide resources within the scope of the charter and contract, as well as within his authority, to keep the project on schedule.

Address project issues as they arise.

Project Team – Assuming American Bantam Car Company Awarded Contract

The Project Team will perform the work of the project. The roles and responsibilities of the Project Team comprise the following:

Role	Responsibility
United States Army, Customer Infantry Cavalry Ordnance Field Artillery Quartermaster	Provide a vision for the project Provide general vehicle characteristics Provide detailed vehicle specifications Coordinate procurement of vehicle Test the prototype Be available to answer questions, provide input, deal with issues, etc. Provide prompt payment as requested Attend meetings and other progress meetings
American Bantam Car Company – Executive Team Roy S. Evans, Chairman of the Board Frank Fenn, President Charles "Harry" Payne, Assistant to the President	Primary contact(s) for the customer Organize the project, hire subcontractors, etc. Be available to answer questions, provide input, deal with issues, etc. Attend meetings and other progress meetings as needed Coordinate all administrative work Coordinate relationship between Customer and Contractor
American Bantam Car Company – Core Project Team Harold Crist, Factory Manager Chester Hempfling, Subject Matter Expert Karl Probst, Engineering Head Ralph Turner, Subject Matter Expert	Design, develop and build the prototype Be available to answer questions, provide input, deal with issues, etc. Attend daily and other meetings, as needed

Risk Identification and Management

The Project Team will identify and analyse risks to the project.

Tradeoff Matrix

Managing a project requires the balancing of three constraints: resources, schedule and scope. These three constraints are interrelated in that a change in one will cause the others to change. The Project Tradeoff Matrix shows the relative importance of each constraint for this project.

The bolded area designation within the Project Tradeoff Matrix below indicates the level of flexibility for the particular constraint.

	Not Flexible	Somewhat Flexible	Most Flexible
Resources (Costs)	**Cannot be exceeded**	Willing to exceed original budget estimated by small amount, only if necessary	Willing to exceed original budget estimates if necessary
Schedule	**Cannot be exceeded**	Willing to exceed original schedule by small amount of time, only if necessary	Willing to exceed original schedule if necessary
Scope	**Cannot be expanded or reduced**	Willing to expand/reduce original requirements somewhat, without compromising quality, only if necessary	Willing to expand/reduce original requirements, without compromising quality, if necessary

For this project all factors are not flexible to meet the objectives and deliverables of the project; thereby making this a high risk project.

Critical Success Factors

The following outlines several critical success factors related to this project. Substantial impacts to the project budget and schedule can occur if these critical success factors are not achieved.

Project team with the perspective and diversity of skills necessary to successfully manage a large scale, high impact project.

Clearly defined roles and responsibilities of all key project team members.

A consistent and lasting project goal that remains the same throughout the life of the project.

The necessary resources.

Project Charter Modifications

All Project Team members and sponsors must approve modifications to this Project Charter.

Signatures

____

George C. Marshall
Chief of Staff
United States Army

____

Roy S. Evans
Chairman of the Board
American Bantam Car Company

Bantam Reconnaissance Car Project
Work Breakdown Structure (WBS)

Truck 4 X 4 Light Project
February 1940 - October 30, 1940

ID		% Comple	Task Name	Duration	Start	Finish	Predece	Resource Names
1	✓	**100%**	**Truck 4 X 4 Light Project**	**174 days**	**Thu 3/1/40**	**Tue 10/30/40**		
2								
3	✓	**100%**	**General Conception Phase (From Colonel Van Deusen) - Quartermaster**	**80 days**	**Thu 3/1/40**	**Wed 6/20/40**		
4								
5	✓	**100%**	**General Characteristics Phase**	**70 days**	**Thu 3/1/40**	**Wed 6/6/40**		
6	✓	100%	Conceive Vehicle General Characteristics	66 days	Thu 3/1/40	Thu 5/31/40		Oseth,Payne
7	✓	100%	Document Vehicle General Characteristics	2 days	Fri 6/1/40	Mon 6/4/40	6	Oseth
8	✓	100%	Obtain Signoff and Send to Using Arms (Ordnance / Cavalry)	2 days	Tue 6/5/40	Wed 6/6/40	7	Oseth
9	✓	100%		1 day	Thu 3/1/40	Thu 3/1/40		
10	✓	**100%**	**Using Arm Phase**	**0 days**	**Sun 6/17/40**	**Sun 6/17/40**	**5**	
11	✓	100%	Review General Characteristics at Assigned Using Arm (Ordnance)	1 day	Sun 6/17/40	Sun 6/17/40		Ordnance Technical Committee
12	✓	100%	Determine Next Steps in Vehicle Development	1 day	Sun 6/17/40	Sun 6/17/40		Ordnance Technical Committee
13								
14	✓	**100%**	**Butler Visit Phase**	**2 days**	**Tue 6/19/40**	**Wed 6/20/40**	**10**	
15	✓	100%	Travel To Butler	1 day	Tue 6/19/40	Tue 6/19/40		Ordnance Technical Committee
16	✓	100%	Bantam Roadster Demonstration	1 day	Tue 6/19/40	Tue 6/19/40		Bantam,Ordnance Techical Committee
17	✓	100%	Tour Plant	1 day	Tue 6/19/40	Tue 6/19/40		Bantam,Ordnance Techical Committee
18	✓	100%	Conduct Chassis Sandbag Test	1 day	Tue 6/19/40	Tue 6/19/40		Bantam,Ordnance Techical Committee
19	✓	100%	Discuss / Agree on Futher Detailed Vehicle General Characteristics	1 day	Tue 6/19/40	Tue 6/19/40		Bantam,Ordnance Techical Committee
20	✓	100%	Develop Conceptual Vehicle Sketch	1 day	Tue 6/19/40	Tue 6/19/40		Beasley,Brown
21	✓	100%	Discuss Front Axles Specifications	1 day	Wed 6/20/40	Wed 6/20/40		Fenn,Crist,Brown,Beasely,Hall
22								

Page 1

Truck 4 X 4 Light Project
February 1940 - October 30, 1940

ID		% Comple	Task Name	Duration	Start	Finish	Predece	Resource Names
23	✓	**100%**	**Approximation of Layout Phase (From Colonel Van Deusen) - Quartermaster**	**7 days**	**Fri 6/22/40**	**Mon 7/2/40**		
24								
25	✓	**100%**	**Detailed Specification Development Phase**	**7 days**	**Fri 6/22/40**	**Mon 7/2/40**		
26	✓	100%	Chalk Outline	1 day	Mon 6/25/40	Mon 6/25/40		Brown,Engler,Dowd
27	✓	100%	Cardboard Mockup	1 day	Tue 6/26/40	Tue 6/26/40	26	Brown,Engler,Dowd
28	✓	100%	Wooden Mockup	1 day	Wed 6/27/40	Wed 6/27/40	27	Brown,Engler,Dowd
29	✓	100%	Confer with Bantam - Fenn	1 day	Thu 6/28/40	Thu 6/28/40		Brown,Fenn
30	✓	100%	Confer with Bantam - Crist	1 day	Sun 7/1/40	Sun 7/1/40		Brown,Crist
31	✓	100%	Review specs with Using Arms	7 days	Fri 6/22/40	Mon 7/2/40		Quartermaster,Tompkins,Oseth
32	✓	100%	Wooden Mockup Test	1 day	Sun 7/1/40	Sun 7/1/40		Quartermaster,Payne,Oseth,Tompkins
33	✓	100%	Develop Detailed Specifications	4 days	Wed 6/27/40	Mon 7/2/40	28	Brown,Engler,Dowd
34	✓	100%	Develop Vehicle Drawing	4 days	Wed 6/27/40	Mon 7/2/40	28	Engler
35								
36	✓	**100%**	**Bid - Contract Phase**	**25 days**	**Mon 7/2/40**	**Sun 8/5/40**		
37	✓	100%	Complete Bid Package	7 days	Mon 7/2/40	Tue 7/10/40		Quartermaster
38	✓	100%	Obtain Permission to Request Bids	7 days	Mon 7/2/40	Tue 7/10/40		Quartermaster
39	✓	100%	Final Review of Specifications	1 day	Thu 7/5/40	Thu 7/5/40		Quartermaster
40	✓	100%	Send out Bid Forms	1 day	Wed 7/11/40	Wed 7/11/40	37,38	Quartermaster
41	✓	100%	Receive Bid Forms	1 day	Tue 7/17/40	Tue 7/17/40		Fenn
42	✓	100%	Obtain Engineering Consulting Assistance	1 day	Tue 7/17/40	Tue 7/17/40		Fenn,Probst
43	✓	100%	Develop Bid Drawing	3 days	Wed 7/18/40	Fri 7/20/40	42	Probst,Crist
44	✓	100%	Complete Bid Forms	1 day	Sat 7/21/40	Sat 7/21/40	43	Fenn,Probst,Crist
45	✓	100%	Bid Opening Meeting	1 day	Sun 7/22/40	Sun 7/22/40	44	Quartermaster,Fenn,Probst,Payne
46	✓	100%	Award Bid	1 day	Sun 7/22/40	Sun 7/22/40		Quartermaster
47	✓	100%	Complete Bid Technical Analysis	1 day	Mon 7/23/40	Mon 7/23/40	46	Quartermaster
48	✓	100%	Develop Contract	10 days	Tue 7/24/40	Sun 8/5/40	47	Quartermaster
49	✓	100%	Complete Signed Contract	0 days	Sun 8/5/40	Sun 8/5/40	48	Quartermaster,Bantam
50								

Page 2

Truck 4 X 4 Light Project
February 1940 - October 30, 1940

ID		% Comple	Task Name	Duration	Start	Finish	Predece	Resource Names
51	✓	**100%**	**Engineering Phase (From Colonel VanDeusen) - Manufacturer**	**35 days**	**Sun 8/5/40**	**Sun 9/23/40**	**36**	
52	✓	100%	Obtain Engineering Dept.	5 days	Sun 8/5/40	Thu 8/9/40		Bantam
53	✓	100%	Obtain - Build Parts	32 days	Sun 8/5/40	Mon 9/17/40		Bantam
54	✓	100%	Build - Deliver Axle	32 days	Sun 8/5/40	Mon 9/17/40		Lewis,Hall
55	✓	100%	Build Frame	32 days	Sun 8/5/40	Mon 9/17/40		Turner
56	✓	100%	Build Chassis	32 days	Sun 8/5/40	Mon 9/17/40		Turner,Hempfling,Crist
57	✓	100%	Create Parts Blue Prints	32 days	Sun 8/5/40	Mon 9/17/40		Probst,Engineering Team
58	✓	100%	Assemble Vehicle	4 days	Tue 9/18/40	Fri 9/21/40		Crist,Turner,Hempfling
59	✓	100%	Test Vehicle	1 day	Sat 9/22/40	Sat 9/22/40	58	Bantam,Suppliers
60	✓	100%	Deliver Vehicle	1 day	Sun 9/23/40	Sun 9/23/40	59	Turner,Fenn,Crist,Probst
61								
62	✓	**100%**	**Vehicle Testing Phase**	**26 days**	**Sun 9/23/40**	**Mon 10/29/4(**	**51**	
63	✓	100%	Initial Test By Colonel Lawes	1 day	Sun 9/23/40	Sun 9/23/40		Lawes
64	✓	100%	General's Test	1 day	Mon 9/24/40	Mon 9/24/40		Lawes,Moesley
65	✓	100%	Infantry Test	1 day	Tue 9/25/40	Tue 9/25/40		Lawes,Moesely
66	✓	100%	Holabird Testing	19 days	Wed 9/26/40	Mon 10/22/4C	65	Moesely
67	✓	100%	Initial Approval of Vehicle	1 day	Tue 10/23/40	Tue 10/23/40	66	Quartermaster Technical Committee
68	✓	100%	Complete Test Reports	4 days	Tue 10/23/40	Fri 10/26/40	66	Quartermaster
69	✓	100%	Review Test Reports	1 day	Mon 10/29/4C	Mon 10/29/4C	68	Quartermaster Technical Committee
70								
71	✓	**100%**	**Project Closeout**	**1 day**	**Tue 10/30/40**	**Tue 10/30/40**	**62**	
72	✓	100%	Final Vehicle Acceptance	1 day	Tue 10/30/40	Tue 10/30/40		Quartermaster,Using Arms,Chief of Staff

Page 3

Bantam Reconnaissance Car Project
Risk Register

#	Risk Description	Probability	Impact	Total Score Probability X Impact	Risk Management Strategy
1	Front Axle – failed to deliver in time	5	5 – Project fails	25	Work closely with Spicer Manufacturing
2	Pilot Model Delivery Time Frame – 49 Days	5	5 – project fails if pilot model not delivered in 49 days	25	Prepare early, work large amounts of overtime
3	Weight	5	5 – will reject vehicle	25	Ignore
4	Obtaining Parts	3	5 – cannot complete vehicle	15	Order early, work closely with suppliers to make sure arrive on time
5	Key Resource Unavailable	3	3 – could miss 49 day deadline	9	Have backup resource; however short project life lessens this risk
6	Inability to Build Vehicle	1	1	1	Resources obtained that are skilled to build the prototype

Bibliography

Books

A Guide to the Project Management Body of Knowledge (PMBOK® Guide) 5th Edition. Newtown Square, Pennsylvania: Project Management Institute, 2013.

Carr, E. H. *International Relations Between The Two World Wars – 1919 – 1939.* New York, New York: Saint Martin's Press, 1961.

Kerzner, Harold R. *Project Management: A Systems Approach to Planning, Scheduling, and Controlling, 11th Edition.* Hoboken, New Jeresey: John Wiley & Sons, Inc., 2013.

McElvaine, Robert S. *The Great Depression: America, 1929 – 1941.* New York, New York: Times Books, 1993.

Mitchell, Brodus. *Depression Decade: From New Era through New Deal 1929 – 1941.* New York, New York: Harper & Row Publishers, 1947.

Overy, R. J. *The Origins of the Second World War, Second Edition.* London and New York: Addison Wesley Longman Limited, 2013.

Rifkind, Herbert R. *Jeep – Its Development and Procurement Under the Quartermaster Corps, 1940 – 1942.* Tallahassee, Florida: Robert V. Nortman, 2011.

Risch, Erna. *United States Army in World War II – The Technical Services – The Quartermaster Corps: Organization, Supply and Services – Volume 1.* Washington, D.C.: Center of Military History – United States Army, 1995.

Taylor, Blaine. *Volkswagen Military Vehicles of the Third Reich.* Cambridge Center, Massachusetts: Da Capo Press, 2004.

Thomson, Harry C. and Linda Mayo. *United States Army in World War II – The Technical Services – The Ordnance Department: Procurement and Supply.* Washington, D.C.: Office of the Chief of Military History – Department of the Army, 1960.

Underwood, John W. *Whatever Became of the Baby Austin.* Sun Valley, California: Heritage Press, 1965.

Watson, Mark Skinner. *Chief of Staff: Prewar Plans and Preparation.* Washington, D.C.: Historical Division United States Army, 1950.

Articles

Bennett, Ralph Kinney. "The Elegant Jeep." *American Magazine,* 9 April 2010.

Chet Hempfling as told to Bob Lindsey. "A Personal Interview of Chet Hempfling." 27 July 1988.

Domer, George Edward. "Good Things Did Come in Small Packages – The History of the American Austin and Bantam." *Automotive Quarterly,* XIV, no. 4 (Fourth Quarter, 1976), 404 – 429.

Domer, George Edward. "Harold Crist – The Man and His Machines."—http://www.willys-overland.com/documents/198203-04%20-%20Looking%20Back%20-%20Harold%20Crist%20-%20The%20Man%20and%20His%20Machines%20-%20George%20Domer.htm

Johnson, Wendell G. "The Howie Machine-Gun Carrier." *Infantry Journal,* (November – December 1937).

Probst, Karl K. with Charles O. Probst. "One Summer in Butler – Bantam Builds the Jeep." *Automotive Quarterly,* XIV, no. 4 (Fourth Quarter, 1976), 430– 439.

Ralph Turner as told to Bob Lindsey. "We Were Beaten by the Roosevelt's." December 1982.

Rolls, Duncan. "Bantam Pilot Reconnaissance Car Recreation." *Army Motors: Journal of Military Vehicles Preservation Association,* (Summer 2009), 21 – 28.

Public Documents

Bantam Jeep Festival, www.bantamjeepfestival.com/about/history

Federal Trade Commission, In the Matter of Willys-Overland Motors, Inc., Toledo, Ohio, *United States National Archives, College Park, Maryland.*

http://en.wikipedia.org

United States National Archives, College Park, Maryland.

Other

Kim and Duncan Rolls. *Interview.* January 14- 15, 2013, Longview, Texas.

Index

A

B

C

D

E

F

G

Q

R

S

T

Paul R. Bruno

Endnotes

Chapter 1

[1] George Edward Domer, "Good Things Did Come in Small Packages – The History of the American Austin and Bantam," *Automotive Quarterly*, Vol. XIV, no. 4, (Fourth Quarter 1976), 405.

2 Ibid.

3 Ibid.

4 Ibid.

5 Ibid.

6 Ibid.

7 Ibid.

8 Ibid.

9 Ibid.

10 John W. Underwood, Whatever Became of the Baby Austin?, (Sun Valley, California: Heritage Press, 1965), 8.

11 Domer, 405.

12 Underwood, 8.

13 Ibid., 8 – 9.

14 Domer, 407.

15 Underwood, 9.

16 Domer, 408 – 409.

17 Ibid.

18 Ibid., 411 – 413.

19 Ibid., 413.

20 Ibid.

21 Underwood, 12.

22 Ibid., 16.

23 Domer, 417.

24 Ibid., 417 – 418.

25 Underwood, 16, 20.

26 Domer, 418.

27 Ibid.

28 Ibid.

29 Ibid.

30 Ibid.

31 Ibid.

32 Ibid., 422-423.

33 Ibid., 423.

34 Underwood, 21.

35 Ibid.

36 Domer, 423.
37 Ibid.
38 Ibid., 425.
39 Ibid.
40 Ibid.
41 Ibid.
42 Ibid.
43 Ibid.
44 Ibid., 425 – 426.
45 Ibid., 426.
46 Ibid.
47 Ibid., 426 – 428.
48 Underwood, 28.

Chapter 2
49 Brodus Mitchell, Depression Decade: From New Era through new Deal 1929-1941, (New York, New York: Harper & Row Publishers, 1947), 3.
50 Robert S. McElvaine, The Great Depression: America, 1929-1941, (New York, New York: Times Books, 1993), 63.
51 Ibid., 65 – 73.
52 Ibid., 82 – 84.
53 Ibid., 77,89.
54 Ibid., 89 – 90.
55 Ibid., 84 – 85.
56 Ibid., 137 – 138, 163 – 168.
57 Ibid., 148 – 149.
58 Ibid.
59 Ibid., 155 – 168.
60 Ibid.
61 Ibid., 152 – 159.
62 Ibid.
63 Ibid.
64 Ibid.
65 Ibid., 164 – 165.
66 Ibid.
67 Ibid., 253.
68 Ibid., 256 – 257.
69 Ibid.
70 Ibid., 265 – 274.
71 Ibid.
72 Ibid., 158 – 161.
73 National Industrial Recovery Act, Ch. 90, 48 Stat. 195, Title I, Sec. 7(a).
74 Ibid., 158 – 161, 258 – 259.
75 Ibid., 258 – 259.

76 Ibid.

77 Ibid., 290 – 291.

78 Ibid.

79 Ibid.,

80 Ibid., 283 – 287.

81 Ibid., 302 – 304.

82 A Guide to the Project Management Body of Knowledge (PMBOK® Guide) 5th Edition, (Newtown Square, Pennsylvania: Project Management Institute, 2013), 563.

83 Harold R. Kerzner, Project Management: A Systems Approach to Planning, Scheduling, and Controlling, 11th Edition, (Hoboken, New Jersey: John Wiley & Sons, Inc., 2013), 6.

84 http://en.wikipedia.org/wiki/Causes_of_World_War_I#Over_by_Christmas; http://en.wikipedia.org/wiki/World_War_I.

85 http://en.wikipedia.org/wiki/George_Washington%27s_Farewell_Address; http://en.wikipedia.org/wiki/The_war_to_end_all_wars.

Chapter 3

86 http://en.wikipedia.org/wiki/Treaty_of_versailles; http://en.wikipedia.org/wiki/Fourteen_points; http://en.wikipedia.org/wiki/Ferdinand_Foch.

87 http://en.wikipedia.org/wiki/Fourteen_points.

88 http://en.wikipedia.org/wiki/Woodrow_Wilson.

89 R. J. Overy, The Origins of the Second World War, Second Edition, (London and New York: Addison Wesley Longman Limited, 2013), 8 – 9; http://en.wikipedia.org/wiki/Warren_Harding.

90 Ibid., http://en.wikipedia.org/wiki/Calvin_Coolidge; McElvaine, 23.

91 Overy, 11; E. H. Carr, International Relations Between The Two World Wars (1919 – 1939), (New York: Saint Martin's Press, 1961), 93 – 98, 117.

92 McElvaine, 89 – 90, 163 – 164, Mitchell, 10 – 16, Overy, 8.

93 Overy, 8.

94 Overy, 12, 36 – 42.

95 Overy, 12 – 18, 25 – 32.

96 Overy, 16 – 22.

97 Overy, 39 – 42.

98 Overy, 25 – 32.

99 Overy, 25 – 32, 63 – 84.

100 Overy, 63 – 84.

101 Overy, 84 – 87.

102 Mark Skinner Watson, Chief of Staff: Prewar Plans and Preparation, (Washington, D.C.: Historical Division United States Army, 1950), 15-56.

103 Ibid., 23.

104 Ibid., 24.

105 Ibid., 23 – 31.

106 Ibid., 23 – 36.

107 Ibid., 24, 31 – 33; http://www.history.army.mil/books/AMH-V2/AMH%20V2/chapter2.htm, 59.

108 Ibid., 34.

109 Ibid., 43.

110 Ibid., 37-38.

111 Ibid., 30.

112 http://en.wikipedia.org/wiki/Neutrality_Acts_of_1930s

113 Watson, 209.

114 Ibid.

115 Ibid., 209-210.

116 Ibid., 52.

Chapter 4

117 Herbert R. Rifkind, Jeep–Its Development and Procurement Under the Quartermaster Corps, 1940-1942, (Tallahassee, Florida: Robert V. Notman, 2011), 6.

118 Ibid.

119 Chief of Infantry to Adjutant General, 26 July 1938, United States National Archives, College Park, Maryland.

120 Rifkind, 6 – 7.

121 Ibid., 7, 11.

122 Ibid., 8.

123 Federal Trade Commission, In the Matter of Willys-Overland Motors, Inc., Toledo, Ohio, United States National Archives, College Park, Maryland, 2410 – 2411.

124 Ibid., 2412.

125 Ibid., 2412-2414.

126 Ibid., 2418.

127 Ibid., 2420-2421, 2432-2437.

128 Ibid., 2437-2438.

129 Ibid., 2439-2441.

130 Ibid., 2451-2454.

131 Federal Trade Commission, In the Matter of Willys-Overland Motors, Inc., Toledo, Ohio, Respondents Exhibit 203 – Report 850 Dated 3-26-36, United States National Archives, College Park, Maryland.

132 Ibid.

133 Rifkind, 10.

134 Captain Wendell G. Johnson, Infantry, "The Howie Machine-Gun Carrier," Infantry Journal, (November – December 1937).

135 Ibid.

136 Ibid.

137 Ibid.

138 Chief of Infantry to Adjutant General, 26 July 1938, United States National Archives, College Park, Maryland.

139 The Infantry Board to Chief of Infantry, 12 February 1938, United States National Archives, College Park, Maryland.

140 Ibid.

141 The Infantry Board to Chief of Infantry, 1 March 1938, United States National Archives, College Park, Maryland.

142 Ibid.

143 Chief of Infantry to Adjutant General, 26 July 1938, United States National Archives, College Park, Maryland.

144 Blaine Taylor, Volkswagen Military Vehicles of the Third Reich, (Cambridge Center, Massachusetts: Da Capo Press, 2004), 15.

145 Ibid.

146 Ibid., 53 – 59.

147 Quartermaster General to Commanding Officer Holabird Quartermaster Depot, 2 June 1938, United States National Archives, College Park, Maryland.

148 Ibid.

149 Quartermaster General to Commanding Officer Holabird Quartermaster Depot, 10 August 1938, United States National Archives, College Park, Maryland.

150 The Cavalry Board to Chief of Cavalry, 8 November 1938, United States National Archives, College Park, Maryland.

151 Ibid.

152 Adjutant General to Chief of Infantry, 13 October 1938, United States National Archives, College Park, Maryland.

[153] This same report detailed the problem as discussed in the Introduction to this chapter and the report's conclusion that the Marmon-Herrington ½ ton 4 X 4 truck met Infantry needs was presented in the "1938: Vehicle Testing" section of this chapter.

154 Ibid.

155 Ibid.

156 Frank H. Fenn to Col. H. C. Lawes, 25 September 1939, United States National Archives, College Park, Maryland.

157 Ibid.

158 Ibid.

159 Ibid.

160 H. J. Lawes to Quartermaster General, 12 December 1939, United States National Archives, College Park, Maryland.

161 Erna Risch, United States Army in World War II–The Technical Services–The Quartermaster Corps: Organization, Supply and Services–Volume 1, (Washington, D.C.: Center of Military History–United States Army, 1995), 246, 253.

162 Harry C. Thomson and Lida Mayo, United States Army in World War II–The Technical Services – The Ordnance Department: Procurement and Supply, (Washington, D.C.: Office of the Chief of Military History–Department of the Army, 1960), 268.

163 Ibid., 267.

164 Ibid., 268 -269.

165 Ibid., 270.

166 Ibid., 267.

167 Rifkind, 16.

168 Thomson and Mayo, 271 – 272.

169 Risch, 51 – 52.

170 Rifkind, 13.

171 Ibid., 13 – 14.

172 Ibid., 15 – 17.

173 Ibid.

Chapter 5

174 Federal Trade Commission, In the Matter of Willys-Overland Motors, Inc., Toledo, Ohio, United States National Archives, College Park, Maryland, 2924.

175 Ibid.

176 Ibid., 2928.

177 Ibid., 2931 – 2936.

178 Ibid., 453.

179 Ibid., 460 – 463.

180 Ibid., 383.

181 Ibid., 454.

182 Ibid., 363 – 365.

183 Ibid., 457, 463 – 464.

184 Ibid., 369 – 370.

185 Ibid., 467.

186 Ibid., 365 – 366.

187 Ibid., 465 – 466.

188 Ibid., 366.

189 Ibid., 366 – 367.

190 Ibid., 1650.

191 Ibid., 1632 – 1634.

192 Ibid., 1636 – 1637.

193 Ibid., 1641.

194 Ibid.

195 Ibid., 1645.

196 Ibid., 1645 – 1646.

197 Ibid., 1648.

198 Ibid., 1648 – 1649.

199 Ibid., 1650 – 1652.

200 Ibid., 1652.

201 Ibid., 1654 – 1656.

202 Ibid., 1656 – 1659.

203 Ibid., 1660.

204 Ibid., 1661 – 1662.

205 Ibid., 1737.

206 Ibid., 1740.

207 Ibid., 1743.

208 Ibid., 1663.

209 Chief of Infantry to Adjutant General (THROUGH The Chief of Cavalry), 6 June 1940, United States National Archives, College Park, Maryland.

210 Ibid.

211 Ibid.

212 Ibid., 1665 – 1666.

213 Ibid.
214 Federal Trade Commission, 1652 – 1653.
215 Ibid., 1664.

Chapter 6

216 Chief of Cavalry to Adjutant General, 8 June 1940, United States National Archives, College Park, Maryland.

217 Adjutant General to The Quartermaster General AND the Chief of Ordnance, 14 June 1940, United States National Archives, College Park, Maryland.

218 Federal Trade Commission, In the Matter of Willys-Overland Motors, Inc., Toledo, Ohio, United States National Archives, College Park, Maryland, 2935-2936.

219 Quartermaster General to Commanding Officer, Holabird Quartermaster Depot, Baltimore, Md., 14 June 1940, United States National Archives, College Park, Maryland.

220 H. J. Lawes to Quartermaster General, 12 December 1939, United States National Archives, College Park, Maryland.

221 War Department General Staff to Adjutant General, Quartermaster General, Chief of Cavalry, Chief of Infantry and Chief of Ordnance, 15 June 1940, United States National Archives, College Park, Maryland.

222 Adjutant General to Chief of Ordnance and The Quartermaster General, 15 June 1940, United States National Archives, College Park, Maryland.

223 Ordnance Sub-Committee on Ordnance to The Ordnance Committee, Technical Staff, 17 June 1940, United States National Archives, College Park, Maryland.

224 Adjutant General to Chief of Ordnance, 18 June 1940, United States National Archives, College Park, Maryland.

225 Federal Trade Commission, 2752-2753.
226 Ibid., 481-482.
227 Ibid., 2936-2942.
228 Ibid., 2943-2947.
229 Ibid., 2943, 2947-2949.

230 Sub-Committee on Automotive Equipment to The Ordnance Committee, Technical Staff, 22 June 1940, United States National Archives, College Park, Maryland.

231 Ibid.
232 Ibid.
233 Federal Trade Commission, 1442, 1438.
234 Ibid., 1438-1439.
235 Ibid., 1442-1449.
236 Ibid., 1455.
237 Ibid., 1456-1457.
238 Ibid., 1460-1463.
239 Ibid., 1465-1466.
240 Ibid., 1669-1672.
241 Ibid., 1672-1674.
242 Ibid., 2961-2964.
243 Ibid., 2776-2768.

244 Quartermaster General, Specification ES–No. 475, 2 July 1940, United States National Archives, College Park, Maryland.

245 Federal Trade Commission, 1675.

Chapter 7

246 War Department General Staff to Adjutant General, Quartermaster General, Chief of Cavalry, Chief of Infantry and Chief of Ordnance, 27 June 1940, United States National Archives, College Park, Maryland.

247 Federal Trade Commission, In the Matter of Willys-Overland Motors, Inc., Toledo, Ohio, United States National Archives, College Park, Maryland, 1724.

248 Ibid., 2949.

249 Ibid., 1561.

250 Ibid., 1573.

251 Holabird Quartermaster Depot to Quartermaster General, 3 July 1940, United States National Archives, College Park, Maryland.

252 Quartermaster General to Chief Motor Transport, 5 July 1940, United States National Archives, College Park, Maryland.

253 Adjutant General to Chief of Ordnance and The Quartermaster General, IN TURN, 5 July 1940, United States National Archives, College Park, Maryland.

254 Charles H. Payne to Colonel J. H. Johnson, 9 July 1940, United States National Archives, College Park, Maryland.

255 Chief of Infantry to The Quartermaster General, 9 July 1940, United States National Archives, College Park, Maryland.

256 Quartermaster General to The Assistant Secretary of War, 10 July 1940, United States National Archives, College Park, Maryland.

257 Quartermaster General to Commanding Officer, Holabird Quartermaster Depot, 11 July 1940, United States National Archives, College Park, Maryland.

258 Federal Trade Commission, 1534.

259 Ibid., 676, 689.

260 Karl K. Probst with Charles O. Probst, "One Summer in Butler-Bantam Builds the Jeep" Automotive Quarterly, Vol. XIV, no. 4, (Fourth Quarter 1976), 432.

261 Ibid.

262 Ibid.

263 Federal Trade Commission, 213, 255.

264 Ibid., 689, 696.

265 Probst, 432.

266 Ibid., 433.

267 Federal Trade Commission, 695.

268 John W. Underwood, Whatever Became of the Baby Austin?, (Sun Valley, California: Heritage Press, 1965), 30.

269 Federal Trade Commission, 708-709.

270 Probst, 433.

271 Ibid.

272 American Bantam Car Company reply to Invitation to Bids No. 398-41-9, 22 July 1940, United States National Archives, College Park, Maryland.

273 Ibid.

274 Ibid.

275 Ibid.

276 Ibid.

277 Ibid.

278 Quartermaster General, Specification ES–No. 475, 2 July 1940, United States National Archives, College Park, Maryland.

279 American Bantam Car Company reply to Invitation to Bids No. 398-41-9, 22 July 1940, United States National Archives, College Park, Maryland.

280 Probst, 433.

281 D. G. Roos to J. Van Ness Ingram, Q.M.C, 20 July 1940, United States National Archives, College Park, Maryland.

282 Probst, 432.

283 Ibid., 433.

284 Ibid.

285 Underwood, 31.

286 Federal Trade Commission, 1720–1721.

Chapter 8

287 Technical Analysis of Bids Submitted in Response to Invitation to Bids No. 398-41-9, 23 July 1940, United States National Archives, College Park, Maryland.

288 Quartermaster General to Commanding Officer, Holabird Quartermaster Depot, 25 July 1940, United States National Archives, College Park, Maryland.

289 Contact No. W-398-qm-8269 (O.I. #137) Invitation to Bids No. 398-41-9, 1 August 1940, United States National Archives, College Park, Maryland.

290 Ibid.

291 Ibid.

292 Ibid.

293 Federal Trade Commission, In the Matter of Willys-Overland Motors, Inc., Toledo, Ohio, United States National Archives, College Park, Maryland, 2952-2960.

294 Ibid., 2961.

295 George Domer, "Looking Back: Harold Crist–The Man and His Machines," http://www.willys-overland.com/documents/198203-04%20-%20Looking%20Back%20-%20Harold%20Crist%20-%20The%20Man%20and%20His%20Machines%20-%20George%20Domer.htm

296 Federal Trade Commission, 680.

297 George Edward Domer, "Good Things Did Come in Small Packages–The History of the American Austin and Bantam," Automotive Quarterly, Vol. XIV, no. 4, (Fourth Quarter 1976), 418, 422.

298 Ralph Turner as told to Bob Lindsey, "We Were Beaten by the Roosevelt's", December 1982, http://www.willys-overland.com/documents/198212%20-%20We%20Were%20Beaten%20by%20the%20Roosevelts%20-%20%20as%20told%20by%20Ralph%20Turner%20-%20by%20%20Bob%20Lindsey.htm

299 Karl K. Probst with Charles O. Probst, "One Summer in Butler-Bantam Builds the Jeep" Automotive Quarterly, Vol. XIV, no. 4, (Fourth Quarter 1976), 435.

300 Probst, 433.

301 Ibid., 432.

302 John W. Underwood, Whatever Became of the Baby Austin?, (Sun Valley, California: Heritage Press, 1965), 31.

303 Chet Hempfling as told to Bob Lindsey, "A Personal Interview of Chet Hempfling," 27 July 1988, http://www.willys-overland.com/documents/19880726%20-%20A%20Personal%20Interview%20of%20Chet%20Hempling%20as%20told%20to%20Bob%20Lindsey.htm

304 Underwood, 31.

305 Ralph Kinney Bennett, "The Elegant Jeep," American Magazine, 9 April 2010.

306 Turner to Lindsey.

307 Domer, "Looking Back: Harold Crist–The Man and His Machines."

308 Turner to Lindsey.

309 Hempfling to Lindsey.

310 Probst, 435.

311 Underwood, 431.

312 Bennett, "The Elegant Jeep."

313 Probst, 432.

314 Ibid.

315 Federal Trade Commission, 235.

316 Probst, 432.

317 Federal Trade Commission, 221- 222.

318 Ibid., 214, 255.

319 Ibid., 255 – 260.

320 Probst, 435.

321 http://www.bantamjeepfestival.com/about/history/

322 Probst, 435.

323 Underwood, 32.

324 Domer, "Looking Back: Harold Crist–The Man and His Machines."

325 Federal Trade Commission, 682, 2846, 2967.

326 Probst, 435.

327 Underwood, 32.

328 Federal Trade Commission, 682.

329 American Bantam Car Company reply to Invitation to Bids No. 398-41-9, 22 July 1940, United States National Archives, College Park, Maryland.

330Federal Trade Commission, American Bantam Car Company, ¼-Ton, 4 x4 Truck ("JEEP") First 70, Contract W-398-QM-8269, United States National Archives, College Park, Maryland.

331 Federal Trade Commission, In the Matter of Willys-Overland Motors, Inc., Toledo, Ohio, United States National Archives, College Park, Maryland, 2906, 2908, 2912.

332 Ibid., 3415, 3432, 3443.

333 Ibid., 3415-3416.

334 Ibid., 3417.

335 John W. Underwood, Whatever Became of the Baby Austin?, (Sun Valley, California: Heritage Press, 1965), 32- 33.

336 Probst, 437.

337 Memorandum For the Chief of Staff: Subject: Demonstration of Light Weapons Carrier, 26 September 1940, United States National Archives, College Park, Maryland.

338 Underwood, 33-34.

339 Federal Trade Commission, 2847.

340 Ibid., 2882- 2883.

341 Ibid., 2910, 3424- 3425, 3435.

342 Inspection Report on Pilot model ¼-Ton, 4 X 4 (Bantam) Chassis Light Reconnaissance and Command Car, 23 October 1940, United States National Archives, College Park, Maryland.

343 Test Report on Bantam, ¼ Ton, 4 X 4, Pilot model Contract No. W-398-qm-8269 (Invitation for Bids 398-41-9) American Bantam Car Company, 23 October, 1940, United States National Archives, College Park, Maryland.

344 Final Inspection Report on Pilot model 1/4-Ton, 4 X 4 (Bantam) Chassis-Light Reconnaissance and Command Car, 29 October 1940, United States National Archives, College Park, Maryland.

345 Quartermaster General to The Adjutant General: Procurement of Fifteen Hundred (1500) Trucks, ¼-ton (4X4) Light Command-Reconnaissance Truck, 22 October 1940, United States National Archives, College Park, Maryland.

Chapter 10

Chapter 9

346 Duncan Rolls, "Bantam Pilot Reconnaissance Car Recreation," Army Motors: Journal of the Military Vehicles Preservation Association, Summer 2009, 21.

347 Kim and Duncan Rolls, "Interview," January 14- 15, 2013, Longview, Texas, 1.

348 Ibid.

349 Ibid.

350 Ibid.

351 Ibid., 2.

352 Ibid.

353 Ibid., 3.

354 Ibid.

355 Ibid.

356 Ibid., 4.

357 Ibid.

358 Ibid.

359 Ibid., 38.

360 Ibid.

361 Ibid.

362 Ibid., 4.

363 Ibid., 38.

364 Ibid., 5.

365 Ibid.

366 Rolls, 22.

---

367 Kim and Duncan Rolls, 13.
368 Ibid.
369 Ibid., 28.
370 Ibid.
371 Ibid., 36.
372 Ibid.
373 Ibid., 28.
374 Ibid., 30.
375 Ibid., 13.
376 Ibid., 25.
377 Ibid., 9.
378 Ibid.
379 John W. Underwood, Whatever Became of the Baby Austin?, (Sun Valley, California: Heritage Press, 1965), 35.
380 Kim and Duncan Rolls, 25.
381 Ibid., 25- 26.
382 Ibid., 25.
383 Ibid., 26.
384 Rolls, 22.
385 Kim and Duncan Rolls, 7.
386 Ibid.
387 Ibid., 8.
388 Ibid.
389 Rolls, 22.
390 Kim and Duncan Rolls, 44.
391 Rolls, 22.
392 Ibid.
393 Rolls, 23.
394 Kim and Duncan Rolls, 39.
395 Ibid.
[396]NOS-New Old Stock which means something was manufactured in the time period, but has never been used.-Kim and Duncan Rolls, "Interview," January 14 – 15, 2013, Longview, Texas, 46.
397 Ibid., 8.
398 Rolls, 22.
399 Kim and Duncan Rolls, 8.
400 Ibid., 37.
401 Ibid., 8- 9.
402 Rolls, 23.
403 Kim and Duncan Rolls, 16.
404 Ibid., 5- 6.
405 Ibid., 6.
406 Ibid., 14.
407 Rolls, 23.
408 Kim and Duncan Rolls, 14.

409 Ibid., 13.
410 Ibid., 20.
411 Ibid., 17.
412 Ibid., 17, 19.
413 Ibid., 20.
414 Rolls, 23- 24.
415 Ibid., 24.
416 Rolls, 24- 25, Kim and Duncan Rolls, 47 – 48, 50.
417 Kim and Duncan Rolls, 16.
418 Ibid., 16,24.
419 Ibid., 19.
420 Ibid., 50.
421 Ibid.
422 Rolls, 25.
423 Kim and Duncan Rolls, 26.
424 Ibid., 26- 27.
425 Rolls, 25- 26.
426 Ibid., 22.
427 Kim and Duncan Rolls, 18.
428 Rolls, 26- 27.
429 Kim and Duncan Rolls, 52.
430 Ibid., 19.
431 Ibid., 12.
432 Ibid.
433 Rolls, 27.
434 Kim and Duncan Rolls, 52.
435 Ibid.
436 Ibid., 53.
437 Ibid., 52.
438 Rolls, 27-28.
439 Kim and Duncan Rolls, 53- 54.
440 Rolls, 28.
441 Ibid.
442 Kim and Duncan Rolls, 19.
443 Rolls, 28.
444 Kim and Duncan Rolls, 10.
445 Ibid., 10- 11.
446 Ibid.
447 Ibid., 54.
448 Ibid., 54- 55.
449 Ibid.
450 Ibid., 56.
451 Ibid., 20.
452 Ibid., 20, 22.

453 Ibid., 20- 21.
454 Ibid., 35.
455 Ibid., 20- 21.
456 Ibid., 33, 48.
457 Ibid., 33.
458 Ibid., 24.
459 Ibid., 24-25.
460 Ibid., 24-25.
461 Ibid., 60.
462 Ibid., 59.
463 Ibid., 41- 42.
464 Ibid., 22.
465 Ibid., 29.
466 Ibid.
467 Ibid.
468 Ibid., 27.
469 Ibid., 38.
470 Ibid., 37.

Chapter 11
470 Federal Trade Commission, In the Matter of Willys-Overland Motors, Inc., Toledo, Ohio, United
471 National Archives, College Park, Maryland, 3420-3422, 3431.
472 http://en.wikipedia.org/wiki/Eugene_the_Jeep 198, 206, 221

About the Author

Paul Bruno, PMP, PgMP works as a program / project management consultant and as a Senior Consultant and Trainer for the International Institute for Learning. He has 25 years' experience in information technology and has held numerous volunteer positions, both at the global headquarters and local chapter level, for the Project Management Institute. He holds Master's Degrees in Business Administration and History, and Bachelor's Degrees in Computer Software and Management. He hosted the *History Czar®*, *Career Czar®* and *Bible Czar®* Internet radio programs and, with his late wife and Max Freedman, has written numerous historically based screenplays.

About the Contributing Editor

Manuel Freedman, known as Max, has been writing since the 1950's. Currently he writes, produces and coaches screenwriters in the movie industry in Los Angeles, as well as writes non-fiction books, of which, this is his seventh participation to be published. Before starting his media company, Mr. Freedman ran his own advertising and publishing company. He authored and edited five college-level textbooks for Adobe Systems, which were translated into eight languages and distributed in 35 countries. Three of them are on the subject of computer-based filmmaking; the other two on desktop publishing. He was born in St. Louis, Missouri, and is a graduate of Stanford University where he was the recipient of a writing scholarship.

Premise of this Volume

The spring and summer of 1940 witnessed the resounding defeats of the French army and British Expeditionary Force at the hands of modernized German troops, designed to take advantage of the latest advances in technology. These included mobile vehicles and tanks used in formation to blast through enemy lines, as well as combined ground and air tactics. The evacuation of the British from Dunkirk and the final defeat of their French allies in June 1940 left only a thin line of English fighter planes between that island nation and total defeat.

Meanwhile, leaders of the United States Army, decimated by demobilization after World War I and budget cuts during the Great Depression, knew they were completely unprepared for this new type of mobile warfare called "blitzkrieg," a German term meaning "lightning war." Though experts in the U.S. Army had worked from the end of World War I to develop a combination light weapons carrier and command and reconnaissance vehicle, no perfect model had yet been developed by 1940. In June of that same year, the Army compiled a list of requirements for a revolutionary new truck to replace the mule as the Army's primary method of moving troops and small payloads.

"Project Management in History: The First Jeep" tells the story of the American Bantam Car Company, which dared to meet the challenge to build the prototype in the impossible timeframe of 49 days. The "¼ ton truck 4x4 light project," as the effort was titled by the Army, represents a textbook case of entrepreneurship and project management that holds lessons for today's business leaders and project managers. Contemporary leaders face a similar environment of rapidly changing technology, volatile economic circumstances and turbulent international relations, forces that assailed the U.S. Army throughout the interwar period.